THE FACTS ON FILE GUIDE TO PHILOSOPHY

Values and the Good Life

THE FACTS ON FILE GUIDE TO PHILOSOPHY

Values and the Good Life

David Boersema
Kari Middleton

Facts On File
An Infobase Learning Company

The Facts On File Guide to Philosophy: Values and the Good Life

Copyright © 2012 by David Boersema and Kari Middleton

All rights reserved. No part of this book may be reproduced or utilized in any form or by any means, electronic or mechanical, including photocopying, recording, or by any information storage or retrieval systems, without permission in writing from the publisher. For information contact:

Facts On File, Inc.
An imprint of Infobase Learning
132 West 31st Street
New York NY 10001

Library of Congress Cataloging-in-Publication Data
Boersema, David.
  The Facts on File guide to philosophy. Values and the good life / David Boersema, Kari Middleton.
    p. cm.
  Includes bibliographical references and index.
  ISBN 978-0-8160-8483-8 (alk. paper)
  1. Ethics. 2. Political science—Philosophy. 3. Aesthetics. I. Middleton, Kari. II. Title. III. Title: Values and the good life.
  BJ1012.B56 2012
  170—dc23   2011029493

Facts On File books are available at special discounts when purchased in bulk quantities for businesses, associations, institutions, or sales promotions. Please call our Special Sales Department in New York at (212) 967-8800 or (800) 322-8755.

You can find Facts On File on the World Wide Web at
http://www.infobaselearning.com

Excerpts included herewith have been reprinted by permission of the copyright holders; the authors have made every effort to contact copyright holders. The publishers will be glad to rectify, in future editions, any errors or omissions brought to their notice.

Text design by Erik Lindstrom
Composition by Hermitage Publishing Services
Cover printed by Yurchak Printing, Inc., Landisville, Pa.
Book printed and bound by Yurchak Printing, Inc., Landisville, Pa.
Date printed: March 2012

Printed in the United States of America

This book is printed on acid-free paper.

Table of Contents

Introduction	ix

Part I: Ethics — 1

Introductory Discussion Questions	3
What Is Ethics?	5
Metaethics	6
Noncognitivism: Prescriptivism and Emotivism	12
David Hume	16
Cognitivism	18
Plato	21
Normative Ethics	26
Virtue Theory	28
Divine Command Ethics	33
Utilitarian Theory	36
Duty Theory (Deontology)	42
Formalism and Social Contract Theory	52
Feminist Ethics	61
Applied Ethics	66
Applied Ethics: Business Ethics and Media Ethics	94
Concluding Discussion Questions	102

Further Reading	103
Glossary	104
Key People	106

Part II: Political Philosophy — 119

Introductory Discussion Questions	121
What Is Political Philosophy?	123
Normative Disciplines and Politics	128
Classical Greeks: Plato and Aristotle	135
Divine Right: Thomas More	141
Social Contract: Hobbes, Locke, and Rousseau	145
The Nineteenth Century: Socialism	164
The Nineteenth Century: Utilitarianism	176
Inequality, Justice, and Liberty	184
Concluding Thoughts	200
Concluding Discussion Questions	202
Further Reading	203
Glossary	204
Key People	207

Part III: Philosophy of Art — 221

Introductory Discussion Questions	223
Aesthetics: Philosophy of the Arts	225
Plato	230
Aristotle	232
The Emergence of Modern Aesthetic Theory	235
Kant and Schiller	241
Romanticism	245
Expressivism and Definability	254
Challenges in the Twentieth Century	260

Art and Society	268
Concluding Discussion Questions	279
Further Reading	280
Glossary	281
Key People	284
Index	298

Introduction

Every day we face a multitude of choices. Some of those choices are important only in the short run, such as what to have for breakfast or whether or not to see a movie over the weekend. Other choices are more important: What college should I attend? Do I really want to marry this person? Is this the career for me? Even more broadly, we wonder about the really big questions, such as what makes life worth living. Obviously, we make choices, at least in part, based on what matters to us and what we consider at some level to be valuable. Is it worth my time and money to go see that movie this weekend as opposed to doing something else? Is this job, and potential career, really something that I want to spend a large part of my life doing? Am I living the kind of life that I want to?

Philosophers use the term *axiology* to speak of the study of values. Usually when we think of values in the context of philosophy, we think of moral and ethical values. Is it ever wrong to tell a lie or to steal? Why should I not cheat on my taxes if I can get away with it? What makes certain actions right and others wrong? How should I live?

These questions are indeed moral and ethical questions, and they have been the subject of philosophical inquiry for millennia. However, there are other questions about values and living a good life that go beyond these sorts of questions. Besides straightforward moral and ethical values (and questions), there are value concerns that point to our collective, social nature. For example, what does it mean to be a good citizen? What are the appropriate roles and functions of government? What obligations, if any, do I have toward others in the communities in which I live? These sorts of value questions are usually grouped within what is called social and political philosophy. "What is the good life?" is related to, but different from, "What is a good government?" So, axiology includes the study not only of moral and ethical values but also of values related to social and political philosophy.

In addition to questions about what makes a good life and a good government, we also speak of aesthetic values, that is, values related to art. What makes a good movie or a good song? Value questions of these sorts might or might not have anything to do with moral/ethical or social/political values. We might say that a particular movie was good because the actors were especially believable in their roles or because the movie had a lot of action scenes or because we found it visually stimulating or because the story was particularly moving. Philosophers, and people generally, often disagree on whether or not a movie (or other work of art) could be good regardless of its moral or social content, but the point is that we can speak of the aesthetic value of art without necessarily bringing in moral/ethical or social/political values.

This book, then, is about the philosophical study of values, from the perspective of ethics, political philosophy, and aesthetics. It is one volume in the Facts On File Guide to Philosophy set, which is designed to provide an accessible and engaging introduction to philosophy for students.

Note that, because major ideas can be important in different contexts and because certain thinkers made important contributions in more than one area, material within the set is occasionally repeated, with the intention of providing full context for each discussion.

David Boersema
Kari Middleton

PART I
Ethics

Introductory Discussion Questions

1. Do you think morality is subjective or objective? For example, does the nature of what is moral only depend on what people feel or think?
2. When you say that something is morally wrong, what do you mean when you say it? Are you describing a fact or just expressing your feelings? Do you mean to influence others to behave in certain ways?
3. What do you think are the traits of a morally good person?
4. Do you think men and women think about ethical issues in different ways? For example, do some virtues matter more to men than to women, or vice versa? If not, why not? If yes, what are the differences?
5. Do you think capital punishment is ever morally justified? Why or why not?
6. What do you believe euthanasia is? Do you think euthanasia is ever the right thing to do? Why or why not?

What Is Ethics?

Also termed *moral philosophy*, ethics is the philosophical study of right action and moral values. For example, How should one live? Is abortion wrong? and Are there facts about morality? are all ethical questions. Philosophers working in ethics sometimes make claims about what is the right thing to do or even, broadly, how a person ought to live. Of course, thinkers outside philosophy have often commented on ethical matters and made claims about what counts as moral behavior and what does not. What is distinctive in philosophy is that philosophers not only examine ethical questions systemically, such as through analysis, but also try to give good reasons for their views. That is, philosophers try to *justify* their claims about right action and moral values.

As this suggests, ethics is related to morality, but it is not the same. Morality consists of values concerning what is good and evil, right and wrong. Morality imposes limitations on how we can behave (for example, it is morally wrong to set a person on fire just to watch her suffer). Ethics examines the nature and basis of morality; so, ethics *studies* morality.

Traditionally, ethics is divided into three subareas: metaethics (which concerns the nature of moral values and the language used to express moral judgments), normative ethics (which concerns theories about what right action is or how one ought to live), and applied ethics (which applies normative ethics to particular practical issues, such as abortion and capital punishment).

Metaethics

Metaethics is the philosophical study of the nature of the right and the good. Rather than saying what right action is or how one ought to live—rather than saying what we ought to do—metaethical views say something broadly about the nature of morality. Put another way, metaethics concerns the nature of moral judgments themselves. For example, a metaethical question is whether morality is objective or subjective. Suppose, for instance, that everyone believed that child abuse was morally acceptable; would that make child abuse morally acceptable? Someone who believes that what is moral does not wholly depend on what people think and feel about the matter might answer no, on the grounds that something can be morally wrong even if no one believes it is. So, in this view, morality is not entirely subjective; that is, it is not just a matter of opinion, belief, or feelings. Other philosophers deny that morality is objective in various ways. Yet others deny that there really are moral values at all: That is, some moral skeptics deny that moral values have any basis in reality at all. Of course, people make moral judgments, claiming some actions are good and some are bad; for some skeptics, however, those judgments are simply false.

Because we use language to express moral judgments, language is also an important topic in metaethics. For example, philosophers concerned with metaethics consider whether statements that express moral judgments (such as "Child abuse is wrong") are true and why or why not. For instance, if the statement "Child abuse is wrong" is true, in virtue of what is it true? As a way of better understanding the concepts named by such words, philosophers concerned with metaethics consider the meanings of words such as *good* and *moral*.

One common distinction in metaethics is the distinction between the moral concepts of *good* and *right*. *Good* is contrasted with *bad*, and *right* is contrasted with *wrong*. Likewise, we speak of "goods" often in the sense of products that people want or need (such as food products or clothing), and we speak of "rights" often in the sense of entitlements that we have or limits on what others can do (such as rights to free speech or a fair trial). These ways that we speak of good and right point to the difference between them. Good has to do with what is beneficial to, or in the interests of, something, while right has to do with an appropriate choice among options. (Bad, then, has to do with what is not beneficial to, or not in the interests of, something, while wrong has to do with an inappropriate choice among options.) For example, some foods are good for people, and other foods are not. The foods themselves are neither right nor wrong, but the decision to consume one food option over another can be right or wrong (for example, arguably the decision to eat an animal that belongs to an endangered species is wrong). One result of the fact that good and right are not the same thing is that there might be situations when the right thing to do is actually to do something bad. If one is faced with several bad choices, the right thing to do might be to choose the least bad among those choices. For instance, in hard economic times an employer might need either to lay off some employees or to reduce their wages. Neither option is good, but one might be less bad than the other, and that option would be the right thing to do.

Sometimes what philosophers believe is the good shapes what they consider is right. For example, some philosophers believe what is good is happiness (and what is bad is unhappiness). This, in turn, suggests that right actions are actions somehow involved in producing happiness.

Also relevant in metaethics is the issue of who, or what, matters morally. Most people agree that humans have moral standing: We cannot morally treat them any way we like. Especially in the 20th and 21st centuries, philosophers have discussed whether nonhuman animals also have moral standing. Are there moral restrictions on the ways we can treat pigs or donkeys or oysters? Also of interest are features of the natural environment, such as ecosystems. Perhaps, for example, it is immoral to destroy ecosystems for no good purpose. What these questions point to is the issue of what gives any person, or any thing, moral standing. In other words, what is it about some beings, or some things, such that there are moral restrictions on how we can treat them? Different answers to this question imply different answers to the issue of which beings (or things) matter morally and which do not. For instance, if all that matters for moral standing is the ability to reason, then most humans have moral standing, but many nonhuman animals do not. If all that matters is sentience (the capacity for pleasure and pain), then many nonhuman animals have moral standing, but trees do not.

An important distinction related to this issue is the distinction between a moral *agent* and a moral *patient*. To say someone is an *agent* in the philosophical sense is to ascribe responsibility to that person. For instance, to say that a person is the *causal agent* in a house fire is to say that she caused the fire; she is causally responsible in the sense that it was her action that started the fire. So, to say someone is a *moral agent* is to ascribe moral responsibility to that person. Moral agency requires the ability to think about the morality of an action and to freely choose to act or not act; a being that is not capable of doing these things cannot be a moral agent. For instance, suppose a normal adult human deliberately set a house on fire as an act of revenge. As someone perfectly capable of reasoning about the morality of her actions, and someone who freely chose to set the house on fire, she is a moral agent. So, she is morally responsible for setting the fire; if there is blame to be cast for setting the fire, it belongs to her. (Moral agents can be praised for their actions as well as blamed. For instance, a normal adult who freely chooses to rush into the burning house to save someone else, despite the risk to himself, is appropriately praised for his action.)

In contrast, moral *patients* are not morally responsible; they cannot think about the morality of their actions or choose to act (or not to act). For example, infants, young children, and people in comas are moral patients. If a baby kicked over a candle and started a house fire, the baby is not morally responsible for the fire (the baby had no conception of the morality of starting a fire, after all). However, moral patients can be the *objects* of moral acts. That is, there are right and wrong ways of treating moral patients, in spite of the fact that they are not morally responsible. It is wrong to cause a baby needless pain, for example. Similarly, some philosophers argue that even though nonhuman animals, the environment, or features of the environment are not moral agents, they are moral patients: There are morally right and wrong ways of treating them.

Cultural Relativism

In addition to the question of whether statements that express moral judgments are true or false (as cognitivists would claim) or neither (as noncognitivists hold), an important question in metaethics is the relation between moral values and culture. Sometimes what one culture considers morally acceptable, another finds morally wrong: For example, in some African cultures, female circumcision is considered morally acceptable, but in the United States it is considered wrong. In some cultures, child marriages are acceptable; in others they are not. So, it is plain that sometimes cultures have moral disagreements. This simple fact raises two important questions. The first is whether the moral disagreements between cultures are often very deep and fundamental (whether they are disagreements about the very basics of morality). The second question is what the fact that there are moral disagreements between cultures tells us about the nature of morality, if anything. The view that cultures commonly have fundamental disagreements about morality is called *descriptive* cultural relativism. Descriptive cultural relativism is meant to describe a fact about the world, the supposed fact that there are such disagreements. The view that morality is relative to a culture we can call *philosophical* cultural relativism. This view is one way we can answer the question regarding what the existence of moral disagreements between cultures tells us about the nature of morality: It tells us that morality is relative to a culture.

Philosophical cultural relativism is a form of moral relativism, the view that what is moral is relative to some standard or another. So, philosophical cultural relativism is a view about the nature of morality itself. For the philosophical cultural relativist, nothing is just simply right or wrong. By way of analogy, suppose it is illegal in some states to shoot off certain types of fireworks, but shooting off these same fireworks is legal in other states. So, it is not simply legal or illegal to shoot off those fireworks; rather, it is legal or illegal only relative to a particular code of laws (and it so happens that those laws vary from state to state). Similarly, according to philosophical cultural relativism, what is right or wrong is relative to a particular cultural standard of morality. Moral questions such as, Is slavery wrong? do not have a simple yes or no answer. The answer depends on a cultural standard; according to some standards, the answer is yes, and according to others, the answer is no. Philosophical cultural relativism, then, is not the view that nothing is either right or wrong. For the cultural relativist, some behaviors really are right, and some behaviors really are wrong; it is just that they are not right or wrong absolutely. For many versions of philosophical cultural relativism, there is no rational way of evaluating one cultural standard of morality as better than another. If, for instance, culture A says slavery is moral, culture B says slavery is immoral, and culture C says that slavery is sometimes immoral, there is no way of standing outside *all* these cultural standards and rationally judging any one standard as better than another. All cultural standards of morality are equal. Outside philosophy, it is common to associate moral relativism with the value of tolerance, the idea that one should be tolerant of values, beliefs, and practices different than one's own. From this perspective, for instance, no one culture occupies a privileged perspective on morality. However, if philosophical cultural relativism is true, tolerance itself is morally valuable only relative to a culture—not absolutely.

Descriptive cultural relativism and philosophical cultural relativism are distinct views, but they are closely related. Thinkers who believe that descriptive cultural relativism is false are less likely to believe that philosophical cultural relativism is true. After all, if cultures agree on moral values more often than not, then there does not seem to be much point in insisting that morality is relative to a culture. It is controversial whether descriptive cultural relativism is true. Some critics argue that, despite the fact that different cultures have different practices, cultures very often share moral values. However, because their particular circumstances differ, how cultures apply those values might differ accordingly. For example, a shared value between two cultures might be modesty. In some cultures, modesty might mean wearing clothes that cover most of one's body. In another culture, in which people must have great freedom of movement to go about physically active lives, such long clothes might be an inconvenience, and modesty might require covering only select parts of the body.

Even if descriptive cultural relativism is true, this does not necessarily mean that philosophical cultural relativism is true. This is because merely disagreeing does not mean that there is no culture-independent standard of morality. Analogously, cultures disagree about the origin of the universe. This in itself, however, does not mean that there is no culture-independent standard of truth; on the contrary, it appears that there is a correct scientific account about the origin of the universe (whatever that account turns out to be), and some cultures are simply wrong about it. Similarly, there could be a single correct standard of morality, even if cultures disagree about what is moral.

Philosophical cultural relativism has been the subject of much disagreement in ethics. One criticism of philosophical cultural relativism is that, if it is true, it is difficult to make sense of moral disagreement. Suppose Tabitha, from culture A, claims that slavery is morally acceptable, and Tom, from culture B, claims in response that slavery is immoral. According to the objection, for the philosophical cultural relativist, it looks as if Tabitha's claim "Slavery is moral" is really a way of saying "Slavery is moral according to the moral standards of my culture." Similarly, it appears that Tom's claim "Slavery is immoral" is really a way of saying "Slavery is immoral according to the moral standards of my culture." So, they are not really disagreeing. Yet on an ordinary understanding, Tabitha and Tom do disagree—they disagree about the morality of slavery in general, even if they agree that their different cultures have different standards of morality. Moreover, what this suggests is that people often seem to believe that their moral judgments are independent of culture; indeed, they might even judge cultures other than their own to be morally superior in some respects. Tom, for instance, thinks that slavery is wrong, period, regardless of a culture's standards (and it is reasonable to suppose that some people who disapprove of slavery would do so even if their own culture approved of it).

Noncognitivism: Prescriptivism and Emotivism

One broad division among metaethical views is between noncognitivism and cognitivism. Noncognitivism is the view that statements that express moral judgments are neither true nor false; in this view, these statements do not report on anything factual. Cognitivism is the view that (at least some) moral claims can be either true or false. So, for example, consider the statement "Murder is wrong." According to the noncognitivist, this statement is neither true nor false (philosophers put this point by saying it has no truth-value). For the noncognitivist, this statement has no *cognitive* content; it is not saying anything about factual matters (this does not necessarily mean that the statement has no content at all, however). For the cognitivist, on the other hand, the statement "Murder is wrong" does have cognitive content, and it has a truth-value. The statement might be true, and it might be false; cognitivism itself does not say which. It just says that it has some cognitive content and some truth-value (whatever that truth-value is). Note that noncognitivism is *not* the view that it does not matter how people behave. Noncognitivists might (and most do) have specific ideas about how people ought to behave, such as that they ought to refrain from lying and stealing. A noncognitivist will just deny that statements such as "Murdering, lying, and stealing are wrong" state facts. But that does not mean that it is okay for people to murder, lie, or steal.

As a version of noncognitivism, prescriptivism is a view about the meaning of moral language. That is, it is a view about the meaning of what we say when we express moral judgments, such as the meanings of the statements "Stealing is wrong" and "Donating to charity is good." According to prescriptivism, statements that express moral judgments should be understood as prescriptions. In other words, such statements give commands. For example, the statement "Stealing is wrong" is at least in part a way of saying "Don't steal"; the statement does not actually express a belief (the belief that stealing is wrong). However, for at least some prescriptivists, the commands expressed by moral judgments are not like any other kind of command. Moral commands are special in the sense that they are universal commands, commands that apply in all situations or all situations of the same kind, rather than in just one situation. For example, the command, "Open the window" is not a universal command. It applies only in a particular circumstance, namely the particular circumstance in which it is uttered. Put another way, when a person says, "Open the window," the command is just to open a particular window in that situation, not to open windows in future situations. But when a person says in a given context "Murder is wrong," the command she is giving not to murder applies in all relevantly similar situations, not just in that particular situation. That is, the command is intended to be followed whenever a person is in a situation that is importantly similar to the situation in which the utterance is first made. Prescriptivism has been defended by philosophers such as Rudolf Carnap (1891–1970) and R. M. Hare (1919–2002).

A closely related view in metaethics is emotivism, a form of noncognitivism. According to emotivism, statements about moral matters primarily do two things: First, they express the attitude of the speaker; second, they attempt to influence others to share that attitude. Emotivism comes from the idea that such statements express *emotive meaning*, as opposed to descriptive meaning. A statement with descriptive meaning describes a state of affairs; for instance, "Oregon is in North America" has descriptive meaning. A statement with only emotive meaning expresses emotion (or arouses emotion) but does not describe a state of affairs. For example, "Drat!" expresses frustration or disappointment, but it does not describe a state of affairs. So, according to emotivism, saying "Stealing is wrong" is rather like "Stealing—boo!" and saying "Donating to charity is good" is rather like saying "Donating to charity—hurrah!" Emotivism is sometimes called the "boo-hurrah" theory, because according to it, statements expressing moral judgments are expressions of attitudes, like the words *boo* and *hurrah*. A person making a moral claim is not reporting how she feels, she is expressing how she feels (it is like the difference between saying, "I disapprove of that call" and "boo!" at a sporting event). Statements that express moral judgments have emotive meaning, but they do not describe states of affairs.

The British philosopher A. J. Ayer (1910–89) defended an early version of emotivism. According to Ayer, statements are meaningful only if they are verifiable or if they are analytically true (roughly, true either by definition or because of the grammar of the statement). Ayer believed that there are no moral facts. There are facts such as that the Earth revolves around the Sun and that water is composed of hydrogen and oxygen, but there are no facts such as that murder is wrong or that being kind is good. For Ayer, then, statements expressing moral judgments are not verifiable. So, they are not literally about anything, although they are used to express one's emotions about something.

The American philosopher Charles L. Stevenson (1908–79) developed a more detailed version of emotivism. In defense of emotivism, Stevenson noted that when a person judges that something is good, she is typically more likely to behave in certain ways—for example, when a person judges that donating to charity is good, she is more likely to donate to charity than she would otherwise. Yet just having a belief does not typically motivate one to act. One's belief that it is sunny, for instance, does not by itself motivate a person to go outside. To do that, a person must also have an attitude or an interest regarding the sunny weather, such as an interest in warming up or an approving attitude toward weather that is perfect for playing Frisbee. If beliefs alone do not motivate one to act, why does the judgment that something is good tend to go hand in hand with the tendency to behave in certain ways? Stevenson's answer is that when one makes a moral judgment, expressing it with a statement such as "Donating to charity is good," the statement does not express a belief at all. Rather, it expresses the speaker's attitude about donating to charity—specifically, it expresses her approval. This explains why someone who announces "Donating to charity is good" is more likely to donate to charity. In short, Stevenson thought that emotivism accounted for the close connection between our moral judgments and how we are motivated to behave.

For Stevenson, moral disagreements are often disagreements in attitude. That is, they are differences of approval or disapproval about a particular matter. For example, when someone says "Capital punishment is wrong," she is expressing her disapproval of capital punishment (and hoping to influence others to share her disapproval), and when someone says "Capital punishment is right," he is expressing his approval of capital punishment (and hoping to influence others to share his approval). Of course, two people who make different moral judgments might also disagree about empirical matters. For instance, one person might think that capital punishment deters crime and another person might not. For Stevenson, sometimes people can settle disagreements in attitude by settling related disagreements about empirical matters. Two people might, say, come to an agreement about the morality of capital punishment if they each learn whether capital punishment does in fact deter crime. But Stevenson thought that people cannot always resolve moral disagreements by appealing to empirical facts.

Like Ayer, Stevenson believed that one purpose of moral language was to influence others: to get them to share one's own approval or disapproval or even to get them to behave in certain ways. So, for Stevenson, any point that one might think will likely change someone else's attitude counts as a reason for a given moral judgment. For example, suppose Alex wanted to convince George that vandalism is wrong. If Alex thinks that pointing out that vandalism hurts innocent people will likely cause George to change his attitude about vandalism, then that vandalism hurts innocent people counts as a reason for the judgment that vandalism is wrong. But if Alex threatens to hit George unless George agrees with him, this threat is also a reason for the moral judgment that vandalism is wrong. This is just because the threat is likely to cause George to change his attitude.

This points to a common criticism of emotivism: that emotivism cannot adequately account for the role of reason in moral judgments and moral disagreements. Few people believe that moral judgments are (or should be) arbitrary or based on just any reason. Rather, they are (or should be) based on *good* reasons. Contrary to Stevenson, threatening someone with harm unless he adopts one's own attitude does not seem to count as a good reason for adopting any moral judgment.

David Hume

The Scottish philosopher David Hume (1711–76) was one of the most important moral philosophers. Hume has sometimes been considered a noncognitivist, but whether his view is really a version of noncognitivism is controversial. Hume did regard moral judgments as subjective in the sense that, according to him, they are ultimately based on feelings rather than on reason. In particular, according to Hume, we regard some character traits as virtues because we find them useful or agreeable (they give us pleasure); we judge other traits as morally wrong because we find them disagreeable (we disapprove of them, and the disapproval makes us feel uneasiness, a form of pain). For Hume, this does not mean that reason plays no role at all in moral judgments; a person might believe that capital punishment is morally acceptable because it helps deter people from committing certain kinds of crimes, for instance—so, her moral judgment about capital punishment is based in part on her reasoning about the effects of capital punishment. However, Hume thought that ultimately moral judgments are based on feelings rather than on reason. One argument Hume gave for this claim is that reason alone is not motivating, but moral judgments are. That is, reason alone does not motivate a person to act. Suppose, for instance, a person's reason tells her that lying to a friend will hurt the friend's feelings. That in itself would not motivate one to refrain from lying to her friend; motivation to act (to refrain from lying) requires what Hume called "the passions," such as desires, fears, and hopes. In this instance, one might refrain from lying to one's friend out of a desire to spare the friend's feelings and the fear of causing pain. Moral judgments, however, are motivating: If one judges, for example, that lying to one's friends is wrong, in making that judgment she is motivated not to lie to her friends. The moral judgment is motivating in a way that reason alone is not. What this shows, Hume thought, was that moral judgments cannot be based on reason alone. Reason, he said, "is and ought to be the slave of the passions."

In addition, Hume thought, we cannot infer just from statements about what *is* the case statements about what *ought* to be the case. Consider, for instance, the fact that many people enjoy watching television. That is what *is* the case—it is just a matter of fact that many people enjoy watching television. However, just because many people enjoy watching television does not mean they *ought* to watch television. There seems to be no logical connection between the statement about what *is* the case— that many people enjoy watching television—and the moral claim that people *ought* to watch television. The general idea here is often put like this: You cannot derive an *ought* from an *is*. In other words, we cannot logically deduce what is moral or immoral just on the basis of claims about facts. Just because something *is* the case does not mean that something or another *ought* to be the case.

Although Hume believed that moral judgments are based on feelings rather than on reason, Hume did not regard moral judgments as arbitrary or groundless. Rather, he thought that there are some character traits (the "natural" virtues) for which people instinctively have feelings of approval or disapproval; the moral judgments of these traits are rooted in human nature itself. By nature, for instance, people disapprove of pointless, wanton cruelty. Approval of other character traits ("artificial" virtues, such as justice) is based more on convention, or social rules. However, even in these cases, according to Hume, the approval is ultimately related to finding traits agreeable or useful.

Of course, Hume was aware that people do sometimes disagree about moral matters. Sometimes such disagreements are rooted in disagreements about related empirical facts, and they can be resolved if people come to agree about those facts. In addition, people might disagree about moral matters because people sometimes have a biased view in favor of themselves or their own interests (for instance, a person might be less inclined to view cheating unfavorably if she herself stands to benefit by cheating).

Cognitivism

According to cognitivism, at least some statements that express moral judgments are either true or false. For cognitivists, such statements can have cognitive content: They purport to say something factual (this does not mean all that statements that express moral judgments are true; it just means such statements concern matters of fact in the sense that they state something is the case). They can have descriptive meaning, not simply emotive meaning. As there are varieties of noncognitivism, there are varieties of cognitivism. One primary form of cognitivism is moral realism, the view that there are moral facts. On this view, there are at least some moral claims that are true, and there are at least some moral claims that are false. This is so even if people disagree about what those moral facts are—and, for the moral realist, it is possible for some people to be mistaken about what those moral facts are. Indeed, it is possible for everyone to be mistaken about the moral facts, but this does not make moral facts any less factual. Moral realists typically view moral facts as facts that do not depend on our beliefs for their existence; they are what they are independent of what we might think about them. Arguably moral realism explains why we make at least some of our moral judgments: We judge the Holocaust as evil, for instance, because as a matter of fact the Holocaust was evil.

One area of concern for moral realists is the nature of moral facts. In particular, a basic issue is how moral facts are similar to or different from facts about the physical world. For instance, in what ways is the fact that plants need water to live similar to or different from the apparent moral fact that slavery is wrong? A second area of concern for moral realists is how it is possible for us to come to know what moral facts there are. Moral realists address these concerns in different ways. One approach to moral realism identifies moral facts with "natural" facts, facts about the empirical, physical world. For example, suppose that morally good actions are actions that produce the most happiness for the people affected by that action. It is an empirical fact that some actions produce more happiness for people than other actions. To learn which actions produce the most happiness, we can research the facts about human psychology and needs, and this will help us learn that, say, giving a child regular meals will make her happier than refusing to feed her at all. So, on the view under consideration, it is a moral fact that the right thing to do in this instance is to give the child regular meals. Moreover, that moral fact is the *same* fact as the fact that giving the child regular meals will produce the most happiness for the people affected.

The approach of identifying moral facts with natural facts supplies a ready answer to the question of how we can come to know the moral facts: If moral facts just *are* natural facts, then we can learn what moral facts there are just by investigating the natural facts. And we investigate the natural facts just by investigating the empirical world, using the methods of science. However, one influential objection to this *naturalist* approach in moral realism is that identifying a moral fact with a natural fact always leaves an open question of whether the moral fact really is that natural fact. For instance, it always makes sense to ask, "Is the moral good really what produces the most happiness for the people concerned?" What this shows, according to the objection (posed by the British philosopher G. E. Moore [1873–1958]), is that the good cannot be identified with any natural fact; the term *good* just does not mean the same thing as any term regarding a natural fact (such as *produces happiness*). Although many philosophers believe that developments in philosophy of language have weakened this objection, it has remained influential.

An alternative approach to moral realism is to identify moral facts with nonnatural facts. In this view, moral facts cannot be identified with or explained only in terms of natural facts (such as facts about what produces happiness, how people mature, and so on). This view avoids Moore's open question objection, but it also raises the question of how it is possible to come to know about such nonnatural facts. They cannot be investigated through the methods of science, which investigates only facts of the natural, physical world. It would seem, then, that perhaps instead one learns about moral facts through intuition, or through one's reason. However, critics charge that such methods are unsatisfactory. Some philosophers have also found the concept of nonnatural facts to be somewhat mysterious.

A general concern for both naturalists and nonnaturalists about moral facts is the relation between moral facts and moral motivation. It is often thought that moral judgments motivate a person to act, in and of themselves; for instance, a person who makes the moral judgment that murder is wrong is motivated to refrain from murdering just in virtue of making that judgment. Along these lines, J. L. Mackie (1917–81) argued that moral facts (or, as he put it, moral properties) must necessarily be peculiar (Mackie used the term *queer*). This is because they must be motivating in and of themselves: that is, moral facts would motivate a person to act in certain ways just in virtue of a person's recognition of those facts (recognizing the supposed fact that murder is wrong motivates a person to refrain from murdering). But, Mackie thought, other facts are not like this: The fact that plants need water to live, for instance, does not in itself motivate one to water plants. Naturalist and nonnaturalist moral realists respond in various ways to Mackie's point that moral facts must be very peculiar sorts of facts. Some, for example, deny that moral judgments must be motivating in and of themselves. Mackie's point can also be taken as a reason to reject the belief that there are moral facts in the first place.

Plato

The ancient Greek philosopher Plato (ca. 428–348 B.C.E.) was a cognitivist: He believed that at least some moral claims are either true or false and that some things really are morally good and some things really are morally bad. Of particular concern to Plato was justice and the nature of justice, and he addressed the question of whether people do what is right (behave justly) for its own sake or only because it is advantageous to do so. It seems evident that most people, most of the time, behave in certain just ways: They refrain from taking what is not theirs, for instance, and do not murder others. It is also apparent that, by doing so, they avoid certain bad consequences of unjust behavior, such as legal consequences (e.g., fines, imprisonment, and even the death penalty) and certain social consequences (loss of respect, friendship, and love, for instance). By behaving justly, people are also likely to reap certain benefits, such as the benefit of others' esteem and affection. In probably his most famous work, *The Republic,* Plato asked whether these are the real reasons people behave justly, to avoid bad consequences and enjoy good ones—in short, whether people behave justly because doing so is useful, rather than for the sake of justice itself. To illustrate, Plato told the tale of the Ring of Gyges, the story of a shepherd (Gyges) who finds a ring that has the power to make him invisible. Using the ring, Gyges is able to seduce the queen, kill the king, and take over the throne. So, the ring allows Gyges to behave unjustly without suffering negative consequences—indeed, the ring allows him to reap the apparent benefits of behaving unjustly. (Contemporary readers will perhaps recognize similar themes from *The Lord of the Rings* by J. R. R. Tolkien.)

Plato, Aristotle, Hippocrates, and Galen play instruments in this woodcut from 1516.

A philosophical question raised by this story is simply: Why be moral? One answer is simply that it is advantageous to do so. This answer implies that when it is *not* advantageous to do so, one might just as well stop being moral, and this, of course, is exactly what Gyges does. However, this is not Plato's own answer. Plato believed that behaving morally (justly) is rational, and not simply because behaving morally (justly) is useful. Rather, when a person understands the nature of justice and the nature of the good, she is motivated to behave justly for its own sake.

To see why Plato thought this, it is worth considering Plato's view of reality. Plato claimed that there are different levels of reality. Shadows are real, but they are not as real as the objects they are shadows of. For instance, a shadow of a dog is real (there really is a shadow of a dog, say, on a sunny day). However, if a cloud comes by and blocks the sun, causing the shadow to go away, the dog itself does not disappear! The dog's shadow is real, but the actual, physical dog is even more real; it exists even when the shadow does not. For Plato, however, while actual, physical, individual dogs are real, they are not as real as the concept of Dog (or what he called the Idea of Dog). For example, if we had a concept of Dog, that concept could exist even if all the actual, physical dogs died off. (We have the concept of Dinosaur even though there are no actual dinosaurs.) Just as an actual, physical dog is more real than a shadow dog so, the concept, or Idea, of Dog is even more real than actual, physical dogs. For Plato, then, there are degrees of reality, and what is most real are not the everyday objects of common experience; instead, Ideas are the most real things. Plato further claimed that the Ideas are like ideal, perfect objects and actual, physical individuals are like imperfect copies of these ideal Ideas. For instance, we normally think of and experience many different breeds of dogs as well as individual dogs. All of these dogs have lots of features that are particular. That is, one dog might be black, while another is brown or multicolored; one dog is large, while another is small, etc. But, for them all to be dogs, there must be something they have in common (or some set of things they have in common) that makes them dogs. There must be some set of features, or conditions, that things have in order for them to be dogs rather than cats or trees. Those features are the essence of Dog, and they are what constitute the Idea of Dog.

To return to what is good, then, Plato believed that is what most real of all is the Idea of the Good (the essential features of goodness). Knowledge of the Good (and of any Idea) requires reason. We can come to know the Ideas, but it takes an effort, said Plato; it is even likely to be painful. As a result, knowledge of Ideas must be gained in a thoughtful way. But a person who does have such knowledge, and in particular knowledge of the Good, would have both knowledge of what is good and right as well as the love and desire to be just. Such as person, even if she acquired a ring like the ring of Gyges, would not thereby live unjustly. She would not do what is wrong for her own advantage, even if she knew she could get away with it.

The central question of Plato's *Republic* is, "What is justice?" According to Plato, living well is the soul's function and to fulfill this function requires justice. To live well, to do the right thing, he said, requires knowledge of what is true and real—that is, knowledge of the Ideas. Plato claimed that we can think of justice itself as applying to individual people and also to a society, or State, collectively. That is, we speak of an individual as being just (or unjust) and a State as being like an enlarged individual (so we can speak of a State also as being just or unjust). In either case, justice is a matter of the harmony of the different parts of something. With individuals, Plato said, there are different parts of the "soul" (which, for him, meant the person). In some respects, people want whatever they think will please them, but, in addition, people also feel the need to be fair and do the right thing. A just person is someone who balances his various urges, responsibilities, etc. The soul, Plato said, was like a chariot driver trying to steer two horses. One horse is spirit, and the other horse is reason. So, our bodily senses (spirit) move us in one direction, while our reason moves us in another. The harmonious soul brings these into balance and steers the right course; this is what a just person is.

With regard to the state, it, too, is a combination of different parts, such as workers and soldiers and administrators, etc. A just state, said Plato, is one in which there is a balance and harmony among these various groups. In particular, each group needs to fulfill its appropriate function or role. For example, soldiers need to protect the state from those who might harm it, while workers need to provide the goods and services that are needed by people. Administrators, or rulers, need to govern well. Plato called these administrators "guardians," because they have the role of guarding the well-being of the state. In a just society, the guardians act like the chariot driver in Plato's metaphor of the soul; they control the other parts of the state by making sure that they all operate in harmony. The best state, then, is one in which each group performs its appropriate role (and does not try to do the job of another group), and those people who are best suited for the duties of a particular group are in fact part of that group. In other words, those people who are best at producing things should be workers, while those who are best at protecting should be soldiers, and those who are best at guiding should be guardians/rulers.

Who would be best at ruling? For Plato, it is philosophers. The reason for this is because philosophers are those who are concerned with true wisdom and with knowing what real justice is. Philosophers, he claimed, focus their lives not merely on the particular things and events of everyday experience but on the essence, or core nature, of things. Their concern is not simply about short-term personal benefit but truly living well. A philosopher-king, then, would focus on living well for the whole state, not just himself. While many people think of philosophers are being impractical and abstract, Plato thought that their devotion to the general, essential nature of things was, rather, what made them the most practical of guardians, because philosophers would have both knowledge of justice and love of justice.

Normative Ethics

Normative ethics gives accounts of what is right and why (a norm is a standard; normative theories give standards for what is right). Scientists study how people actually behave; ethicists study how people *ought* to behave, morally speaking. Yet moral psychology (how people actually think and feel about moral matters) matters in ethics. One reason moral psychology is important is because of a principle known as *ought implies can.* According to this principle, to say that one *ought* to do something makes sense only if one *can* do that thing (if one is capable of doing that something). For example, it would seem silly to say that people ought to fly faster than the speed of light in order to protect people who are in danger on the other side of the Earth. It would be silly because people are not capable of flying faster than the speed of light; a moral principle that requires the impossible is not a very good moral principle. What this suggests is that how people are by their very nature motivated to behave is relevant to a theory about how they *ought* to behave. As an example, suppose that people always act out of a desire to further their own interests and that they cannot help doing otherwise (a view known as psychological egoism). If this is so, any moral principle that required one to act contrary to her own interests would be a bad theory. So, perhaps ethical egoism is true, the view that people ought to act to further their own interests. Similarly, according to psychological hedonism, as a matter of fact people always seek pleasure; so any moral principle that required one not to do so would be a bad theory, and perhaps ethical hedonism is true (the view that one *ought* to seek one's own pleasure). Whether either psychological egoism or psychological hedonism is true is a matter of disagreement. The point here is just that facts about moral psychology are relevant to normative ethics. Sometimes such facts even count as reasons for accepting or rejecting a particular normative theory.

Virtue Theory

Virtue theory, or virtue ethics, is often seen as an alternative to accounts of normative ethics that are based on principles, or rules (such as consequentialism and deontological ethics). Rather than formulating ethical principles (as those views do), virtue ethics focuses instead on virtues and what it is to live a good life. One way of putting this point is that whereas principle-based ethics addresses the question, what should I do? virtue ethics concerns the question, what kind of person should I be?

Modern virtue ethics has roots in ancient Greek philosophy, especially in the work of Aristotle (384–322 B.C.E.). In the 20th century, especially with the 1958 publication of the essay "Modern Moral Philosophy" by G. E. M. Anscombe (1919–2001), philosophers began to draw on Aristotle's ideas about ethics in part out of dissatisfaction with principle-based ethical accounts. One criticism of such accounts is that morality cannot be accounted for just in terms of ethical principles. Put another way, the concern is that rules cannot adequately capture what it is to live morally. This is because rules are rigid, and life's actual situations are nuanced: That is, they take place with particular people in particular situations and contexts, to which rigid moral principles do not always readily apply. For example, one principle is that one should treat others as one would like to be treated. But it is not obvious that one can mechanically apply this rule to all situations—for example, in a situation where one must decide whether to tell a dying person just how ill she is, knowing that hearing the truth will likely worsen her already fragile health. Arguably, resolving this dilemma requires some knowledge not only of the dying person's health but of her state of mind, desires, and values (which might be different than one's own), and the various likely consequences of telling the truth or refraining from doing so. Making the decision seems to require identifying, sorting out, and weighing all these factors against each other in order to decide the right thing to do. So, in this view, the notion that the right thing to do is just a matter of following a rule such as "Treat others as one would like to be treated" does not capture the complexity of moral behavior.

A second criticism of principle-based ethical theories is that they do not adequately account for the role of emotions and motivations in moral behavior. Imagine, for instance, that a friend visits you while you are in the hospital, and when you thank her for visiting, she replies seriously that she was just doing her moral duty (this example is given by contemporary philosopher Robert Stocker). Such a motivation for her visit seems morally wrong—your friend should visit you because she *wants* to, because she is your friend and cares about you, not because she is acting out of duty to a moral principle. What this shows is that *why* we do what we do, as well as our personal relationships, are important factors in moral behavior. An ethical theory that evaluates the moral worth of an action just in terms of whether a person is doing one's duty, or just in terms of following an ethical principle, is mistaken. Arguably, virtue theory can account for the role of emotions in ethical life: Virtues, for example, can include kindness, benevolence, and even friendship itself.

A central question for virtue theory is what a virtue *is*. One way of understanding virtue is that a virtue is, roughly, a character trait, such as honesty, kindness, and courage. A virtuous person is disposed to behave virtuously and is motivated to do so by virtue itself. In other words, a virtuous person has the tendency to behave virtuously, and she does so out of a desire to be virtuous. So, to have the virtue of kindness, for example, it is not enough always to act kindly: One must act kindly *to be kind* (rather than to get something in return, say). In addition, a virtuous person is attentive to the complexities of particular situations and knows how to act accordingly. She knows how to behave morally even in complicated situations. For example, although it is generally a virtue to be honest, the virtuous person knows when it is better not to tell the whole truth in order to avoid causing pointless harm. Using Aristotle's term, such a person has *practical wisdom*—together with courage, justice, and temperance, one of the four virtues of ancient philosophy.

30 VALUES AND THE GOOD LIFE

For Aristotle, a virtuous life is a life of *eudaemonia,* a key concept in virtue ethics. *Eudaemonia* is Greek for happiness, or flourishing. In ancient philosophy, eudaemonia was considered the ultimate purpose and the ultimate good in human life. So eudaemonia is the state of living the good life for humans (it does not apply to nonhuman animals or inanimate things). Although eudaemonia involves happiness, this does not mean a short-lived feeling (the way a person might feel, for instance, during a pleasant evening spent with friends). Rather, happiness has to do with the way one lives one's life as a whole. Moreover, eudaemonia is objective; it is not based on a person's individual preferences. Rather, the idea of eudaemonia is that there is a way of living that is good for all humans. This does not mean that everyone must behave exactly the same way in order to live well and be happy—that everyone must pursue sports as a hobby, for instance. It does mean, however, that there are certain components of human flourishing and human happiness that are objective in the sense that they apply to every person's flourishing and happiness. Aristotle believed living virtuously was one necessary component of eudaemonia. That is, he believed it was not possible for a person to flourish and be happy unless he lived virtuously. In addition, Aristotle believed that the function, or purpose, of human beings was to reason and that exercising one's reason involves practicing the virtues. For Aristotle, then, it is rational to be virtuous.

Aristotle's teacher, Plato (ca. 428–348 B.C.E.)—as well as Plato's teacher, Socrates (469–399 B.C.E.)—had said that virtue is knowledge. This view included the notion that no one does what she truly believes is wrong. If someone does what is wrong, then she must have simply been mistaken, or ignorant. Aristotle, however, claimed that there are both virtues of intellect and virtues of character (such as courage or modesty). It is not enough to know the good or to know the right thing to do: One must also *act* well. The study of ethics, then, is to become good. To become good, one must know the good, so virtues of the intellect are important. To become good, in its turn, requires good habits. That is, in order to have a virtue of character such as courage, one must habitually act in courageous ways (a person cannot be said to be courageous if she has impulses to behave courageously but never actually behaves courageously or behaves courageously only intermittently when given the opportunity).

Fundamental to Aristotle's views of virtues of character is what is called the doctrine of the mean. The word *mean* means "middle point." For example, mathematicians talk about the mean number of a set of numbers (7 is the mean of the set "6,7,8" and of the set "1,4,6,7,8,10,13"). The emphasis is on moderation, finding a middle point, or moderate action, among different possible actions. Aristotle claimed that virtue involved the mean action among a set of actions connected to some feeling. For example, courage is the mean between two excesses: (1) too little bravery (or, cowardice) and (2) too much bravery (or, foolhardiness). Likewise, with respect to shame, modesty is the mean between bashfulness and shamelessness. While virtue is the mean, what counts as an appropriate mean will vary depending upon contexts. For instance, what might be a rash or foolhardy action for someone might be a courageous action for someone who has relevant training or experience (such as a firefighter trying to save someone in a burning building). Or, less dramatically, what might be a moderate amount of food to eat could be different for a young child as opposed to a full-grown adult. Nonetheless, for Aristotle, given any relevant context and circumstances, moderation is the appropriate action.

Like other ethical views, virtue theory has been criticized on various grounds. One criticism is that virtue theory does not tell a person what to *do*. The concern is that because virtue theorists avoid formulating general principles, it is not always obvious how one should behave according to virtue theory. One possible response to this concern is that one should act like a virtuous person (however, it is not always clear how a virtuous person would act). Another possible response is that in real life there are no easy answers, and therefore it is not a fault of virtue theory for failing to provide them. A second criticism of virtue theory is that even good (virtuous) people can encounter moral dilemmas, and that faced with such dilemmas, sometimes they need principles for determining right action. To return to the dilemma of whether to tell a very sick friend the true extent of her illness, for instance, a critic of virtue theory might argue that what is needed to determine the right course of action (to tell the friend or not to tell the friend) is a principle, such as perhaps the principle that it is wrong to lie or the principle that one should respect others' autonomy. A third criticism of virtue theory is that sometimes virtues conflict. The virtue of honesty, for instance, might sometimes conflict with the virtue of kindness; in such cases, how should one behave? One answer is that is there *is* no single answer, but that one can gradually attain practical wisdom, which will allow one to decide the right thing to do in each particular situation where virtues conflict.

Divine Command Ethics

Divine command ethics is the view that moral behavior consists of obeying God's commands. This type of ethical philosophy is often avoided by modern philosophers—though by no means all—but was much more prevalent in earlier times. As an ethical theory, it does not attempt to say exactly what God commands; the answer to that question varies according to religious doctrine. It does provide one answer to a very old philosophical question: What is the relation between morality and religion? According to divine command ethics, morality depends on God (if there were no God, there would be no morality). Divine command ethics provides an objective ground for ethics. If right actions are just those actions commanded by God, then it seems that right actions are objectively right—it is not just a matter of personal preference or opinion that some actions are morally right and some actions are morally wrong. Morality is also universal: God's laws would seem to apply to everybody.

Divine command ethics has also long been a matter of controversy. Perhaps the most important criticism of it comes in the form of a question posed by Plato in the *Euthyphro*. In that work, Socrates asked, "Is what is holy holy because the gods approve it, or do they approve it because it is holy?" The question can be rephrased like this: Is right action right because God commands it, or does God command right action because it is right? The problem for divine command ethics is that the two most obvious ways of answering this question are not very attractive answers, at least by the lights of divine command theory. If right action is right because God commands it, then it looks as if God's commands are arbitrary. This is because if what makes actions right is just that God commands them, then God could just as well have commanded other actions, and *those* would have been right, because God commanded them. God could well have commanded us to murder our firstborn children, for example. However, something seems wrong with the view that murdering all firstborn children would be good just because God commanded it. If *that* could count as right action, then it does not seem to make much sense to say that God is good; rather, it seems that God just commands. Because of these apparent consequences, many philosophers deny that actions are right just because God commands them.

Suppose instead, then, that God commands right actions *because* they are right. This eliminates the problem that God's commands seem arbitrary. Moreover, the notion that God commands us to do certain things because those things are morally right fits with the traditional belief that God is morally good. However, answering Socrates' question this way is also problematic. If God commands certain actions *because* they are right, then it looks as if God is really irrelevant to the morality of that action. This is because those actions would have been right whether or not God commanded them—in this view God commanded them, after all, *because* they were independently right. Moral behavior, then, is less a matter of obeying God's commands than it is a matter of doing what is right in any case. But this view is contrary to divine command ethics.

Some philosophers, noting that both answers to Socrates' question seem unacceptable for divine command ethics, believe that divine command ethics is not a good theory: Although religion might be related to morality in various ways (for example, religious doctrines often include moral teaching), morality is not *dependent* on religion.

However, other philosophers have attempted to respond to Socrates' question in a way that is still consistent with divine command ethics, without claiming either that God's commands are arbitrary or that morality is independent of God. For example, some have argued that divine commandments are unlike any other kind of commandment. If God is truly the source of these commandments, then that matters; their divine source *is* all that is needed to justify them. Bad commandments simply cannot come from an all-good source.

In addition to the question posed by Socrates, there are other important issues related to divine command ethics. One issue is the view that morality is a matter of obedience. Some philosophers believe that it is a mistake to view morality as consisting of obeying commands (divine or not), arguing instead that moral maturity requires more than just obedience for the sake of obedience. A child obeys commands. But one might expect an adult to reason thoughtfully about ethical issues and make moral decisions on the basis of that reasoning. Along these lines, one criticism of divine command theory is that it is contrary to human flourishing, which requires skills and abilities beyond simple obedience to commands. One defense of divine command ethics is that one can freely and autonomously choose to obey God's commands, and that doing so actually demonstrates moral maturity in the sense that one acts on the basis of recognizing certain facts (for instance, that one needs God's help to be moral) and takes responsibility for one's actions.

There are also issues related to the content of what God demands. First, how does one know what God commands, and hence how to behave? Second, do God's commands tell us everything we need to know to behave morally? Suppose, for instance, God's commands are just the Ten Commandments of the biblical Old Testament. These commands do not seem to provide answers for every moral question one might face—for example, whether one should go to war to fight for a just cause or stay at home to care for one's ailing mother; whether to vote for one political candidate or another; or whether to disobey a racist law.

Utilitarian Theory

Utilitarian theory, or utilitarianism, is one version of consequentialism, the view that what makes an action morally right (or wrong) is the value of its consequences. It seems plausible that the consequences of actions do matter, from a moral point of view. For instance, one reason it is wrong to torture animals is because it hurts them; one reason it is wrong to burn down people's houses is because it leaves people homeless. What is distinctive about consequentialism is the view that consequences are *all* that matter, morally speaking. That is, an evaluation of whether an action is morally right or wrong just depends on the consequences of that action. This contrasts with the view that an action is morally right (or wrong) depending on whether performing it fulfills one's duty or what someone's intentions were. For instance, a consequentialist would say that rescuing a child from drowning is morally right because it had the right sort of consequences—making the child and her family very happy, say—not because doing so fulfills one's duty or because someone wanted to do something good.

One issue for consequentialism is whether the consequences that matter morally are the *actual* consequences of an action. Suppose a person gave a ride to someone else, and that during the trip, there was an accident that resulted in the passenger being severely injured. If it is the actual consequences that are morally important, then giving the passenger a ride in this case was morally wrong. Yet it seems odd to suppose that the driver behaved immorally by giving the passenger a ride. On another view, what matters morally are the consequences that a person reasonably could have foreseen. It seems unlikely that the driver could have foreseen the accident, so, on this view giving the passenger a ride was *not* morally wrong.

Consequentialists differ about which consequences are morally important. One might think, for instance, that what is morally important is keeping the Earth as pollution-free and beautiful as possible, or that what is morally important is converting as many people to a religion as possible. Utilitarianism is perhaps the most prominent version of consequentialism. A brief statement of classical utilitarianism is that morally right actions are those that produce as much happiness as possible (or, at least, minimize unhappiness as much as possible) for as many people (or beings) as possible. This point is often expressed in the phrase that what is morally right is what produces the greatest good ("utility") for the greatest number. Classical utilitarianism, then, is closely associated with hedonism. *Psychological* hedonism is the view that people always seek pleasure. *Normative* hedonism is the view that pleasure or happiness is the only intrinsic good (the only thing that is good in and of itself). So psychological hedonism is a view about what actually motivates human behavior, whereas normative hedonism is a view about what *ought* to motivate human behavior. Classical utilitarianism is linked to both forms of hedonism: According to classical utilitarianism, not only do people in fact seek pleasure or happiness, but they ought to do so.

Jeremy Bentham (1748–1832) and John Stuart Mill (1806–73) are credited with formulating classical utilitarianism. According to Bentham, when a person must make a moral decision, she should calculate how much pleasure and pain her possible actions would produce for those involved. He called such calculation of pleasures and pains "the hedonic calculus." Moreover, to Bentham, all pleasures are equal: The pleasure of eating a fine meal, for instance, is no better or worse than the pleasure of solving a difficult intellectual problem. Famously, Bentham said that push-pins (an old name for bowling) is as good as poetry. So the hedonic calculus did not distinguish between different *kinds* of pleasures but only between different *quantities* of pleasures. In contrast, Mill thought that there were some pleasures that were more valuable than other pleasures; for instance, the pleasure of viewing fine art is a superior pleasure to the pleasure of taking a hot bath, and in general, intellectual and aesthetic pleasures ("higher" pleasures) are superior to bodily pleasures ("lower" pleasures). In a well-known remark, Mill said that it was better to be Socrates dissatisfied than a pig satisfied. Mill based the distinction between higher and lower pleasures in part on the claim that people who had experienced both sorts of pleasures regarded high pleasures as superior. Mill also acknowledged that sometimes people act, not for pleasure or happiness itself, but rather for the sake of something else: For example, a person might work to become an accomplished pianist for its own sake rather than for the sake of being happy. In such a case, being an accomplished pianist is desired as a *part* of happiness, not as a means for happiness. For Mill, then, people do desire happiness and act to attain happiness, but they desire some things as part of happiness (and they do not desire those things for themselves unless they also desire them as part of happiness).

However one understands pleasure and pain, according to utilitarianism everyone's happiness counts equally; no one's happiness is more important than anyone else's. So when a person undertakes a hedonic calculus, no one takes priority over anyone else. Also, it is not enough to take an action that would make one person very, very happy at the cost of making others rather unhappy. Instead, one must try to make as many people as happy as possible.

There are two main versions of utilitarianism. According to *act utilitarianism*, right actions are those that produce the greatest good for the greatest number. According to *rule utilitarianism*, right actions are those that follow *rules* that produce the greatest good for the greatest number. There are some cases in which a particular action might be right according to act utilitarianism but wrong according to rule utilitarianism (or vice versa). Suppose, for example, a person lied under oath during a murder trial, with the result that the accused murderer was convicted. Suppose, in this case, that the accused murderer was guilty, likely would have offended again, yet would not have been convicted of the crime without the false evidence. In this case, it looks as if according to act utilitarianism, lying under oath was the right thing to do. This is because it produced the most happiness: It helped secure the murderer's conviction, without which he would likely have murdered more people, causing a great deal more unhappiness than any unhappiness caused by his conviction. However, the rule utilitarian is likely to view this case rather differently. Plausibly, the person who lied under oath could be said to be following a rule to the effect that one should lie under oath

Peter Singer speaking at MIT in 2009 *(Photograph by Joel Travis Sage)*

to secure guilty convictions when otherwise the guilty would go free. Yet it is not clear that this rule would produce the greatest happiness for the greatest number. If people followed this rule, it seems likely that people would lose faith in the justice system, never knowing for sure when people are telling the truth or not. And if people lost faith in the justice system, then it seems likely the justice system would collapse, which would cause a great deal of social unrest and ensuing unhappiness. So, it looks as if following the rule "Lie under oath to ensure guilty people are convicted when otherwise they would go free" would have very bad consequences: Far from maximizing happiness, it would cause a lot of unhappiness. Since the rule utilitarian believes that right actions are those that follow *rules* that would produce the greatest good for the greatest number, then according to rule utilitarianism, our person testifying during the murder trial should not lie after all—contrary to act utilitarianism.

Unlike many doctrines in philosophy, utilitarianism has had a noticeable impact on thinking outside philosophy. Of particular note are views about animals and how we ought to treat them. Utilitarianism requires treating everyone's happiness equally. Today, this is sometimes put in terms of preferences, or interests: Every sentient being (that is, being capable of pleasure and pain) has interests, and those interests count equally. The Australian utilitarian philosopher Peter Singer (1946–) has argued that this principle of impartiality applies to the interests of sentient animals as well as of people. If the interests of sentient animals should be counted as equal to the interests of human beings, this suggests that practices such as intensive factory farming to produce meat are morally wrong: The suffering they inflict on animals outweighs the pleasure they produce for humans. Singer's utilitarian-based arguments are often considered the spark to the modern animal rights movement.

Although utilitarianism continues to be influential, there have been many objections to utilitarianism. Among the most important is the claim that utilitarianism conflicts with widely accepted views about justice and rights. Suppose, for example, that executing one innocent person would make a great many people very happy, people who believe the person is guilty and are likely to riot unless she is executed. It appears that, according to act utilitarianism, the right thing to do would be to execute the innocent person, because doing so would maximize happiness for the greatest number of people. The unhappiness of the innocent person is outweighed by the happiness of those who want to see her executed. Yet many people find it very unlikely that the morally right thing to do in this case would be to execute an innocent person. First, not executing an innocent person is a matter of justice; an innocent person does not deserve execution. Second, some people argue that executing an innocent person would violate that person's right to life. Although this example is imaginary, the point is that utilitarianism sometimes tells us that the right thing to do is an action that violates ordinary notions of justice and human rights. To that extent, according to objectors, utilitarianism is wrong: No accurate moral theory would ever tell us to violate our sense of justice and rights, whether in real cases or imaginary ones. Note that this objection seems to apply to act utilitarianism more than rule utilitarianism. This is because rule utilitarians might deny that it would ever be right to violate a person's rights; rather, the rules that produce the most happiness might be those that tell us to respect each other's rights. So a rule utilitarian might say that *those* rules are the rules that we should follow.

Another concern regarding utilitarianism is that there are times when it seems wrong to treat everyone's happiness (or everyone's interests) equally. We have special relationships with some beings and not others, and in one view this means we ought to give moral priority to those people or beings. That is, when we must make a moral decision, we ought to count the interests of some beings (say, the interests of one's family and friends) as more important than those of others. Another objection is that utilitarianism is too demanding: It just asks too much of us. There are many ways one can spend one's spare time, and if right actions are those that produce the greatest happiness for the greatest number of people, then it appears that one should spend one's spare time doings things like volunteering to help abused children and raising money to combat world hunger, rather than surfing the Internet or practicing with one's rock band. Yet it does not seem wrong to spend one's time doing things just for one's own personal enjoyment. One response to these objections is just to deny that one should give moral priority to certain beings (say, one's friends and family) and to claim that one *should* spend one's spare time maximizing happiness for the greatest number possible.

Another objection to classical utilitarianism takes issue with hedonism, as some philosophers argue that things other than pleasure—such as friendship or intellectual artistic achievement—are intrinsically good. Finally, in opposition to Bentham, some philosophers have argued that it seems to be difficult to measure pleasure, but normative hedonism seems to require that some measurement be possible (if it is not clear what actions provide the most pleasure, it is not clear what actions one should take). Utilitarians have refined utilitarianism and responded in various ways to these criticisms. Modified versions of utilitarianism continue to be influential.

Duty Theory (Deontology)

One general approach in normative ethics is the approach of deontology. The term *deontology* comes from the Greek word *deon,* meaning "duty," and the Greek word *logos,* meaning "study of." So deontology is, literally, the study of duty. Deontology specifically concerns moral duties: Deontological views of ethics are views that evaluate the rightness or wrongness of some actions (or kinds of actions) in terms of a person's moral duties. This contrasts with consequentialist views, which evaluate the moral rightness or wrongness of an action (or kind of action) just in terms of an act's consequences. For instance, in a case where telling a lie might make a lot of people very happy and just one person a little sad, one consequentialist view is that telling the lie is the morally right thing to do. This is because all that matters for the morality of an action is its consequences, and in this case the consequences are more good than bad. However, the deontologist is likely to disagree. Deontologists typically believe that it is intrinsically right to do some things and intrinsically wrong to do other things, no matter the consequences (that is, some actions are good or bad in and of themselves, just by their very nature). Lying is usually taken in deontological views to be an action that is intrinsically wrong. So, one has a duty not to lie, even if telling a lie will make a lot of people very happy and just one person a little sad. Philosophers often associated with deontological ethics are Immanuel Kant (1724–1804) and W. D. Ross (1877–1971).

There are at least three features of deontology that are often taken to be advantages of deontological views. First, many people believe that there are some moral duties we ought to follow even when doing so results in bad consequences; deontological views are consistent with this belief. For instance, many people believe it would not be okay to torture an innocent person even if *not* torturing means that others will suffer as a result. Second, deontological views are consistent with the ordinary belief that it makes a moral difference *who* performs a particular action. It seems that some of our moral duties are based on the fact that we have certain relationships with particular people. For instance, parents have a duty to care for their children. Not just anyone has a duty to care for a child; parents have that duty because *they* are the parents. Not just anyone has a duty to help someone else move; sometimes one has a duty to help another person move because one is *that* person's friend. Philosophers put this point by saying that deontological views are *agent-relative*. In other words, who the moral agent of an action is matters morally, because moral duties are sometimes based on particular relationships. This contrasts with many versions of consequentialism, which tends to be *agent-neutral* (if all that matters for the morality of an action is that action's consequences, it does not matter who performs that action). Third, deontological views typically distinguish between moral duties a person is required to follow and moral actions that go above and beyond a person's duties. These actions are supererogatory as opposed to obligatory: They are very highly morally good, but no one is required to do them. For example, suppose a person devotes her life to working to end poverty. Her actions are supererogatory because they go above and beyond her moral duties (such as the duty not to lie). The ability of deontological views to distinguish between obligatory and supererogatory acts is often contrasted with consequentialism. This is because one common criticism of consequentialist views—especially classic utilitarianism—is that it demands too much. If, for instance, right actions are those that produce the most happiness, then it looks as if devoting one's life to end poverty rather than, say, reading books, is the right thing to do and therefore morally required; working to end poverty is likely to produce more happiness than spending most of one's time reading books. So, some philosophers view it as a good thing that deontology usually does not make similarly strict demands.

Deontological views involve a number of different issues. First, there is simply the issue of what moral duties a person has. Refraining from lying and refraining from murdering are usually considered moral duties, but what about paying one's taxes or maximizing one's potential? Are these moral duties also? A second issue is whether there are different kinds of moral duties. Kant, for instance, argued that some duties are direct and some are indirect: The former we owe directly to someone or something, and the latter we have only for the sake of someone else (for example, according to Kant, one's duty to treat animals humanely is an indirect duty, a duty we have only for the sake of people, not for animals themselves). Another topic is what makes moral duties moral duties. Consequentialists explain the morality of an action by pointing to its consequences; deontologists need some other explanation for the morality of an action. In addition, what should a person do when her moral duties conflict? Deontologists offer various answers to these questions.

Kant is perhaps the most important philosopher in deontological ethics. Kant believed morality was a matter of reason; that is, it is rational to be moral, and moral principles are themselves based on reason. Kant formulated a moral principle he believed applied universally, a principle he called the *categorical imperative*. For Kant, moral behavior is behavior in accordance with the categorical imperative; immoral behavior is contrary to the categorical imperative. Because the categorical imperative is based on reason and because humans are rational, autonomous beings, the categorical imperative is a principle we can freely impose on ourselves.

The categorical imperative contrasts with a *hypothetical imperative*. An imperative is just a command, such as, "Take out the garbage." A hypothetical imperative is an imperative that is based on having a particular end, or goal. It is hypothetical because it depends on having that goal; if a person does not have a particular, relevant goal, then a given hypothetical imperative does not apply to that person. For example, if someone's goal is to come to school on time, it is a good idea for her to set her alarm clock. So in this instance, a hypothetical imperative is, "If you desire to come to school on time, set your alarm clock." In contrast, a categorical imperative is a command that does not depend on having a particular goal. The categorical imperative applies *categorically*, without exception and without regard to a person's goals. It applies to everyone; that is, everyone ought to behave according to the categorical imperative.

Kant gave several different versions of the categorical imperative, which he believed were equivalent to each other. Perhaps his most famous version is, "Act only according to that maxim by which you can at the same time will that it should become a universal law." By *maxim*, Kant meant principle, or rule. According to this version of the categorical imperative, one should behave only according to principles that one can rationally will that *everyone* should follow in similar circumstances. That is, one should act according to rules that are universalizable. Suppose, for example, someone must decide whether to promise to pay back money she knows she cannot actually repay. To see whether making such a promise is morally acceptable, she must determine what rule she would be following in making that promise. Then she must decide whether she could consistently will that everyone in similar circumstances follow that same rule. If she made a false promise, it looks as if the rule she would be following would be something like, "When you desire a loan but cannot repay it, make a false promise to repay the loan." However, by Kant's lights, this rule is not universalizable: One cannot rationally will that everyone should follow the same rule in similar circumstances. To see why this is so, consider what would happen if everyone followed this rule. Eventually people would stop believing promises made to them about repaying loans. If people stopped believing promises, people would also stop making promises, because there would be no point in making promises if no one believed them. So, if everyone followed the rule "When you desire a loan but cannot repay it, make a false promise to repay the loan," the very practice of promise-keeping would be destroyed. This contradicts the reason for making the false promise in the first place: to take advantage of the practice of promise-keeping. For Kant, then, one cannot rationally will that everyone follow such a rule. Because the rule is not universalizable, it would be a violation of the categorical imperative to make the false promise to pay back the loan. So, one has a moral duty to refrain from making a false promise, not just in this instance, but in *all* instances. Kant called duties that one always has an obligation to follow, such as the duty not to make false promises, *perfect duties*. Another example of a perfect duty, according to Kant, is the duty not to lie. So, for Kant, moral behavior involves universal moral rules that should not ever be broken.

Kant also formulated the categorical imperative this way: "Act so that you treat humanity, whether in your own person or in that of another, always as an end and never as a means only." To treat someone as an end is contrasted with treating someone as a means only, that is, only as a tool for some purpose or other. For example, to spend time with a person only for the sake of borrowing money from her, or only for one's own sexual pleasure, are instances of treating a person as a means only. Kant believed that humans are intrinsically valuable: That is, they are valuable in and of themselves, not just because they are useful for fulfilling some purpose or another. He also believed that humans are uniquely valuable because of the human capacity for rationality and autonomy. According to Kant, because humans have these traits, they have a certain dignity, and treating people as a means only wrongly ignores that dignity. To treat a person as an *end*, then, is to treat her as valuable in and of herself, respecting her dignity, rationality, and autonomy. This does not mean that one cannot ever morally treat a person as a means, as when one uses the services of a clerk in order to buy groceries, say; it just means that one cannot ever morally treat a person as a means *only*.

So, for Kant, morality is rational, and moral actions must be consistent with the categorical imperative. Yet Kant believed that just because an action is consistent with the categorical imperative does not in itself make that action morally valuable. Kant wrote that the only thing that is (morally) good without qualification is a good will. Put another way, only a good will can be said to be simply, unreservedly good. To have a good will in performing some action is to perform that action with the intention of doing one's duty for the sake of doing one's duty. To return to the example of making a false promise, if a person refrains from making a false promise because she fears that her false promise will hurt her in the long run (say, it will destroy a friendship she values), then for Kant her action lacks moral worth. It is not that her action is immoral (it is, after all, consistent with the categorical imperative). But it is not morally valuable. For Kant, her action would have moral worth only if, in addition to being consistent with the categorical imperative, she performed it out of duty—in other words, only if she chose to tell the truth and refrained from making a false promise because she wanted to do her duty for its own sake. Note that this implies that if a person performs some action because she *wants* to, not for the sake of duty, that action does not have moral worth. For example, suppose a lifeguard rescued a drowning child because she wanted to save the child's life, hating the thought of seeing the child suffer and possibly die. In this instance, saving the child lacks moral worth (again, this is not the same thing as being morally wrong). The lifeguard's action would have moral worth only if the lifeguard saved the child from duty, for the sake of duty.

This might sound odd. Yet to see why Kant believed that only a good will is good without qualification, consider that other character traits can be used for bad purposes. For example, one might think that courage is a virtue, and therefore that courage is of moral worth. Yet a person might be courageous for bad purposes—for instance, a person might deliberately put herself at great risk in order to perform a terrorist act. In this instance, courage does not seem to be a good thing. Courage, then, is not good without qualification. Similarly, in our case of the lifeguard, suppose the lifeguard is motivated by a desire not to see the child suffer—suppose the lifeguard is motivated by compassion. But arguably even compassion can be used to bad ends. For example, it would be bad for a parent to let a child have whatever it wants—such as not to be vaccinated against certain illnesses and to spend all one's time playing—out of a feeling of compassion, so as not to cause the child pain. By contrast, however, a good will is always good.

One important criticism of Kant's ethics, due to Elizabeth Anscombe, is that it seems possible to describe the same action in different ways, so that the same action can be said to be following different rules. For example, making a particular false promise might be said to follow the rule, "Make a false promise when it is convenient," but it might also be said to follow the rule, "Make a false promise when doing so will save an innocent person's life." Whereas the first rule might not be universalizable, perhaps the second one is. This suggests that Kant's universalizability principle is not a very good guide for how one should behave morally (whether an action violates the categorical imperative depends on how the action is described, and it is not always clear how an action should be described). Another criticism is that sometimes absolute moral rules conflict, and in those cases it is not clear how one should behave.

As noted, Kant believed that the categorical imperative applies universally: Under no circumstances is it morally permissible to violate the categorical imperative. In one famous discussion, for instance, Kant thought that it was morally wrong even to lie to a killer about the location of the killer's next intended victim, although telling the killer the truth likely means an innocent person will die. For Kant, lying is not universalizable; as it violates the categorical imperative, it is not morally acceptable to lie even to save a person's life. However, not all deontological theories hold that moral duties can ever acceptably be violated; whether they can is one important issue in deontology. Perhaps it is not morally permissible to lie just for the sake of making people happy. But some people believe it is permissible to lie in order save an innocent person's life. For another example, suppose killing one innocent person will prevent two other innocent people from being killed. Is the first killing morally permissible? The view that sometimes it is morally permissible, or even obligatory, not to do one's usual duty (such as refraining from killing innocent people) is *threshold deontology*. The idea in threshold deontology is that sometimes the consequences of doing one's usual duty would be so bad that one should not do so (there is a metaphorical threshold of bad consequences).

Karl Marx

Historically, some philosophers reacted against deontology. Karl Marx (1818–83), for example, influenced by Georg W. F. Hegel (1770–1831), believed that how we understand the world and how we understand even ourselves is shaped by economic conditions and structures. According to Marx, for any economic base, there is an *ideological superstructure* built upon it. By this he meant that people come to have beliefs and values, but that those beliefs and values are a result of living within certain economic structures. For example, a capitalist economic structure has relations of production that are private (that is, individuals own the factories and the businesses). As a result, Marx claimed, certain beliefs and values arise that reflect this economic structure and that promote this economic structure. Put another way, the moral values that arise within a capitalist system benefit those who are in power (those who own factories and businesses) and serve to keep powerless those who are not in power (the ordinary workers). So, Marx said, within a capitalist system, an emphasis arises on individual priority and privacy, with the result that people value individualism and a political, legal system that protects individual rights and limited government (and downplays community or responsibility to others). Briefly, then, Marx's view is that people must produce in order to survive; in order to produce, there must be some mode of production (that is, means and organization, or materials and relations of production); social relations and patterns result from the mode of production, resulting in political, social, philosophical beliefs and values that reflect and promote that mode of production.

Friedrich Nietzsche

Following Kant, another philosopher critical of Kant and deontology was Friedrich Nietzsche (1844–1900). Nietzsche's view of moral values was complex and cannot be understood wholly without an understanding of his famous claim that God is dead (a claim Nietzsche's character Zarathustra makes in *Thus Spoke Zarathustra* and which Nietzsche repeated in *The Gay Science*). By saying that God was dead, Nietzsche did not mean that God had literally died; he did not believe God literally existed in the first place. Rather, Nietzsche's point was that God had ceased to play a significant role in people's lives. In other words, although people might talk as if they believed in God and lived by God's commands, as a matter of fact belief in God made very little difference to them. Yet the death of God (in this sense) raised a serious question about morality. Many people had once regarded God as the basis for morality. But if God does not tell us what is morally right and wrong, then what does? Nietzsche's answer was that, with the death of God, we are free to create our own values. To put the point another way, because God does not provide the basis for morality, we must decide for ourselves what is good and what is not, what is worth valuing and what is not.

Although Nietzsche believed we are free to create our own values and decide for ourselves what is good and what is not, he clearly thought that some views about what is good (and what is not) are better than others. In *On the Genealogy of Morals* and other works, Nietzsche distinguished between two different kinds of morality: master morality and slave morality. Master morality is positive in the sense that it is concerned mainly with the good, rather than being preoccupied with what it considers bad. For the master moralist, what is good concerns creativity and merit, achievement versus mediocrity. The master moralist is also strong and independent; she does not feel compelled to behave or think as others do but instead has the strength to forge her own path. (Unfortunately, Nietzsche's comments on strength and morality, among other topics, have sometimes been linked to Nazism.

Photograph of Erwin Rohde, Carl von Gersdorff, and Friedrich Nietzsche in 1871 *(Photograph by Friedrich Henning)*

However, Nietzsche consistently opposed anti-Semitism.) Slave morality is a reaction against master morality, and in that sense it is mainly negative. In particular, what motivates slave morality is resentment against the strong. Because the slave moralist fears and resents strength and excellence that it cannot (or perhaps, does not) achieve, the slave moralist values weakness instead. Consider, for example, someone who would like to act as an individual rather than merely going along with the crowd but who does not have the inner strength to do so; she might come to resent the person who does. Similarly, someone who cannot achieve the greatness of a first-class artist or scientist might resent people who can. Reacting against them, she prefers to keep everyone at her level. So, whereas master morality strives for excellence, slave morality prefers that everyone remain mediocre. Whereas master morality is a morality of independence and achievement, slave morality is a morality of the "crowd" in a negative sense, or to use Nietzsche's term, *the herd*.

Nietzsche clearly preferred master morality to slave morality. However, he believed that in a historic struggle against master morality and slave morality, slave morality had won, and he associated slave morality with Christianity in particular. For example, he viewed traditional Christian virtues such as meekness and humility as being motivated by fear rather than by a genuine sense of harmony with others. In general, Nietzsche's critique of Christian morality is based largely on the view that it is life-denying rather than life-affirming. To put the point another way, Nietzsche regarded Christianity as being in opposition to a life of flourishing and achievement and in favor of a meek, passive existence instead. One reason for this is simply Christianity's focus on otherworldly entities such as God and soul; Nietzsche believed these were illusions and that Christianity irrationally focused on them at the expense of our real lives on Earth. In addition, Nietzsche charged Christianity with being life-denying by rejecting human instincts (such as sexuality) and passions. (In his assessment of Christianity, Nietzsche distinguished between Jesus and Christianity as a body of thought and was much more critical of the latter.)

Formalism and Social Contract Theory

Formalist approaches to ethics focus less on content than on the form of an ethical theory, particularly as it relates to ethical issues in social contexts. That is, rather than saying specifically what is right, formalists focus on formal procedures or structures for determining what is right. One version of formalism is social contract theory (also called contractualism). *Social contract theory* is a term both for a view in political philosophy and in ethics. In political philosophy, social contract theory is the view that a government somehow derives its legitimacy from the consent of the people it governs (it is as though there is a contract between a legitimate government and the people). In ethics, social contract theory is the view that morality consists of rules that rational, self-interested people would agree upon (it is as though people agree on a contract about how they can and cannot behave, in order best to promote their own interests). A central idea of social contract theory is that individual people are all better off cooperating with each other than they would be if they did not do so. Social contract theorists typically view humans as rational, self-interested beings who would, therefore, actually be motivated to cooperate with each other.

To illustrate why cooperation is advantageous for everyone, philosophers such as Thomas Hobbes (1588–1679), John Locke (1632–1704), and Jacques Rousseau (1712–78), each very influential in social contract theory, imagined humans living in a state in which people did not cooperate, a state without rules or government. This imaginary state is the state of nature, and philosophers described it in different ways. Hobbes, for example, described the state of nature as a state in which everyone was at war with everyone else. According to Hobbes, people tend to act to further their own interests. The problem is that in the state of nature there are not enough resources to go around; everyone would selfishly compete for the same resources, attacking others to pursue her own ends. Yet no one could ever truly gain the upper hand, for the reason that people are roughly equal in their abilities (even the strongest person would not be safe from harmful attacks). Life in the state of nature, Hobbes famously said, would be "solitary, poor, nasty, brutish, and short." To escape the state of nature, people must agree to cooperate; they must agree to abide by certain rules. They must also agree on a way to enforce those rules, because otherwise people would break them to pursue their own self-interest. In Hobbes's view, a ruler must enforce those rules, and the ruler's political authority must be absolute, for only then could the ruler enforce the rules. Although granting absolute political power to a ruler might sound unattractive today, Hobbes believed that it would be rational: Only by doing so could one escape the state of nature and attain peace and security. So, as rational, self-interested beings, humans would agree to do so.

John Locke offered a more optimistic account of the state of nature. According to Locke, in the state of nature, people are equal and enjoy perfect freedom. Locke also believed that people have natural rights, even in the state of nature, such as the right to life, in addition to the moral duties not to attack others, restrict the freedom of others, or harm their property. Yet because people do not always abide by those rights (and because some people are less capable than others of defending their natural rights), people agree to abide by certain rules in order better to ensure the safety and security of each person. Like Hobbes, then, Locke thought of a social contract as an agreement made by rational people who seek to protect their own interests (although, unlike Hobbes, Locke did not think that the social contract should involve ceding power to an absolute monarch).

Social contract theorists disagree about the importance of whether people actually formed a social contract in the past. Those who believe that people did form such a contract face the question of why the contract would apply to the descendants of the people who initially made the contract (if the descendants never agreed to the contract, why should they be bound by its rules?). For other social contract theorists, the important point is that a social contract provides a good way of understanding what morality consists of. In this view, the contract is hypothetical: Historically speaking, people never made such a social contract to escape the state of nature, but the notion of a social contract clarifies the nature of morality (or the legitimacy of a government).

More contemporary proponents of social contract theory are David Gauthier (1932–) and John Rawls (1921–2002). Rawls used social contract theory to give an account of justice as fairness. He was concerned to rule out built-in biases that make society unjust, for instance, racism, sexism, etc. He was also specifically concerned with social institutions related to the distribution of wealth and opportunities in society (for example, related questions include, Who should get to fill certain professions or hold political office? Who should be taxed, and how much?). Rawls proposed that just social institutions are those that abide by principles that free, rational people would agree on under certain conditions. To illustrate, Rawls posed a hypothetical situation, which he referred to as the original position. In the original position, people are assumed to be self-interested and rational. That is, they are concerned about their own well-being and interests (not necessarily at the expense of others), and they are usually quite clever about how to advance their own well-being and interests (that is, they are rational). Rawls asked what sorts of principles of justice rational, self-interested people would adopt and accept if they knew nothing about themselves other than that they will live under these principles that they establish. That is, they would not know if they were male or female, young or old, white or black (or some other race), gay or straight, etc. Rawls referred to this as being behind a veil of ignorance, meaning ignorance concerning these details about oneself. For example, if someone suggested that only whites could hold elected offices, would a rational, self-interested person agree to this—not knowing whether or not he was white? Rawls thought that, no, a rational, self-interested person would not accept such a suggestion. After all, once the veil of ignorance is lifted, if that person turned out not to be white, he would be barred from holding political office.

Rawls claimed that from behind such a veil of ignorance, rational, self-interested people would formulate two fundamental principles of justice. The first he called the equality principle. This principle states that each person is to have an equal right to the most extensive basic liberty compatible with a similar liberty for others. This simply means that everyone is socially and politically equal with respect to what rights and liberties they have. However, people are different, and unequal, in various ways. A rational, self-interested person would want to acknowledge and accept many of those differences and would not consider some differences to be the cause of injustice. For example, one person might not care to make a lot of money, while another person might be very interested in making money. If so, there is nothing inherently unjust about one person working hard to make a lot of money while another person spent time relaxing and not making a lot of money. There would result an unequal distribution of wealth, but in itself that would not be unfair or unjust. So, Rawls said that behind the veil of ignorance, rational, self-interested people would come up with a second principle of justice, which he called the difference principle. This principle states that social and economic inequalities are to be arranged so that they are both (a) reasonably expected to be to everyone's advantage, and (b) attached to positions and offices open to all. This simply means that rational, self-interested people would accept differences in terms of having social goods as long as those differences served their self-interest.

Finally, Rawls suggested that people who are behind a veil of ignorance—and, so, cannot build in biases to the basic social systems—would agree to a single, basic principle of justice: All social values—liberty and opportunity, income and wealth, and the bases of self-respect—are to be distributed equally unless an unequal distribution of any, or all, of these values is to everyone's advantage.

As a way of explaining morality, social contract theory enjoys certain attractions. First, people do commonly act in self-interested ways. A theory that takes that fact into account is a good theory in the sense that it does not make unrealistic demands (say, that people should often ignore their own interests). Second, it also provides a reason for why people ought to behave morally: Doing so is ultimately in one's own best interests. Like other philosophical views, however, social contract theory has its detractors. One significant objection is that, as a theory of morality, social contract theory seems to leave out morally important beings. If morality is a set of rules agreed on between rational, self-interested beings, those rules would not seem to apply to beings who are incapable of forming an agreement in the first place. Nonhuman animals, infants, and severely brain-damaged people, for example, are not capable of agreeing to abide by rules in the way that normally functioning adult humans are. Yet many people believe we have moral obligations to those beings as well: It is not okay to torture animals or infants, for instance, even if they cannot come to an agreement about refraining from torture. Critics charge that insofar as social contract theory does not make room for such moral obligations, the theory is mistaken. Other criticisms of social contract theory come from feminist philosophers and philosophers focusing on race. Some argue that social contract theory is used, not to advance just government or just institutions, but to continue existing social inequalities (for example, inequalities between white people and black people). Another criticism is that the "rational, self-interested" individual so often described in social contract theory is described from a male perspective and therefore does not represent how humans in general actually are; in particular, the concern is that it wrongly ignores qualities and experiences associated with women.

Communitarianism

Communitarianism is the name of a particular political philosophy, but is also relevant in ethics. The root of the name is *community*, and a fundamental focus of communitarianism is the importance and centrality of community. The basic assumption of communitarianism is that individuals live *within* communities, not that communities just happen to be a collection of individuals. An important aspect of our social lives is that both individuals and communities must be respected and valued. Communitarianism includes both a negative, critical part and a positive, constructive part. The negative part focuses on criticisms of other political philosophies, especially libertarianism and liberalism. The positive part focuses on advocating certain social and political policies and practices, specifically, ones that value communities as well as the individuals within them.

For communitarians, liberalism (and the particular version of it called libertarianism) sees individuals as the primary, and perhaps only, things that matter for social and political concerns. Liberalism, they say, sees groups of people—including whole communities and societies and cultures—as just collections of individuals. Individuals are the things that have value and rights; groups have value and rights only to the extent that they derive them from individuals. Communitarians acknowledge that the powers and rights of individuals are very important. However, they claim that the view of liberalism is mistaken about the very nature of individuals. A phrase that communitarians use when they criticize liberalism is "the unencumbered self." By this phrase they mean that liberalism sees individuals as separate, unique, and fundamentally isolated entities who just happen to be part of communities. Communitarians disagree. They say that people are inherently, and always, members within communities. Communities are not simply add-ons, they say; rather, people are at their core communal, social beings.

A consequence of this view that we are not unencumbered selves is, for communitarians, the recognition of a balance between rights and responsibilities. They claim that liberalism only speaks of the rights of individuals, not of their responsibilities—other than not to infringe on the rights of other individuals. There is an overemphasis on individual rights, say communitarians, which is based on this view of the unencumbered self, and the result is that this leads to the neglect of care for others or for the common good. But, they argue, we need to balance the rights and freedoms of individuals with the rights and care of communities. Liberalism focuses on individuals' rights *against* communities. This might include, for example, an individual's right to distribute certain offensive material (such as racist or sexist literature) or say offensive things (such as racist or sexist slurs). Communitarians claim that these rights and freedoms must be balanced with the rights *of* communities and understood always as rights *within* communities.

In addition to claiming that people are not unencumbered selves, communitarians also say that liberalism's emphasis on individual rights and freedoms misses the point of why rights and freedoms matter. Communitarians say that what is important about having rights and freedoms is not simply that other people do not get to tell you what to do (or not do). The real importance of rights and freedoms, they say, is that rights and freedoms help people to fulfill their possibilities and potentials. In other words, what is important about rights and freedoms is not merely being free from the constraints and dictates of others; instead, the importance is that we are free to do and accomplish things. For communitarians, the freedom to simply sit around and watch television or play video games is a freedom that has little purpose or value. Rights and freedoms, they say, should be a basic part of living well, of the quality of life, in other words, of a good life. But a good life, they say, necessarily includes concern for community, because who we are as individuals is not isolated from who we are within communities.

Communitarians emphasize balancing rights with responsibilities and the good of individuals with the good of communities. This is one way that communitarians stress the need to be concerned with what is *good* as much as with what is *right*. These two terms—*good* and *right*—do not mean the same thing, although they are related. Good involves content; that is, some things are good for people and other things are not, they are bad for people. For example, smoking is bad for people. Right, on the other hand, does not necessarily involve content (or goods). Some actions or decisions are right, while others are wrong. For example, we might say that fulfilling one's duties is the right thing to do, whatever the content of those duties are. Communitarians claim that some actions and decisions are bad, even if they might be right in the sense that people are free to perform those actions or make those decisions.

Egoism

Another view in normative ethics is ethical egoism, the view that people should always act in their own self-interest. According to *psychological egoism*, people are always in fact motivated to act to promote their own self-interest. So psychological egoism is a view about how people actually behave, while *ethical egoism* is a view about how people *ought* to behave. The term *egoism* is derived from the Latin word *ego*, meaning "I." So, egoist views are views centered on the individual (an ethical egoist thinks she should act for the sake of *her* interests, not for the sake of others' interests). Egoism is not the same as egotism (when a person regards herself as more important than she really is).

One prominent advocate of ethical egoism was the Russian-American novelist and philosopher Ayn Rand (1905–82), who defended what she called "the virtue of selfishness." According to ethical egoism, the only moral obligation one has is to promote one's own interests (this contrasts with *altruism*, the quality of acting for others' benefit for their own sakes). Precisely what a person's interests are is another issue. Hedonism is the view that one's interests—what is good for one—just consists of pleasure. Another view, associated with ancient philosophy, is that one's interests consist of living virtuously; in this case, acting to promote one's own interests turns out also to be acting in such virtuous ways as being just, courageous, and a good friend. Another view might be that one's interest is to maximize one's potential. Any of these answers (and others) are open to the ethical egoist, who as an ethical egoist need only claim that one's only moral obligation is to promote one's own interest, whatever that happens to be. This does not mean that, according to ethical egoism, one should never help others. One might indeed do so; however, according to ethical egoism, one is morally obligated to do so only if helping others promotes one's own interests. In addition, acting always and only in one's own interests does not necessarily mean acting only for one's short-term interests. For instance, it might be in one's short-term interest to sleep in every day, because it would be pleasurable and afford one plenty of rest. However, it is not in one's long-term interests, because doing well in school and work generally requires getting there on time (and doing well in school and work generally promotes one's long-term interests).

Ethical egoism seems inconsistent with some ordinary moral beliefs—for example, the belief that one should help one's friends for their own sakes, or that one is morally obligated to save an innocent life, at least if one can do so at minimal cost to oneself. (For instance, turning right-side-up a baby who is lying facedown in a puddle would prevent the baby from drowning at no cost to oneself.) One important objection to ethical egoism is based on the principle of impartiality. According to this principle, one should treat people alike unless there is some difference between them that justifies treating them differently. For example, it is not morally justifiable to allow men to vote but not allow women to vote just on the basis of the difference in sex: A person's sex is not morally relevant when it comes to the right to vote. On the other hand, allowing adults to vote while refusing to allow toddlers to vote seems justifiable, because there are morally relevant differences between adults and toddlers (among other differences, adults are typically capable of understanding the consequences of their votes, whereas toddlers are not). What ethical egoism essentially says is that one should put one's own interests ahead of the interests of others. The problem is that there seems to be no reason why one should treat one's interests in a different, better way than the interests of others. Just because one's interests are one's own does not seem to make them more worthwhile. In short, there seems to be no morally relevant difference between oneself and other people that would justify treating oneself differently, and better, than treating everyone else. So, according to the criticism, ethical egoism violates the principle of impartiality.

Feminist Ethics

Like philosophy in general, ethics has historically been dominated by men. In the 20th century, some philosophers have approached ethics in ways intended to respect and incorporate the moral experiences of women, experiences that (according to critics) traditional ethics ignores or regards as inferior. In addition, some philosophers working in ethics have adopted a positive, proactive attitude toward freeing women from social attitudes, beliefs, practices, and institutions that oppress them. We can call such approaches to ethics that share one or both of these characteristics feminist ethics. Feminist ethics includes diverse approaches, views, and perspectives. Some philosophers believe the role of feminist ethics is to enrich and add to traditional views in ethics, such as utilitarianism and deontology. Others believe that feminist ethics should replace these views rather than merely supplement them; on this perspective, feminist ethics is an alternative to other, male-dominated ethical theories.

Alison Jaggar (1942–), a contemporary American philosopher, noted several important ways in which traditional ethics devalues women. First, important philosophers such as Kant explicitly claimed that women were morally inferior to men, on the grounds for instance that women cannot reason about moral issues as well as men. Second, philosophers devalued virtues associated with women (such as cooperation and caring) in favor of virtues associated with men (such as autonomy and reason). Third, they ignored areas of moral concern that are relevant to women in particular, such as issues related to home life (for instance, how should one balance a career with family? how should

Sigmund Freud, ca. 1905 *(Photograph by Ludwig Grillich)*

children be raised?). Fourth, they regarded as less legitimate a feminine approach to ethical issues, an approach involving emotions (not just reason) and focusing on relationships rather than on abstract principles. Many philosophers, including those who do not explicitly identify themselves as feminists, agree with at least some of these criticisms. On the assumption that all or most of Jaggar's criticisms of traditional ethics are sound, it is a further question how to remedy the male-centered focus of traditional ethics.

One influential response has been the ethics of care, often understood as a kind of virtue ethics. Ethics of care focuses on traits such as caring and an approach to moral issues that emphasizes personal relationships and responsibilities. Two important philosophers in the ethics of care are Carol Gilligan (1936–   ) and Nel Noddings (1929–   ). In 1982, Carol Gilligan published *In a Different Voice: Psychological Theory and Women's Development.* In that work, Gilligan charged that some theorists on morality and moral development, including Sigmund Freud (1856–1939) and the psychologist Lawrence Kohlberg (1927–87), viewed women as morally inferior to men because these theorists wrongly privileged a male perspective. Gilligan's critique of Kohlberg has been especially influential. Kohlberg theorized that humans go through six stages of moral development. In the first stage, for example, children do what they are told because they fear punishment and hope to be rewarded. By the third stage (dubbed the "good boy–nice girl" stage), in adolescence, people have advanced morally enough that they are not motivated solely by fear of punishment or hope of reward; instead, they perform their expected social roles to be liked, loved, and approved of by others. Kohlberg's final and sixth stage of moral development is the adoption of universal moral principles, as when adults live by principles such as that one should respect the rights of others. In Kohlberg's view, the sixth stage of moral development represents the highest and best stage of moral development. So, for Kohlberg, it is better to behave on the basis of universal moral principles than for any other reason, such as to maintain positive relationships. Women often stop at stage three of Kohlberg's scale, however, while men usually reach stage four or higher. In Gilligan's view, this was not because men are in fact morally superior to women. Rather, it was because Kohlberg's stages of moral development are biased toward a male perspective. Males, according to Gilligan, are more likely, when they think about ethics, to think in terms of rights and justice. But females, Gilligan argued, are more likely to think in terms of personal relationships and responsibilities. For example, a boy might argue that someone should not steal medicine because stealing is wrong; a girl might say that it is okay for someone to steal medicine if without it his wife would die, or the girl might suggest that the man talk to the people who sold the medicine to see if something can be worked out. What this suggests is that Kohlberg's stages do not accurately represent how humans in general morally develop. They reflect an ethics of justice; but an alternative to the male ethics of rights is a feminine ethics of care. Gilligan noted that males as well as females can view ethical concerns in terms of care, and that females as well as males can view ethical concerns in terms of justice. However, she focused on ethics of care as illustrated by females in particular.

Nel Noddings developed a feminine ethics of care, which in her view better captures our actual moral experiences and our moral obligations than an ethics based on universal moral rules. Indeed, to Noddings, *all* of one's moral obligations can be understood in terms of caring. Noddings distinguished between the one who cares (the *one-caring*) and the one who is cared for (the *cared-for*). Caring does not just mean always giving the cared-for what she wants. For instance, a child might want to eat nothing but candy, but a caring mother is not likely to give in to that desire, because she understands that the child's genuine, objective need is to eat a nutritious diet. For Noddings, caring is also not just a matter of feeling a particular way; rather, caring involves specific actions toward specific people. For instance, a person who professes to care about his mother but never visits or contacts her (although he can) cannot be said actually to care for his mother. Caring involves what Noddings called *engrossment,* a regard for the cared-for and that person's well-being; engrossment involves coming to know the genuine needs, interests, and desires of the cared-for. Caring also involves *motivational displacement,* a desire to act for the sake of those needs, interests, and desires. Moreover, because for Noddings, caring involves specific people with whom one has a relationship, one cannot be said to "care" for refugees in a distant country, for instance. So, actions such as donating money to help starving strangers, for example, are not examples of caring, and according to Noddings one does not have obligations to help people in general, independent of specific caring relationships. Noddings also describes caring as reciprocal: In a genuine caring relationship, the cared-for acknowledges the care of the one-caring.

According to its advocates, one advantage of ethics of care over other ethical theories is that ethics of care does not try to apply abstract rules to every moral situation. This is in line with the common feminist criticism that abstract, universal rules are not a good way of understanding moral experience or approaching moral issues. This is because the actual situations we face involve real people in particular circumstances. Knowing how to respond morally in situations—such as whether to tell a friend a lie, or whether to let a child attend a particular movie—requires knowing and understanding the details of those situations and the people with whom we have relationships. Abstract rules do not capture the particularity of moral experience. In addition, ethics of care takes into account the role of emotion in our moral lives: Sometimes what a person feels matters morally. For example, it is morally good to visit a sick friend because one cares for her friend and wants to see her, and it seems morally wrong to visit a sick friend *only* out of duty. A third apparent advantage in ethics of care is that it accounts for the fact that personal relationships matter morally: We seem to have special moral obligations to friends and family, for instance, in ways we do not have toward strangers (one is not usually morally obligated to visit a sick stranger in the hospital, for instance).

Noddings envisaged ethics of care as replacing traditional ethical theories. For Noddings and other advocates of ethics of care, ethics of care applies to men as well as women. After all, humans are social beings who form personal relationships, so on one view it makes sense that this fundamental fact would provide a basis for ethics. However, critics note that ethics of care tends to focus on women. This is problematic because if women are inherently better at caring than men, then it is not obvious that ethics of care offers an ethics for men *and* women, or whether instead it replaces a female-centered ethics with a male-centered ethics. But if a male-centered ethics is flawed, it is not obvious why a female-entered ethics would be less flawed. One response to this is to see an ethics of care as enriching other ethical theories (but not replacing them). Some feminist critics also charge that there is a danger in focusing too much on women as those who care. By caring too much, women run the risk of losing their own identities and sacrificing their own legitimate needs. On this criticism, the danger is more acute because the status of women is not equal to that of men in the first place, since societies are male-dominated.

Lesbian ethics is another field within feminist ethics. Lesbian ethics has focused on women who love women, as distinct from ethics associated with heterosexual relationships. Thinking of women as simply women, on one view, is associated with particular relationships between men and women, and in particular with men as dominant over women. Because lesbians stand outside heterosexual relationships, the idea is that their values can be distinct from those relationships. One theme in some feminist ethics is the importance of lesbians making choices, with the aim of promoting their own freedom. In addition to ethics of care and lesbian ethics, some feminist philosophers in ethics have also linked feminism to environmental issues. Some argue, for example, that there is a close relationship between the oppression of women and abuse of the environment.

Applied Ethics

Applied ethics is the study of particular, practical ethical issues, such as capital punishment, abortion, or euthanasia. As the label implies, applied ethics applies normative ethical accounts to particular issues. Some philosophers claim that applied ethics is not really a separate area of ethics but is essentially normative ethics focused on particular topics or applications. However, other philosophers say that the focused emphasis in applied ethics is what distinguishes it from normative ethics, in the sense that normative ethics also involves the analysis and evaluation of different normative theories, something that is not the focus of applied ethics. Still other philosophers claim that by applying those normative theories to particular issues, such as abortion or euthanasia, applied ethics actually does engage in the analysis and evaluation of normative theories, since these particular issues provide evidence of the meaningfulness and relevance of those normative theories. That is, if a normative ethical theory, such as utilitarianism, cannot be applied to particular ethical issues or seems to be inadequate in resolving those issues, then the application of that theory to particular issues constitutes an evaluation of it (a negative evaluation). In effect, the applied issues are the tests for evaluating those normative theories. Whether or not applied ethics is a separate area than normative ethics (and whether or not it matters), the focus on applied ethics is addressing particular ethical and moral issues.

Philosophers often speak of various subfields within applied ethics, such as media ethics, business ethics, bioethics, sports ethics, education ethics, etc. The point is that there are particular ethical and moral issues that arise in connection with certain concerns. Media ethics is focused on ethical and moral issues that arise in the context of news media (for example, the appropriate role of the news media or questions of privacy and confidentiality in news reporting), while bioethics is focused on ethical and moral issues that arise in connection with medicine and health care (for example, abortion and euthanasia, as well as stem cell research and appropriate allocation of health resources).

In addition, there are particular topics that are subject to the analysis of applied ethics. Besides some that have already been mentioned, such as euthanasia, there are broad, general social issues that are investigated in applied ethics, such as hunger and poverty, violence and war, and racial and gender discrimination (as well as other forms of discrimination). Applied ethics considers the ethical and moral issues connected to these topics, as opposed to the economic or legal issues (although there is often a great deal of overlap between the ethical/moral issues and the economic/legal issues). For instance, with respect to capital punishment, a purely sociological question might be whether or not capital punishment actually deters future crimes. This is a straightforward empirical, factual question. An applied ethics question might be whether or not capital punishment can be justified, regardless of whether or not it actually deters future crimes. Or another applied ethics question would be what, if anything, justifies capital punishment—for example, would deterring future crimes be enough to justify capital punishment?—as well as how this could be determined.

The method of applied ethics is to investigate how normative ethical theories or principles or concerns relate to the particular issue at hand. For example, with capital punishment, the question might be: Is capital punishment right? The first step is to be clear on what exactly is being asked. This question might mean: Is capital punishment, as opposed to other forms of punishment, a morally acceptable practice? That is different than the question: Is capital punishment, as opposed to other forms of punishment, the morally best practice? Other questions need to be asked that are ethically and morally related, such as: For whom is capital punishment acceptable/best/etc.? (Is it good/best for society generally, for the person being punished, for particular victims of some crime, etc.?)

Usually, what follows is the analysis and evaluation of some particular moral judgment or claim. For instance, someone might say: Capital punishment is right for capital crimes. (This means that the death penalty is right for crimes in which someone killed someone else.) When asked to justify this claim, two sorts of support are usually given. On one hand, there are relevant conditions that are given. As an example, someone who favored capital punishment might provide the factual data that capital punishment (seems to) deter future crimes. It certainly deters that particular individual from committing future crimes! If that person is executed, then she will not commit future crimes. But, furthermore, one might say that the practice of capital punishment deters others from committing future (capital) crimes. This is one sort of support that is given to the moral judgment, namely, relevant conditions or information. However, it is still legitimate to ask why deterring future crimes justifies capital punishment. Here, the second sort of support is given, and this sort of support is some form of normative ethical theory or principle or concern. For instance, someone might say that deterring future crime is good because it makes everyone better off. This claim turns out to be an application of utilitarianism. It is here that the normative ethical matter is applied to this particular issue. That is, it is the application of some ethical norm that shows the relation between the moral judgment and the relevant conditions or information already mentioned. If we did not care for the general happiness of people, then it would not matter that capital punishment deters future crimes (assuming that it actually does). Without the application of some ethical norm, the moral judgment would not be connected to the conditions or information that was offered. This can be seen (again) from the opposite side of this issue of capital punishment. Suppose someone claimed that capital punishment is not right for capital crimes. Why not? This person might argue that if killing is wrong, then it is wrong period; it is wrong for the state to execute someone just as much as it is wrong for that person to have killed someone. If questioned about this view, the person might say that the reason it is wrong is because it violates a person's right to life and rights should not be violated. (Or, perhaps, the person might say that the reason it is wrong is because life is sacred and no one, including the state, should violate the sanctity of life.) Again, the point is that an ethical norm—in this case the norm of respecting rights or respecting the sanctity of life—is being applied to this particular issue in order to justify the particular moral claim. It is in this sense that applied ethics is said actually to apply (normative) ethics. It is said to show how normative ethics relates to particular issues; it relates by providing a necessary component in justifying a moral claim or perspective on some particular topic.

Finally, the method of applied ethics not only asks other relevant ethical questions and shows how ethical norms relate to the justification of particular moral claims but also considers what relevant ethical and moral assumptions as well as implications go along with a moral judgment or claim for a particular issue. That is, in addressing the ethical and moral issues related to a particular topic, there might well be relevant value assumptions that underlie the particular moral claim or issue. In the case of capital punishment, a nonmoral assumption might be that capital punishment is reserved for capital crimes, as opposed to other sorts of crimes. A moral assumption might be that the taking of life is only for God to decide, not for humans, or that a certain level of human life is necessary for the taking of that life to be a moral crime. (For instance, some people claim that the taking of the life of an unborn human fetus is not a crime; others say it is a capital crime and deserves capital punishment.) Besides identifying and evaluating underlying assumptions, another aspect of applied ethics is to identify and evaluate implications of a particular moral claim or judgment. For example, if someone says that capital punishment is legitimate because it deters future crimes and that this itself is legitimate because of its utilitarian value, then one should analyze and evaluate the implications of that justification. Would it then follow, for instance, that if torture deterred future crimes and would have utilitarian value, then torture would be justified? This is the sort of question about implications that would be asked in the context of applied ethics.

Bioethics and Medical Ethics

The term *bioethics* refers to ethical and moral issues that arise in connection with biology. This covers a wide array of topics: cloning, stem cell research and applications, genetically modified organisms (particularly for use in the food industry), the right to life, public health policies, and many others. Although bioethics covers many topics, most of the time the term *bioethics* is used to refer to ethical and moral issues that arise in connection with health care and medicine. *Medical ethics* is a closely related term, regarding ethical and moral issues related to the practice of medicine and health care. Not all bioethical issues are medical ethical issues—for example, the genetic engineering of food is not. (One important topic relating biology to ethics and morality is what has come to be known as evolutionary ethics. Evolutionary ethics is about the development of ethical and moral practices and standards as explained by evolutionary theory. This topic is quite unrelated to what is usually covered within health care or medical ethics.)

Restricting the notion of bioethics to topics connected to health care and medicine, there are many ethical and moral issues that arise. Some of these issues are broadly about the very concepts of health care and medicine. That is, what exactly are health care and medicine? Taking medicine first, people usually think of it as the products and treatments and therapies that are provided for people once they get sick or have an injury or suffer some ailment (either physical or mental). However, there are various different notions of what medicine is, some of them focusing on preventive care (such as good nutrition, healthy living practices, etc.), some of them focusing on health treatment once a person is harmed or impaired in some way or other, and some of them focusing on general maintenance of health. These various notions blend over into general conceptions of health and health care, so that health (and health care) involves more than taking medicines or having certain treatments or therapies. Ethical and moral issues arise here in the sense of an individual's personal responsibility for his or her health as well as with the related issue of having a right to health care. Some people have argued that a right to health care carries with it a responsibility of individuals to engage in actions and practices that do not put them at risk in terms of their health. For example, if a person smokes heavily, eats primarily junk food, and fails to get any exercise, that person is likely to require health care treatment much more than if he had lived a healthier lifestyle. The costs for maintaining and treating such a person will make everyone's costs rise because that person's health care will be funded either by the government (and, so, everyone's taxes) or by private insurance (and, so, insurance rates will rise). If a right to health care means that people can expect programs and treatments and therapies to give them a certain level of health, then there arise value questions about the rights of that person and the responsibilities of that person (as well as the rights of everyone else). Even at the conceptual point of just asking about what health care and medicine are, then, ethical and moral issues arise.

Another major topic within the area of bioethics is the allocation of medical and health resources. That is, there are decisions that must be made about who gets what medical and health resources, especially when those resources are limited. Clearly, value decisions must be made, decisions regarding ethical and moral values as well as social and economic values. Some allocation decisions are said to be macro-level decisions. These are decisions about the broad, social allocation of resources. For example, the government must decide how much and what kinds of resources can go into public health programs or disaster relief or basic research or health education, etc. At a smaller level, decisions must be made about how much and what kinds of resources should go toward, say, nutrition programs versus disease prevention or toward AIDS treatment versus heart disease research, etc. Other allocation decisions are said to be micro-level decisions. These are decisions within, say, a hospital or clinic about who gets access to certain medicines or treatments when there are not enough for everyone who needs them. At a very basic level, for example, if 10 people come into an emergency ward at the same time, but there are medical staff and equipment to handle only five of those people at a time, who will or should get treated first (and on what basis is or should that decision be made)?

Among health care providers themselves, there are many ethical and moral decisions that must be made. As individuals, health care providers themselves have certain rights and values, and they might not agree with the values of the patient whom they are treating. For instance, a pro-life pharmacist might not want to dispense birth control to someone. Does that pharmacist have the right to refuse to provide birth control? In addition, health care workers are employees of hospitals or other organizations. As such, they have obligations and responsibilities to their employers as well as obligations and responsibilities to their coworkers, in addition to their obligations and responsibilities to their patients. These multiple obligations and responsibilities might very well come into conflict with each other, and then a moral decision must be made. For example, a physician might tell another health worker not to provide certain treatments or medications even though that other health worker believes they should be provided.

In addition, there are many ethical and moral decisions that are directly related to patients themselves. There are issues of confidentiality and truth telling. For example, a physician might believe that a patient should be weaned off some addictive substance and, with the patient's health in mind, tell that patient a lie or hide certain information in the hope that it will benefit the patient (or break confidentiality and disclose some information about the patient to someone else, again with the patient's benefit in mind). Although the motivation for such actions might be good, on the surface at least they violate the right of the patient to know what is being done, or not done, on his behalf. A related issue is called *informed consent.* Informed consent is a matter of a patient agreeing to some treatment or procedure or therapy based on having relevant information that she believes helps her to make a genuine decision; that is, she gives her consent based on having been given relevant information. One concern about this issue is that some people cannot give informed consent, for example, young children or people who are in shock or a state of trauma or with serious mental or psychological distress. The ethical and moral issues that arise in the context of bioethics, then, cover broad social matters as well as professional, organizational matters, and individual matters. These are all within the context of health care and medicine, but as noted previously, there are also ethical and moral issues that arise in connection with biology that are not directly about health care or medicine (such as cloning or the use of genetically modified organisms in the food industry).

Finally, there are obvious issues related to "beginning of life" issues and "end of life" issues. Issues related to the beginning of life include the issue of involuntary sterilization and the issue of surrogate pregnancy, or contracting with someone to be pregnant on your behalf; that is, having one woman go through a pregnancy with the intention that when the child is born, the child "belongs" to someone else. This could involve either the father's sperm being implanted in the surrogate mother or even the mother's egg being implanted into another woman for her to carry the fetus during pregnancy. Surrogate pregnancies are usually done because one of the parents is incapable of contributing to a pregnancy or because at least one of the parents is unwilling to contribute to a pregnancy. Surrogate pregnancies have raised legal issues as well as ethical issues about contracting (or trafficking) for human life.

End of life issues are usually labeled as issues of euthanasia, including recent issues about the right to die and physician-assisted suicide. The term *euthanasia* comes from two Greek words, *eu*, meaning "good," and *thanatos*, meaning "death." It refers to the notion of someone experiencing a good death, or at least a form of death that a person would consider to be a good death. Usually, however, the term is used in the context of a deliberate decision to bring about someone's death in a way that the person considers good (or, at least, preferable to other forms of death). Even more, euthanasia usually refers to the intentional and—as much as possible—quickening of someone's death. Although millions of animals are euthanized every year, most people speak of humans when they think of the ethical and moral issues connected to euthanasia.

Different forms of euthanasia are often distinguished from one another. One such distinction is between *active* euthanasia and *passive* euthanasia. Active euthanasia is sometimes spoken of as "killing," and passive euthanasia is sometimes spoken of as "letting die." The point is that with active euthanasia some positive action is taken in order to bring about the death of someone, while with passive euthanasia there is a "negative" action, or deliberate decision to refrain from taking an action to keep someone alive. In both cases, the intent is to have a person die as painlessly as is feasible and perhaps, but not necessarily, sooner than they otherwise might. Although the distinction between active and passive euthanasia seems clear and obvious to some people, others find that there are cases and situations in which the distinction is not straightforward. For example, if someone is put on life-support equipment and then later decides that she does not want to be kept alive by this equipment, would "pulling the plug" at that point in time be a case of active euthanasia (that is, taking a direct, deliberate action knowing this would likely bring about the person's death) or a case of passive euthanasia (that is, no longer taking a direct, deliberate action to keep the person alive)?

A second distinction relating to different forms of euthanasia is the distinction between *voluntary* euthanasia and *involuntary* euthanasia. Voluntary euthanasia is said to be at the request of a conscious, competent person (the person whose life is in question). That is, a case of euthanasia is voluntary when that person makes the genuine decision that she wants to have her life ended (again, as painlessly as is feasible and perhaps sooner than it otherwise would). What has become known as physician-assisted suicide is a form of voluntary euthanasia. This form requires the direct and deliberate cooperation and involvement ("assistance") of a physician in order to bring about the person's death, as opposed to other forms of suicide, in which a person might bring about her own death without involving anyone else. Involuntary euthanasia is said to be against the will or wishes of the person whose life is in question. There are also cases that are said to be *nonvoluntary*. These are cases that are not at the request of the person but also not obviously against the will or wishes of that person. For example, someone might never have expressed or even had a view one way or the other about euthanasia or about being kept alive regardless of her situation. In addition, not all cases of refusing lifesaving treatment are cases of euthanasia. For instance, a Jehovah's Witness or Christian Scientist might refuse medical treatment because of religious convictions, but not necessarily out of a desire to die.

Several ethical and moral arguments have been put forth in support of euthanasia. For example, some people argue that it is a matter of personal liberty. A person has a right to die, they say; it is simply no one else's decision whether or not they live or die. Some have phrased this point as: Whose life is it, anyway? Critics of this argument have said that euthanasia is not merely suicide but a form of suicide that involves other people; as such, the rights and obligations of those other people are also involved. Another argument that some people have given in favor of euthanasia is that it is a matter of human dignity, of allowing a person to decide for herself what quality of life is relevant to her and to respect the decision of that person. Critics have responded by saying that bringing about the death of someone is never a matter of respecting that person; it is valuing human dignity, and human life, that they hold to be important. A third argument that some people give in support of euthanasia is that it is humane; it is a case of reducing the suffering of someone. Critics reply that suffering in itself does not justify killing someone or allowing a person to die when that person could be saved. The focus can and should be on reducing the suffering and trying to end it without ending the person's life.

On the other hand, there are a number of arguments that have been given not only in response to supporters of euthanasia but directly against euthanasia. One argument is the sanctity of life; life is sacred. Often, though not always, this argument is based on religious grounds; God gives life and only God can appropriately take life. Critics reply to this argument that it is those who oppose euthanasia who are "playing

God," in the sense that they are imposing their own values and beliefs on others. Another argument is often called a slippery slope argument, namely, if some cases of euthanasia are allowed, then even other more questionable cases might then be allowed. For example, if passive voluntary cases are allowed, then perhaps active voluntary cases might be allowed, followed perhaps by passive involuntary cases and then finally active involuntary cases of simply killing people who do not want to die. Critics say that this is simply not true; there is no evidence that there would be a slippery slope, and indeed, the principles of human liberty and dignity would preclude such a slippery slope. Still another argument that has been given against euthanasia is that there might be medical progress that could help someone, or possibly even a wrong diagnosis with respect to someone, such that she could have been saved. Critics respond that there are safeguards against acting on the basis of a wrong diagnosis (since a person can easily get other medical and health providers involved) and that the possibility of medical progress does not outweigh the right of the person to decide for herself what she sees as the quality of her own life.

Capital Punishment

Social ethics is a broad subarea of applied ethics related to social issues. One such issue is capital punishment, sometimes called the death penalty. Capital punishment is one form of legal punishment. Other forms of punishment, including fines, mandatory community service, imprisonment, and others, are considered by almost everyone as lesser punishments, and so, capital punishment is a response that is legally restricted to a small group of offenses. As of 2009, the United States was the only Western industrialized nation that allowed capital punishment, and within the United States, capital punishment was allowed in only 38 of the 50 states.

One concern about capital punishment is that it is a form of punishment that is "cruel and unusual." If this were correct, then it would violate the Eighth Amendment of the U.S. Constitution, which prohibits cruel and unusual punishment. This concern has been raised about the very existence and practice of capital punishment. It has also been raised about various forms of capital punishment, such as electrocution, hanging, beheading, firing squad, and even chemical injection.

Besides the concern about capital punishment being cruel and unusual, there are concerns that capital punishment violates "equal protection under the law," which is to say that it is unfair. When this concern has been raised, it has been because the data reveal that a larger proportion of ethnic minority legal offenders have been subjected to capital punishment than have ethnic whites. Supporters of capital punishment have responded by saying that, even if this is true, it shows a problem with fair implementation of capital punishment, not with capital punishment itself.

There are two broad philosophical perspectives on the justification of punishment generally, and on the justification of capital punishment specifically. The first perspective is utilitarianism. Under this perspective, punishment is justified because it helps to deter crime. The second perspective is retributivism. Under this perspective, punishment is justified because offenders deserve to be punished, whether or not future offenses are actually deterred. Each of these perspectives has been used by both supporters and opponents of capital punishment.

Arguments in favor of capital punishment include: (1) offenders of certain crimes deserve to die, (2) capital punishment balances or restores justice, (3) capital punishment deters/prevents future crime, obviously for the person who is punished, but also for others who might commit such crimes, (4) capital punishment is the only way to prevent certain crimes, because lesser punishments do not, and (5) capital punishment is more effective and economical than long-term (perhaps lifelong) imprisonment.

Arguments against capital punishment include: (1) all life is sacred, even the lives of convicted criminals, (2) innocent people might be executed because they can be and sometimes are wrongly convicted of crimes, (3) capital punishment does not actually deter/prevent future crime (except for the person executed), (4) capital punishment desensitizes people to the killing of others, and (5) capital punishment prevents the possibility of reform of convicted criminals.

Abortion

Abortion means the termination, or ending, of something, usually as a result of a deliberate decision by someone. It is the termination, or ending, of a human life—especially that of a human fetus—that is especially relevant in applied ethics. There are spontaneous abortions, cases of human fetuses dying but not because of a deliberate decision by anyone. Such spontaneous abortions are not the kinds of cases that people mean when they speak of abortions as having ethical or social importance.

There are several philosophical issues related to the topic of abortion. One issue is the matter of whether or not an abortion is an act of killing. Some people have argued that what it means to be alive is that a thing has the ability to use resources for both self-maintenance and reproduction, but that some fetuses do not have that ability, such as a fertilized human egg that is less than one day old (what biologists call a zygote). In addition, they say, some crystals have this ability, but they are not living organisms. Furthermore, they ask, is a human sperm cell or a human unfertilized egg alive? Although these concerns point to the difficulty of clearly stating what life is, almost everyone accepts the view that a human zygote is alive, and so, aborting it is indeed an act of killing.

Another question is what is actually killed in an abortion. Assuming that from the moment of conception (that is, the fertilization of the egg) there is a human being, there is the question of whether that organism is fully human, or a person. Many people argue that being human is a biological concept; having the relevant genetic material is what makes something human and, hence, a person, since there are not degrees of being human. Others argue that being a person is not the same thing as being human; a one-day-old zygote is human but not a person, and in addition, some nonhumans (for example, a cat or dog) should be considered as persons, because they have consciousness or a basic level of awareness of themselves and the world around them or because they have the ability to suffer. Yet others claim that being a human and being a person is the same thing; it is to have a soul, not simply to have a particular genetic structure. These various views all point to one philosophical aspect of abortion, which is the nature of the thing that is aborted: Is it a living being and is it a person (along with the questions of what it is to be alive and what it is to be a person)?

Yet another question is whether or not an abortion is ever a justified killing. For some people, no intentional killing of another person is justified. For others, there are cases of intentional killing of other persons that are justified. For example, some cases of self-defense might be cases of justified intentional killing (that is, the only way of saving your own life is to kill another person, the person who is attempting to kill you). Some argue that in cases of combat, some intentional killing of others is justified. With respect to abortion, then, some people have argued that an abortion is justified if the life of the mother is at risk otherwise. Some others, however, have argued that even in those cases, the killing of a human fetus is not justified because—unlike the cases of self-defense or combat—a human fetus is innocent of any wrongdoing.

Often the issue of abortion is framed in terms of rights. Those people who identify themselves as pro-life claim that a human fetus has a right to life and that this right is basic; it trumps other concerns. Those people who identify themselves as pro-choice claim that the mother has a right to self-determination (that is, a right to choose what happens to herself) and that this right is basic; it trumps other concerns. By framing the issue in terms of rights, this points to the question of the hierarchy of rights, in other words, not only what rights persons have, but also what determines which right takes precedence over which other rights.

Philosophers usually group people's views about abortion into the categories of conservative, liberal, or moderate. Those who are most conservative about abortion tend to claim that abortion is never justified, while those who are most liberal about abortion tend to claim that abortion is always justified. Those who are moderate span the gap between those two extremes. For instance, some claim that abortions are acceptable until a human fetus is said to be viable (meaning that it could survive outside of the mother's womb); the timing of viability is usually said to be around the sixth month of pregnancy, although changing technology has made that timing sooner. Others claim that abortions are acceptable in cases of unwanted pregnancies (for example, as a result of rape). Still others claim that abortions are acceptable if not aborting the fetus would create undue hardship on the mother or parents.

Because the issue of abortion involves rights, as well as questions of limitations of choices, many people see this issue as being not only about the fetus or even about the relationship between the mother and the fetus but also about social power. That is, some people have argued that opponents of abortion (or, at least, of the liberal view about abortion) also oppose other forms of birth control and, so, are actually concerned about limiting women's choices. Many opponents of abortion reject this argument, claiming that some conservatives about abortion oppose many other forms of birth control, but that some moderates about abortion do not oppose them.

Abortion can be understood as a social ethics issue because it affects society as a whole. It is also related to the ethics of sex in the sense that it is concerned with human reproduction.

Ethics of Sex and Love

Philosophers address various questions regarding sex and love. Central in the ethics of sex are issues regarding the morality of certain sexual behaviors. Some people believe, for example, that certain sexual behaviors are immoral, ought to be illegal, or both. Incest and polygamy (the practice of one man having multiple wives), for instance, are illegal in the United States, and many believe these practices are immoral. Other sexual behaviors discussed include homosexual sex, group sex, adultery, and sex that is not intended for procreation. In the discussions of the morality of certain sexual behaviors, a key issue is treating a sexual partner (or partners) as a means only, in other words using a person as a tool for one's own purposes. Like Immanuel Kant, many people believe it is wrong to treat another person merely as a means to one's own gratification. Some philosophers have argued that some sexual behavior involves just that: It objectifies a person, or in other words, treats a person as an object rather than as a person. For example, perhaps group sex, insofar as it is performed without love between all the partners, involves objectifying at least some of the people involved. Another topic in the ethics of sex is sadomasochism (the consensual and intentional giving and/or receiving of pain and/or humiliation during sexual intercourse, for the purpose of sexual pleasure). Some thinkers argue that sadomasochism is wrong because it is demeaning, physically harmful, or both. Others believe that sexual behavior between consenting adults (perhaps provided that no one gets injured), whatever form it might take, is morally acceptable and should not be subject to legal restrictions.

In recent years ethical issues related to gays, lesbians, and transgendered people have also attracted much attention (transgendered people are those who regard their actual gender as not being identical with their biological sex, and act accordingly; for instance, one might be born with male sex organs but identify oneself as female and behave in some ways that are traditionally associated with females). Gay marriage, for example, is a hotly debated ethical issue. Supporters of gay marriage see it as a matter of civil rights; on this view, not allowing women to marry women and men to marry men discriminates against gays and lesbians. Opponents claim that gay marriage is immoral, on the grounds that homosexual sex is immoral, that gay marriage threatens traditional, heterosexual marriages or families, or both.

Another issue in the ethics of sex and love is pornography. The word *pornography* comes from two Greek words, *porné,* meaning "harlot," and *graphein,* meaning "to write." One difficulty in considering pornography is that the term is vague, not only conceptually, but also socially and politically. It is generally agreed that pornography involves some form of representation or depiction of sexuality and that this representation or depiction includes at least one human. There are three separate points here. First, pornography must be a representation or depiction; sexual behavior in itself is not what is considered pornographic, but the representation or depiction of it might be. Second, the representation or depiction must be sexual in nature. Third, pornography must include at least one human in that representation or depiction. Although some people might think of representations or depictions of nonhuman sexuality as being offensive, pornography is taken to involve at least one human.

The first two points above are not precise, which is why it is difficult to explicitly define or characterize pornography. With respect to representation or depiction, there are questions of what is represented or depicted, how it is represented or depicted, and why it is represented or depicted. In term of what is represented or depicted, the notion of sexuality is quite broad. The most obvious cases involve sexual behavior or interactions; yet many people resist regarding some sexual behavior, such as kissing, as pornographic. In addition, many people regard the representation or depiction of nudity as itself pornographic. For instance, even if photographs in an adult magazine such as *Playboy* do not involve sexual behavior but simply a nude person posing, some people include this in the concept of pornography. Or the representation or depiction might be of specific sexual organs, such as genitalia, although there is no explicit sexual behavior. So, sexuality and not necessarily sexual behavior might be what is represented or depicted in order for something to be pornographic. A difficulty about characterizing pornography as the representation or depiction of sexuality is that this is quite broad and would include what many people phrase as erotica or even simply the representation or depiction of human sexual nature.

Besides vagueness about what is represented or depicted, there are questions concerning *how* something is pornographic. Usually, people think of pornography in terms of visual images, but there can also be representations or depictions of sexuality that are nonvisual, such as written words or certain sounds, and even musical arrangements that are intended or interpreted as representing or depicting sexuality (as well as sexual behavior). There are also questions of whether the pornographic nature of such images or sounds are the result of the intentions of the persons making those images/sounds or are the result of the interpretations of the persons "receiving" those images/sounds. That is, is pornography (say, as opposed to erotica) in the eye of the beholder? This also points to questions concerning why sexuality is represented or depicted, along with the issue of who and what determines whether the reasons or motivations for such representations or depictions count as pornography. These three issues (what, how, and why) are not necessarily separate or unrelated. For example, what is represented or depicted might be not actual sexual behavior but a simulation of some sexual behavior, perhaps involving no actual humans but computer-generated images of people with sexual props or toys. Because of the difficulties in defining pornography, courts of law have generally focused on three aspects of representations or depictions in order to classify them as pornographic: what community standards would find as appealing to prurient interests, that the work depicts or describes in a patently offensive way sexual conduct specifically defined by applicable laws, and that the work, taken as a whole, lacks serious literary, artistic, political, or scientific value. These three aspects are themselves, of course, imprecise. Many people have argued that a distinguishing characteristic of pornography is the degrading and demeaning portrayal of the role and status of women in particular, and that this feature separates pornography from erotica. In this respect, they say, pornography is akin to hate speech, where the goal is not merely to represent or depict something but to harm certain people. With this aspect, they argue, erotica, which does not degrade or demean, is an acceptable representation or depiction of sexuality and differs from pornography.

There have been a number of arguments against pornography. The primary one is that it is harmful. As just noted, some people claim that it is harmful to women generally. Some people have argued that it is harmful not only to women but to society generally, because it dehumanizes and desensitizes everyone. In addition, they say, it not only harms women by portraying them in degrading and demeaning ways, but it also leads to crime by promoting a sexual predator attitude (with increased sexual assaults and prostitution as a result). Critics of this argument have stated that there is not clear and sufficient evidence that pornography leads to crime. For example, they claim, in some European countries, there is less sexually related crime than in the United States even though pornographic works are readily available. Indeed, these people argue, pornography can actually be liberating because it decreases sexual inhibitions and repression. Opponents of pornography counter this claim by saying that erotica could serve these same functions but that pornography does not.

The main argument that is usually given for pornography—that is, in opposition to restricting it—is that restricting it is a violation of people's freedom of expression. Supporters of this view claim that no one is required to sell or distribute or purchase or view pornography. Exposure to it is a matter of choice, and people have the right to express themselves however they want to as long as they do not harm others. Restricting pornography is simply censorship. Not only is this wrong, they say, but censoring pornography is just the first step on a slippery slope of further censorship of things that some people find offensive. Some opponents of pornography claim that the existence of pornography (including its creation, distribution, and availability) is harming others, as was mentioned above. Other opponents of pornography claim that even if it only offended, there are good reasons for restricting it on that basis. That is, there are good reasons for restricting at least some offensive actions, for the same reasons that hate speech should be restricted; even if it does no direct, physical harm to a person, it does lessen the quality of people's lives. Once again, they say, erotica is one thing, but pornography is something else. Opponents of this view respond that appealing to something as being offensive is subjective and too broad; it can lead to the slippery slope of greater censorship. For the most part, the courts of the United States have agreed with this latter view and have been quite hesitant to restrict the creation, sale, or distribution of pornography and almost always on the basis of freedom of expression.

Environmental Ethics

Environmental ethics is the field of philosophy that investigates ethical issues concerning human relationships with the environment. Properly speaking, environmental ethics is a subfield of the broader area of environmental philosophy. For many philosophers, however, the terms *environmental ethics* and *environmental philosophy* are taken to be synonymous. While environmental ethics focuses on ethical issues connected to human relationships with the environment, there are also basic conceptual issues that are also addressed. The first such conceptual issue is what does the term *environment* mean or refer to? At first glance, most people think the term *environment* refers to nature, that is, to the nonhuman, nonsocial world. However, a person's environment includes humans. Indeed, people live in the midst of many environments. For example, a person living in the United States in the year 2001 lived in the midst of a natural environment (that is, on a particular landmass on the Earth, containing various plant and animal life). That person also lived in the midst of a historical environment (that is, in a context that was different in various ways than someone living in the same natural environment, say 100 years earlier or 1,000 years earlier). That person also lived in the midst of a social environment (that is, human institutions and relations that were different in various ways that someone living at the same time in, say, Saudi Arabia or North Korea). There are, then, multiple environments in which a person lives at any given point. Beyond the fact of multiple kinds of environments in which people live, there is also the matter of local environments and a global environment. That is, a person's local environment might include a fairly definite geographical setting, as opposed to a global environment, namely, the Earth as a whole. In addition, while people usually think of the environment as nature, the environment for, say, a tree or a tiger includes humans; we are part of their environments. The very term *environment*, then, is broader and more complex than simply the notion of nature (which, itself, is a very complex term).

In spite of the complexity of the nature of environment, a fundamental question that philosophers ask with respect to environmental ethics is: What is the nature of the value of the environment? Another way of phrasing this is to ask: Is nature intrinsically valuable? (Yet another phrase among environmental ethicists is: Do trees have moral standing?) In other words, if nature (or the environment) has value, does it have value in itself (that is, intrinsically) or does it have value only in relation to humans (that is, extrinsically)? Is the environment, or particular aspects of the environment, worth protecting or preserving or restoring, only because it is useful for humans to do this or because nonhumans (including nature as a whole) have value just as much as humans do? One perspective that argues in favor of nature having intrinsic value is often called deep ecology. The emphasis is on ecosystems, or nature as a whole, and it is said to be deep in the sense that these ecosystems have as much value as do the organisms and species (including humans) that live in them. Some deep ecologists speak of environmental rights, claiming that the environment itself has rights, and those rights must be protected and respected just as much as human rights. Most deep ecologists do not claim that ecosystems themselves are moral agents, that is, things capable of making moral choices and having responsibility for those choices. Rather, ecosystems are "moral patients," meaning that they are deserving of moral treatment by humans. So, while ecosystems cannot themselves act in good or bad ways, they can be treated by humans in good or bad ways, and they should be treated in good ways, namely, protected and preserved and restored, etc.

One view about the value of nature, then, is that it is intrinsically valuable. Many other people, however, claim that nature is not intrinsically valuable. Among those people, some say that nothing is valuable in itself; all value is in relation to some agent and some goal. Others claim that moral and ethical value only makes sense in connection with humans, because only humans can act in moral or ethical ways (that is, only humans can act in ways that are right or wrong). In either case, those who claim that nature has only extrinsic (or relational) value can and do take a variety of positions with respect to the environment. Some claim, like the deep ecologists, that humans must protect and preserve and restore the environment as much as possible—not because the environment deserves it, but because this is the wisest way to deal with the environment, where wisest means that it is the way that benefits humans the most. An analogy would be that one should protect and preserve and (if needed) restore one's teeth by practicing good oral hygiene, not because one's teeth have any special moral standing, but because doing that is good for the person. Or one should keep one's house well-kept (for example, do regular maintenance and upkeep), not because a house has any intrinsic value, but because it is better for the person to have a well-preserved house than one that is falling down. Some philosophers refer to this view as anthropocentric, meaning human-centered, noting that an anthropocentric view is not necessarily one that finds little or no value in the environment; rather, the value that the environment has, it has because humans value it. For those who hold this anthropocentric view, some claim that humans have dominion over nature, while others claim that humans have a stewardship with nature. Having dominion is to be in charge, in a sense to dominate. This view sees nature as having value only in relation to human needs and wants. Having stewardship is to be in charge in the sense of having the responsibility for something (much like a gardener is responsible for keeping a garden well cared for).

Others who do not hold an anthropocentric view but also deny that nature is intrinsically valuable often are labeled as having a biocentric view. This view holds that nature (or the environment) has value but only in relation to other life-forms, that is, other nonhumans (such as wildlife). This view holds that the notion of value applies only to living organisms, so it is not nature itself that has value but those living organisms in nature that have value. What distinguishes this view from the anthropocentric view is that this view sees other species as having equal value to humans. So, a particular habitat for some species should be protected and preserved and restored, they claim, not because this would be useful for humans, but for the sake of other living organisms. One particular concern of this view is the issue of biodiversity. Biodiversity, they say, is important not because of its value to humans but because of its value to living species generally (including humans).

The question of whether nature is intrinsically valuable, while a basic question in environmental ethics, is only one question among many. Another important question is: What is the nature of the relationship between humans and the environment? For example, should humans protect the environment? If so, how should they do so and protect it from what? What does it mean to say that humans should protect the environment? Another way to ask this is: What does it mean to say that the environment is harmed (and, so, not protected)? There are fairly clear and obvious examples of harming the environment, such as dumping toxic chemicals into waterways or into the atmosphere (keeping in mind that what is toxic to one organism or species might not be toxic to another). But there are many cases that are not clear and obvious. For instance, if humans cut down trees and plant crops, is this a case of harming (and, therefore, not protecting) the environment? Besides the notion of protecting the environment, there are related notions that also need clarification, such as preserving the environment or restoring the environment or maintaining the environment. Does preserving the environment mean not changing it? Few people would say yes, since natural processes themselves often result in changes in the environment. The point is not that these various notions are confused or confusing, but that a major aspect of environmental ethics is to help make them clear and meaningful, especially with respect to particular human practices, such as specific farming practices or use of chemical products.

Typically the way that environmental ethicists approach these various issues—and other related issues, such as energy consumption, consumerism, population control, economic development, etc.—is to apply ethical theory to them. For example, one basic ethical theory is utilitarianism. This theory holds that the right thing to do is whatever will maximize the good, that is, create the greatest happiness or, at least, the minimum unhappiness, among the various options that are faced. If it turns out that there is greater overall good that results from using mass transportation than from using personal transportation (that is, individual cars), then there should be policies and practices that lead to the greater use of mass transportation. This claim, however, immediately produces a number of questions: Whose happiness matters (for instance, it might be very inconvenient for some people to use mass transportation, since it is much more limited in where it can go than individual cars); how would the overall happiness be determined (many taxpayers would pay for mass transportation even if they never used it; some people might have their property or livelihoods negatively affected by mass transportation); how would this relate to other values, such as people's rights? The point here is not to settle these questions but to note that applying utilitarian moral theory to a particular environmental issue is the sort of thing that environmental ethicists investigate and analyze.

Animal Ethics

An important issue in applied ethics relates to animals. At the heart of animal ethics are these questions: Do animals deserve moral consideration, and why or why not? Animal ethics relates closely to the metaethical issue of who (or what) matters morally. Some thinkers have argued that although animals are not moral agents (they are not morally responsible for any actions), they are moral patients (there are moral restrictions on how we can treat them); others disagree. The questions of whether animals deserve moral consideration and why or why not are not just abstract, for the simple reason that humans make use of animals in a variety of ways, and depending on how these questions are answered, some of these uses might turn out to be morally wrong. If animals deserve moral consideration, then we cannot morally treat them any way we like; there are morally right and wrong ways of behaving toward them. For instance, if animals deserve moral consideration, then there are reasonable grounds that people should stop eating them. Other practices, such as using animals for research or for entertainment (such as in rodeos and circuses), might turn out to be immoral as well. So, answering the central questions in animal ethics has potentially significant implications for common human behavior.

One traditional view has been that although there are moral restrictions on how we can treat humans, there are far fewer restrictions on how we can treat animals (and perhaps there are no restrictions at all). For example, many practices often considered acceptable when applied to animals, such as eating them, would be considered reprehensible if applied to humans. What justifies this difference in moral consideration, if anything? Many philosophers have answered this question by arguing that humans have some trait(s) that animals lack, such as consciousness or the ability to reason. The ancient philosopher Aristotle, for example, believed that because humans can reason and animals cannot, humans are superior to animals and are therefore justified in using animals for human purposes; Thomas Aquinas (1225–74) defended a similar view. René Descartes (1596–1650) regarded animals as mindless automata (that is, machines of flesh and blood), a view that implies that animals do not deserve moral consideration. For example, in Descartes's view, if a dog yelps when pricked with a needle, then the dog is reacting mechanically rather than because it feels pain, somewhat in the same way a car starts when the key is turned in the ignition. Another historically important view was Immanuel Kant's. Kant believed that animals are not capable of acting from a good will, as a human is. For instance, consider the human who sees someone drowning and, overcoming her impulse to give in to her own fear of water and do nothing, instead acts out of duty to try to rescue the drowning person. Animals, Kant believed, are not similarly capable of overcoming an impulse and acting out of duty; they lack autonomy and therefore do not deserve moral consideration for their own sake. Kant believed we do have duties to animals but that these duties are indirect. For instance, one has a duty not to be cruel to animals because (Kant believed) if one is cruel to animals one is likely to become cruel to people. So the duty not to be cruel is a duty to people, not a duty to animals themselves.

In contemporary philosophy, an influential argument known as the argument from marginal cases has been used to oppose the claim that a being has inferior moral status if it lacks qualities such as consciousness or the ability to reason. A version of the argument is this: There are some people, such as newborns, severely disabled people, and people in comas, who are not conscious or who lack the ability to speak or reason (these people are marginal cases in the sense that they are at the "margins" of humanity). Nonetheless, these people deserve moral consideration; it is not okay to cause them pointless suffering, for instance, just because they lack consciousness or the ability to reason. If such people deserve moral consideration, then animals deserve moral consideration as well. So, what the argument is said to show is that qualities such as consciousness or the possession of reason are not necessary for something to count morally. If we extend moral consideration to nonconscious, nonreasoning humans, then it seems we cannot arbitrarily deny moral consideration to nonconscious, nonreasoning animals. To put the point another way, if we are justified in giving moral regard to such humans and not to animals, then there must be some morally relevant difference between such humans and animals. Many proponents of the argument from marginal cases argue that there is no morally relevant difference. For example, perhaps it does not matter that the nonconscious, nonreasoning animals happen to be human and that animals are not. Many philosophers (although not all) deny that a being's species makes a difference in how it ought to be treated. Treating an animal differently *merely* on the basis of its species, in this view, is an unjustifiable prejudice analogous to treating a person differently *merely* on the basis of her race; speciesism is no less wrong than racism.

Related to the argument from marginal cases is the view that when it comes to whether a being deserves moral consideration, what matters is not whether a being can reason but whether it can suffer (a point famously made by the utilitarian philosopher Jeremy Bentham). In his influential 1975 book, *Animal Liberation,* Peter Singer elaborated this view, giving a version of the argument from marginal cases and introducing the concept of speciesism to a mass audience. Singer argued that the interests of animals (what matters for their well-being) deserve equal consideration as the interests of humans. Singer's point was not that animals should be treated exactly the way humans should be treated; it does not make sense, for instance, to give a chicken the legal right to vote and it does not make sense to build nesting perches for humans. Singer acknowledged that animals and humans have different interests (and different abilities); Singer's point, however, was that animal interests are no less important than human interests. Singer's view is utilitarian. In his view, what is morally right is what produces the most benefit for the greatest number of beings, and he believes that when we are totaling the possible benefits and detriments of an action, animal interests and human interests should count equally. Consider factory farms, for example, large institutions that produce relatively inexpensive mass volumes of eggs and meat. Factory farms inflict great suffering on animals who live in them, as the animals are typically very tightly confined and are denied the opportunity to engage in activities that come naturally to them. According to Singer, giving up eggs and meat produced by factory farms would cause little harm to humans (humans can live happy, well-nourished lives without eating eggs and meat) while it would greatly reduce the suffering of animals. Because the benefit to animals will outweigh any harm to humans, the right thing to do is for humans to stop eating factory farm–produced eggs and meat. As a utilitarian, Singer also believed that sometimes the right thing to do might involve harming (or even killing) an animal. For example, research that causes a small amount pain to a small number of animals might be justified if the research benefits a great many humans in significant ways.

Although Singer's work gave impetus to the animal rights movement, Singer himself did not regard animals as having moral rights,

Photograph of Peter Singer at the College of New Jersey in 2009 *(Used under a Creative Commons license)*

strictly speaking (nor is he the only philosopher to argue that animals deserve moral consideration while denying that animals have moral rights). However, in addition to utilitarian viewpoints such as Singer's, an important view in animal ethics is that not only do animals deserve moral consideration but also that animals have moral rights. In discussions of animal rights, it is usually moral rights, not legal rights, that are at issue. Whereas whether someone or something has a legal right depends on whether the law says so, a moral right is held independently of a legal right. For example, if a farm horse has a moral right to water, it has that right whether or not the law says so (in the same way, a human is often thought to have the moral right to be free from random imprisonment, even if her government does not acknowledge that right). Here, right will be used as shorthand for moral right. In addition, a right is often understood as a kind of moral claim. For instance, to say that a horse has a right to water is to say that the horse has a moral claim to water, that it is owed water as a matter of morality (not just as a practical matter). In addition, this claim is justified on rational grounds—it is not simply arbitrary. As rationally justified moral claims, rights govern behavior, sometimes requiring someone (or something) to do something and sometimes requiring someone (or something) *not* to do something. If a horse has a right to water, then someone (likely the owner) is obligated to provide the horse with water. If a horse has a right not to be tortured, then someone (in this case, everyone) is obligated not to torture the horse. So, on this understanding, the question of whether animals have rights is the question of whether animals have rationally justified moral claims that require others to behave (or refrain from behaving) in certain ways.

Two other distinctions are worth making. First, the claim that some animals have rights is not the same as the claim that *all* animals have rights. Whether a being has rights is sometimes thought to depend on that being's cognitive capacities. For instance, one might deny that a tapeworm has rights while claiming that an elephant does, on the grounds that an elephant's cognitive capacities are much richer and more sophisticated than a tapeworm's (perhaps the elephant is able to suffer, and the tapeworm is not). Similarly, the claim that some animals have rights is not the same as the claim that all animals have exactly the same rights. It seems absurd, for instance, to suppose that a cow has the right to vote, because a cow is not the sort of creature who is capable of voting. But this does not mean that a cow has, for instance, no right to life.

Animal rights views tend to value more highly than utilitarian accounts the individual animal's well-being. For instance, whereas a utilitarian might advocate painful research on a chimpanzee if the research would have significant benefits to many human beings, an

Tom Regan in 2008 *(Photograph by Bryan Regan)*

advocate of animal rights would be more inclined to view such research as an unacceptable violation of the chimpanzee's right not to be harmed. Of philosophical views advocating that animals have moral rights, an account by the contemporary American philosopher Tom Regan (1938–) has been the most influential. Regan believed that animals have inherent value, value in and of themselves, and not just because they serve some purpose. He argued that at least some animals (those with certain characteristics, such as a sense of self and the possession of beliefs and desires) have the moral rights not to be harmed and to be treated with respect. Other philosophers have offered different accounts in favor of animal rights. For example, some believe that animals have a right to life (although this right might reasonably be overridden in some circumstances), as well as rights based on their specific natures. Others have argued that animals capable of experiencing pleasure and pain (animals who are sentient) have rights, but that these rights are weaker than the rights of humans.

One critic of Regan's view is the American philosophy professor Carl Cohen (1931–). Cohen argued that rights simply do not apply to animals. They do not apply to animals because, according to Cohen, animals lack autonomy. What this means in particular, for Cohen, is that animals lack moral agency: They cannot make moral choices and therefore cannot carry out moral acts. Neither can they make immoral choices or carry out immoral acts. Animals are simply amoral, outside the realm of morality altogether. For Cohen, this is crucial because he regards rights as a moral concept. If the concept of rights is a moral concept, and animals are amoral, then for Cohen rights simply do not apply to animals. For example, if a zebra has a right to life, then it appears that a lion would have an obligation to respect that right. However, Cohen argued, it is evident that the lion has no such obligation; a lion does not violate a zebra's right to life by killing it. On this view, it is nonsensical to claim that a lion has moral obligations and equally as nonsensical to claim that lions and zebras—or any animals—have rights. (Cohen agreed that there are restrictions on how we can morally treat animals; he simply did not believe these restrictions were based on rights.)

Other critics of animal rights, such as the American philosophy professor Jan Narveson (1936–), base their views that animals do not have rights (and cannot have rights) on social contract theory. According to social contract theory, morality is a set of rules agreed on by rational, self-interested people. For instance, people might agree to respect each other's property because this is a rational way of keeping their own property safe. However, it seems that animals cannot enter into agreements; they cannot be party to a social contract. If animals cannot enter into an agreement, then a social contract does not apply to them, which is to say (in Narveson's view) that morality does not apply to them. This does not necessarily imply that there are no restrictions on how we can treat animals, however. It does mean that those restrictions are based on our obligations to other people, not to animals themselves. For instance, perhaps one is obligated not to torture one's neighbor's cat. But this is because one has obligations to one's neighbor (who presumably does not want her cat tortured), not because one has obligations to the cat.

Applied Ethics: Business Ethics and Media Ethics

The field of business ethics deals with ethical and moral issues that arise within the context of business. These issues occur in the context of the relationship of business to society as a whole (such as concerns about pollution and sustainability), business practices (such as concerns connected to advertising and product safety), and the interactions among the different people and roles within businesses (such as rights and responsibilities of employers and employees). As with any area of ethical and moral concern, value issues that arise in the context of business ethics are not simply about what is legal or illegal. Instead, they are about what is ethically justifiable, what ethical principles and arguments are relevant and reasonable in addressing and resolving such concerns.

With respect to ethical and moral issues that relate to business as a social institution, one focus is on the nature of economic systems themselves. Business, in the sense of economic exchange—buying and selling of goods and services—occurs in all cultures and societies, regardless of particular economic systems. How this exchange is organized and conducted, however, can and does vary, from free market capitalist systems to state-controlled systems. There are ethical questions about the very nature of these different economic systems. For example, some people have argued that free market capitalism is morally the best system because it is the economic system that is most consistent with individual personal freedom and liberty. Others, such as Karl Marx, have argued that a free market system is not morally the best because it results in an undesirable distribution of wealth, with some people (the business owners) unjustly getting far more wealth than the majority of people (the workers). While it would be difficult, if not impossible, to find a pure free market system or a completely state-controlled system, there is, of course, a spectrum of systems in the world ranging from more or less governmental regulation of business. So, there are ethical questions about the very justice of a given economic system, as well as about the justice of types and specific regulations of business within an economic system. For example, there are ethical and moral questions about the nature of governmental oversight and regulation of business. For instance, should the government be allowed to require someone to get a license in order to conduct a certain business? What kinds or levels of sanctions or punishments should the government be allowed to impose on business? Should the government be allowed to establish certain standards of worker safety or impose standards of safety for the products that businesses create and sell?

Besides broad ethical and moral issues related to the very nature of economic systems within which business functions, there are other value issues that arise because of the relation between business and society as a whole. For instance, there are questions about what responsibilities businesses have toward society broadly speaking or the particular communities in which they exist. The issue of sustainability is especially noted today. Sustainability is usually understood in terms of environmental degradation and resource depletion. What obligations or responsibility, if any, do businesses have with respect to environmental sustainability? Some people argue that the function of business is to make a profit, and that the primary (perhaps even the only) responsibility that a business has is to make a profit for its stockholders. If, they say, the practices of a business can be shown to harm people, then there are appropriate laws (and ethical principles) to regulate those practices. In addition, if being environmentally sustainable makes smart business sense, then, yes, a business has such a responsibility. However, they claim, a business has no such responsibility unless sustainability meets this condition. Others claim that businesses have more of an impact on the environment than do individuals, so businesses do have greater obligations and responsibilities with respect to sustainability concerns.

In addition, there are questions of business obligations and responsibilities beyond that of environmental sustainability, at least according to some people. Businesses also have obligations and responsibilities to the particular communities in which they exist. For example, some people argue that businesses have an obligation to support their communities and, especially, to maintain jobs within their communities to the extent possible, even if this means smaller profits for the business. Others argue that businesses have no special obligations or responsibilities to their communities. Again, if it makes smart business sense (that is, if it contributes to profit) to support the community, then, yes, a business should do that. However, there is no other basis for such obligations or responsibilities.

Another area, other than that of the relation of business to society as a whole, where ethical and moral issues arise in the context of business is the relation of business to consumers. One issue here is the issue of advertising. Advertising, of course, is a means for a business to make consumers aware of its products or services. The intention of advertising, obviously, is to encourage consumers to purchase those products or services. Ethical and moral questions arise especially in terms of how a business's products and services are advertised and to whom they are advertised. For example, how much and what kinds of information should be included in advertisements? There is a well-known phrase, caveat emptor, Latin for "let the buyer beware." The sense is that consumers are responsible for their purchases; if they purchase a cheap product and are unhappy about it, then they have no one to blame but themselves, because it was their free choice to make the purchase. Some people argue that advertising is intended to get people to buy products and services but not to provide full disclosure to consumers of those products or services. Some people have argued that there is a moral obligation to be truthful in advertising, and truthfulness includes disclosure of information about the products and services. Others argue that, while it is wrong for a business to advertise falsely (for instance, to claim that its product can do something that it cannot do), it is not the obligation or responsibility of a business to provide full information about its products or services. For one thing, they say, the point of advertising is simply to let consumers become aware of their products and services (with the hope that they will purchase them); if consumers have questions about those products or services, they can find out any further information that they believe is relevant to them. For another thing, they say, disclosure of full information is not possible, since there are countless points of information that apply to any product or service, and it is certainly not practical or even desirable by most consumers.

Another area where ethical and moral issues arise with respect to business is in terms of the relations of different groups or roles connected to business. Those groups or roles include owners and stockholders, producers, employers, and employees. In particular, there are many ethical and moral issues that arise with respect to employers and employees. One issue is working conditions. One aspect of the issue of working conditions is the matter of worker safety. In what ways and to what extent, if any, should a business be required to provide for worker safety? The question is not about what laws are in place but about what laws should be in place. That is, what moral requirements are there on businesses to provide for worker safety, even if this means a smaller profit for the business? Some people argue, again, for the equivalent of caveat emptor, but in this context meaning that workers who choose to accept a given job need to take responsibility for any risks that come with that job. The business cannot openly harm the worker, but some say, it is the responsibility of the worker, not the business, to be concerned with safety. Again, if it is good business sense to provide for worker safety, then a business can choose to do so. Others disagree; they claim that businesses have an obligation to provide a safe workplace, knowing that there might always be risks involved with a given job and knowing that workers themselves might ignore those risks. A second aspect of working conditions that is often raised is that of harassment and what is called a hostile workplace environment. This issue usually involves sexual harassment, but is also involves other forms of harassment (for example, racial harassment or gay-bashing). There are clear value issues connected to the presence of harassment in the workplace and about the relevant obligations and responsibilities of a business to deal with harassment and a hostile workplace environment.

Another important moral issue in relation to employers and employees is that of employer monitoring and privacy. When and in what ways, if any, may a business oversee the activities of its employees? Where this becomes particularly important is in terms of where the employee's rights and privacy extend and where the employer's rights extend. For example, may an employer read or have access to an employee's e-mails or phone calls or other communications? In what contexts, if any, are the activities of an employee while not at work relevant to the rights of the employer? For instance, may an employer discipline or discharge an employee who engages in activities outside of work that the employer finds undesirable? On the other hand, there is also the issue of whistle-blowing, that is, an employee making public some activities of the business that the employee finds undesirable. Is a business morally obligated to keep such a person employed (and to ensure good working conditions) if that person blows the whistle on the business? Some argue that, of course, the business is obligated to do so. Others claim that this is a violation of the rights of the business to hire and fire whom it wants.

Media Ethics

Within social ethics, one area is the field of media ethics, which investigates ethical and moral issues that arise both about the media and within the media. That is, there are some ethical and moral issues that arise about the very nature and roles of the media in society (such as being a public watchdog of the government), and also with respect to the content and process of creating and distributing news via the media (such as the reliability of sources of information). Although the term *the media* includes things such as films and books, because these are a public mode of communication, the term *media ethics* is usually restricted to ethical and moral issues that arise in connection with news media, that is, public modes of communication (such as newspapers, television, radio, and the Internet) that have a primary function and goal of informing the public (or its target audience) of relevant news and events. So, while there are ethical and moral issues connected to the creation, content, promotion, distribution, and impact of such media as films and books, the field of media ethics is mostly concerned with news media.

A fundamental question about the news media is what the appropriate role(s) of the news media is. Answering this question requires an additional question: What is the appropriate role(s) of the news media with respect to whom? Usually when people speak of the appropriate role(s) of the news media they mean with respect to society at large. The assumption is that the news media is a social institution, on a par, say, with the military or with health care or education. As such, the social role(s) of the news media is to inform the public about issues and events that are relevant to their lives. In addition, the assumption for some people is that the news media should be a watchdog of other social institutions and of people, especially with respect to how those institutions or people threaten the social good. For example, many people argue that the news media should bring to the public's attention when and if and how the government is wasting taxpayers' money or should inform the public about the wrongdoings of individuals or groups (including corporations) that behave in undesirable ways. On the other hand, some people claim that it is inappropriate for the news media to make public certain events or information that might put the security of the nation at risk (for instance, by publishing photos of American soldiers abusing civilians in Iraq). The role of the news media as a social watchdog, then, is one that is disputed, depending upon who is being watched and why.

In connection to the issue of the watchdog role of the media is a concern that some people express about what is not covered by the news media. That is, some people say that more and more news coverage has become less and less about informing the public on important issues and more on trivial or sensationalistic stories. The term *infotainment* has been coined to suggest that the role of information has been supplanted by that of entertainment, but presented in the guise of news. For example, some people claim that more and more broadcast time (especially, but not only, for television news) is devoted to car chases or stories about entertainment celebrities than to providing relevant information about important political, social, scientific, and artistic matters. As such, some people claim, the news media fail to fulfill the function of informing the public of important information as opposed to trivial information.

Another answer to the question of who the news media are responsible to, and therefore their appropriate role(s), is that they are responsible to their owners and stakeholders. That is, news media are businesses, at least in the United States. As such, they are (mostly) private companies and organizations. Their ultimate goal is to make a profit for their owners and stakeholders. They do this by providing a product—namely, information—that people are willing to purchase. If, in the process of providing this product, they put a particular spin or slant on that information, they are fulfilling their role(s) for their stakeholders as long as they are making a profit.

Because there are different notions of the appropriate role(s) of the news media, there are different views that emerge with regard to particular aspects of the media. For instance, during the military conflicts involving the United States in Iraq during the 1990s and then again in the early 2000s, some news reporters were embedded with various military units. This meant that reporters traveled with soldiers during their assignments and missions. In particular, however, the news coverage that was provided by these reporters was screened by military officials before being released to the general public. Some people thought this screening and required approval were an appropriate precaution by the military to help safeguard soldiers. In addition, they said, these reporters were invited by the military to be involved at the scene. The reporters were, in effect, guests of the military. Other people, however, thought this screening and required approval a form of inappropriate censorship by the military and therefore that it undermined the proper role of the news media being a watchdog of the military.

Also, ethical and moral issues connected to the media at the broad social level are issues of media regulation as well as what is called the fairness doctrine. Media regulation involves government regulation of the media (specifically, the Federal Communications Commission, in the United States). This includes granting licenses for broadcast media (such as television and radio) and also restrictions on "where" they can broadcast (that is, what specific frequencies of, say, radio waves) and restrictions on content, at least in terms of prohibiting profanity and offensive material. This has raised the issue for many people of the right of free speech and expression as well as people's right to know. The fairness doctrine is the governmental requirement that licensed news media should present honest, equitable, and balanced treatment of any controversial issues they cover. Again, some people argue that this is improper governmental restrictions on free speech, while others claim that there is no consensus on what counts as a controversial issue.

Besides ethical and moral issues relating to media in a broad social sense, there are also ethical and moral issues that arise at the more local level. That is, there are value questions involving the day-to-day operations of news media. One such question is in connection to how information is obtained by the news media. What, if anything, are the legitimate limits to the gathering of information by news media? Some people claim that, in its role of informing the public, the news media should gather whatever information they need or want; they need to get the whole story. The result is what some people see as the overly aggressive behavior of news reporters, particularly those who have been dubbed the paparazzi. Ethical and moral questions arise concerning the right to privacy of people who are being investigated or reported on. There are also questions about decency of treatment and even of content of news stories.

Another point of concern with respect to news coverage is the issue of confidentiality. News reporters often claim that in order to maintain the reliability of their information, they have the right of confidentiality with respect to their sources of information. In other words, they argue that they should not be required to reveal where they obtain information, and indeed, if they are required to reveal their sources, some of those sources might not provide them with information. For instance, some people might want their identity kept confidential because they might be at risk by providing news media with certain information. As a result, news media often argue that reliability requires confidentiality. On the other hand, others argue that confidentiality is simply another word for secrecy and runs counter to the public's right to know (and to verify the reliability of the information).

Still another topic within media ethics is the issue of objectivity in news coverage and reporting. One aspect of this issue is whether or not objectivity is possible, while another aspect is whether objectivity is desirable. Some people claim that the role of news reporting is to present facts as objectively as possible, while the role of editorials is to make assessments and evaluations (and, perhaps, recommendations). Reporters, however, should get as much relevant information as possible and report it in as balanced a way as possible. Others claim it is not possible to do this because relevance is itself relative. That is, some information might be relevant to some person in some context but not relevant to someone else or to some other context. There are no simple objective facts say these critics. To claim objectivity is to intentionally mislead people, they claim. Supporters of objectivity respond that it is true that relevant is relative, but that it does not follow from this that all data is equally relevant. For instance, in reporting a house fire, it is more relevant to report the address of the house than the color of the house, so that, even if ideal objectivity is not possible, greater or lesser relevant information is.

Concluding Discussion Questions

1. What is moral realism? What does it mean to identify moral facts with natural facts? What is one objection to doing so?
2. What is descriptive cultural relativism? What is philosophical cultural relativism? Do you think that philosophical cultural relativism is true? Are some practices wrong even if some cultures believe they are right? How do we know?
3. What are some of the main differences between utilitarianism and deontology? Which do you think is the better way of understanding right action? Why?
4. What is morality, according to social contract theory? Why would people agree to form a government (or agree on certain rules) according to social contract theory? Do you think social contract theory is a good view of morality? Why or why not?
5. What does it mean to say that nature has intrinsic value? What does it mean to say it has extrinsic value? Do you think nature has intrinsic value? Why or why not? If nature has intrinsic value, do you think people ought to change some of the ways they behave toward the natural environment? If yes, what should they do differently? If not, why not?
6. What is the argument from marginal cases, in animal ethics? Do you think it is a good argument? Why or why not? If the argument is a good one, do you think people ought to change some of the ways they treat animals? If yes, what should they do differently? If not, why not?

Further Reading

Metaethics

Blackburn, Simon. *Being Good: A Short Introduction to Ethics*. Oxford: Oxford University Press, 2003.

Gensler, Henry. *Ethics: Contemporary Readings*. New York: Routledge, 2003.

Miller, Alexander. *An Introduction to Contemporary Metaethics*. Cambridge: Polity, 2003.

Shafer-Landau, Russ, and Terence Cuneo. *Foundations of Ethics: An Anthology*. New York: Wiley-Blackwell, 2007.

Normative Ethics

Driver, Julia. *Ethics: The Fundamentals*. New York: Wiley-Blackwell, 2006.

Rachels, James, and Stuart Rachels. *The Elements of Moral Philosophy*. New York: McGraw-Hill, 2009.

Shafer-Landau, Russ. *Ethical Theory: An Anthology*. Wiley-Blackwell, 2007.

Tannsjo, Torbjorn. *Understanding Ethics: An Introduction to Moral Theory*. 2nd ed. Edinburgh: Edinburgh University Press, 2009.

Applied Ethics

Lafollete, Hugh, ed. *Ethics in Practice: An Anthology*. New York: Blackwell, 2006.

Mappes, Thomas A., and Janes S. Zembaty, eds. *Social Ethics: Morality and Social Policy*. 7th ed. New York: McGraw-Hill, 2007.

Martin, Mike W. *Everyday Morality: An Introduction to Applied Ethics*. Florence, Ky.: Wadsworth, 2006.

May, Larry, Shari Collins-Chobanian, and Kai Wong, eds. *Applied Ethics: A Multicultural Approach*. 4th ed. Upper Saddle River, N.J.: Prentice Hall, 2005.

Glossary

applied ethics a subarea of ethics, concerned with the application of normative ethical theories to specific, practical issues such as animal testing, euthanasia, and abortion.

communitarianism a view in ethics and political philosophy that regards individuals as beings who are fundamentally members of communities; communitarians seek to balance individual rights with the good of the community and hold that moral judgments are made within the context of a community's values, practices, and beliefs.

cultural relativism, philosophical the view in metaethics that morality is relative to cultural standards; philosophical cultural relativism is a kind of moral relativism.

deontology literally, the study of duty; in normative ethics, deontology evaluates the rightness of actions in terms of moral duty (rather than in terms of the consequences of an action).

divine command theory in normative ethics, the view that right action consists of obeying God's commands.

egoism, ethical the view that moral action consists in pursuing one's own interests or, put another way, that one morally ought to pursue one's own interests.

emotivism the view in metaethics that statements that express moral judgments are neither true nor false but serve to express a speaker's attitude and influence others.

ethics of care in normative ethics and feminist ethics, a school of thought that understands morality and right action in terms of caring relationships and the virtues associated with them.

hedonism, ethical the view that moral action consists in producing or promoting happiness or pleasure, that people ought to promote happiness or pleasure.

metaethics a subarea of ethics, concerned with the nature of moral judgments and the meaning of moral terms (such as *good* and *right*) and moral statements (such as "murder is wrong").

moral realism the view that there are moral facts and at least some moral beliefs and moral statements (such as "kindness is good") are true or false.

moral relativism the view that morality is not absolute but is instead relative to some standard.

noncognitivism, cognitivism *noncognitivism* is a term used for any view in metaethics according to which moral judgments lack cognitive content and statements expressing moral judgments are neither true nor false; cognitivism is the denial of noncognitivism, holding that at least some moral judgments have cognitive content and at least some statements expressing moral judgments are true or false.

normative ethics a subarea of ethics, concerned with norms (standards) of moral behavior, such as right action and how one ought to live.

prescriptivism the view in metaethics that an important component of statements that express moral judgments (such as "donating to charity is good") is that they express commands, rather than a speaker's beliefs.

social contract theory the view that morality consists of an agreement between rational, self-interested people.

utilitarian theory an account in normative ethics that evaluates the morality of an action according to whether it produces the greatest good for the greatest number of people affected by that action (or whether it follows a rule that produces the greatest good for the greatest number).

virtue ethics an account in normative ethics that focuses on virtues, rather than principles, as a way of understanding morality and how one ought to live.

Key People

Aristotle (384–322 B.C.E.) *Greek philosopher who understood moral life in terms of virtues. He defended the doctrine of the mean and viewed a virtuous life as a rational life; he thought one could not live a happy life unless one lived virtuously. In the following passage, Aristotle describes virtue as a kind of moderation.*

> If . . . every art or science perfects its work in this way, looking to the mean and bringing its work up to this standard (so that people are wont to say of a good work that nothing could be taken from it or added to it, implying that excellence is destroyed by excess or deficiency, but secured by observing the mean; and good artists, as we say, do in fact keep their eyes fixed on this in all that they do), and if virtue, like nature, is more exact and better than any art, it follows that virtue also must aim at the mean—virtue of course meaning moral virtue or excellence; for it has to do with passions and actions, and it is these that admit of excess and deficiency and the mean. For instance, it is possible to feel fear, confidence, desire, anger, pity, and generally to be affected pleasantly and painfully, either too much or too little, in either case wrongly; but to be thus affected at the right times, and on the right occasions, and towards the right persons, and with the right object, and in the right fashion, is the mean course and the best course, and these are characteristics of virtue. And in the same way our outward acts also admit of excess and deficiency, and the mean or due amount.
>
> Virtue, then, has to deal with feelings or passions and with outward acts, in which excess is wrong and deficiency also is blamed, but the mean amount is praised and is right—both of which are characteristics of virtue.
>
> Virtue, then, is a kind of moderation, inasmuch as it aims at the mean or moderate amount.
>
> [Aristotle. *Nicomachean Ethics*. Book 2. 5th ed. Translated by F. H. Peters. London: Kegan Paul, Trench, Truebner & Co., 1893.]

Bentham, Jeremy (1748–1832) *British philosopher important in classical utilitarianism. He thought that morally right action is action that produces the greatest good for the greatest number. Bentham was a psychological and ethical hedonist who believed all pleasures were equal, as long their quantity was equal. Bentham describes the avoidance of pain and seeking of pleasure as driving forces in how we behave, claiming also that they ought to guide how we behave.*

> Nature has placed mankind under the governance of two sovereign masters, *pain* and *pleasure*. It is for them alone to point out what we ought to do, as well as to determine what we shall do. On the one hand the standard of right and wrong, on the other the chain of causes and effects, are fastened to their throne. They govern us in all we do, in all we say, in all we think: every effort we can make to throw off our subjection, will serve but to demonstrate and confirm it. In words a man may pretend to abjure their empire: but in reality he will remain subject to it all the while. The *principle of utility* recognizes this subjection, and assumes it for the foundation of that system, the object of which is to rear the fabric of felicity by the hands of reason and of law. Systems which attempt to question it, deal in sounds instead of sense, in caprice instead of reason, in darkness instead of light.
>
> But enough of metaphor and declamation: it is not by such means that moral science is to be improved.
>
> The principle of utility is the foundation of the present work: it will be proper therefore at the outset to give an explicit and determinate account of what is meant by it. By the principle of utility is meant that principle which approves or disapproves of every action whatsoever, according to the tendency which it appears to have to augment or diminish the happiness of the party whose interest is in question: or, what is the same thing in other words, to promote or to oppose that happiness. I say of every action whatsoever; and therefore not only of every action of a private individual, but of every measure of government.
>
> [*The Works of Jeremy Bentham*. Published under the superintendence of his executor, John Bowring. 11 vols. Vol. 1. Edinburgh: William Tait, 1838–1843.]

Epicurus (ca. 341–270 B.C.E.) *Greek philosopher who argued that happiness or pleasure is the goal of life and that it can be attained in part through practicing the virtues; he noted that sometimes one should give up short-term pleasures for the sake of long-term pleasures. Epicurus here explains what he means (and does not mean) in claiming that pleasure is the goal of life.*

> When . . . we maintain that pleasure is the end, we do not mean the pleasures of . . . those that consist in sensuality, as is supposed by some who are either ignorant or disagree with us or do not understand, but freedom from pain in the body and from trouble in the mind. For it is not continuous drinkings and revellings, nor the satisfaction of lusts . . . which produce a pleasant life, but sober reasoning, searching out the motives for all choice and avoidance, and banishing mere opinions, to which are due the greatest disturbance of the spirit.
>
> [*The Epicurus Reader.* Translated by Brad Inwood and Lloyd P. Gerson. Indianapolis, Ind.: Hackett, 1994.]

Hobbes, Thomas (1588–1679) *British philosopher who argued that life without government (in the state of nature) was solitary, poor, nasty, brutish, and short. He believed people were both rational and self-interested and would agree to form a government for the sake of their own security. Hobbes claims that in the state of nature, in which each person vies with all others for his own advantage, people cannot live with safety or security; for this reason, they agree to give up rights enjoyed in the state of nature.*

> And because the condition of man . . . is a condition of war of every one against every one; in which case every one is governed by his own reason; and there is nothing he can make use of, that may not be a help unto him, in preserving his life against his enemies; it followeth, that in such a condition, every man has a right to every thing; even to one another's body. And therefore, as long as this natural right of every man to every thing endureth, there can be no security to any man, how strong or wise soever he be, of living out the time, which nature ordinarily alloweth men to live. And consequently it is a precept, or general rule of reason, *that every man, ought to endeavour peace, as far as he has hope of obtaining it; and when he cannot obtain it, that he may seek, and use, all helps, and advantages of war.* The first

branch of which rule, containeth the first, and fundamental law of nature; which is, *to seek peace, and follow it*. The second, the sum of the right of nature; which is, *by all means we can, to defend ourselves*.

From this fundamental law of nature, by which men are commanded to endeavour peace, is derived this second law; *that a man be willing, when others are so too, as far-forth, as for peace, and defence of himself he shall think it necessary, to lay down this right to all things; and be contented with so much liberty against other men, as he would allow other men against himself*.

[*The English Works of Thomas Hobbes of Malmesbury; Now First Collected and Edited by Sir William Molesworth, Bart*. 11 vols. Vol. 3. London: Bohn, 1839–1845.]

Hume, David (1711–1776) *Scottish philosopher who defended a version of subjectivism about morality, arguing that morality is ultimately based on feelings ("sentiment") rather than on reason. In this passage, Hume claims that because passions (not reason) motivate us to act, morality (which is motivating) is based on passions rather than reason.*

If morality had naturally no influence on human passions and actions, 'twere in vain to take such pains to inculcate it; and nothing wou'd be more fruitless than that multitude of rules and precepts, with which all moralists abound. Philosophy is commonly divided into *speculative* and *practical*; and as morality is always comprehended under the latter division, 'tis supposed to influence our passions and actions, and to go beyond the calm and indolent judgments of the understanding. And this is confirm'd by common experience, which informs us, that men are often govern'd by their duties, and are deter'd from some actions by the opinion of injustice, and impell'd to others by that of obligation.

Since morals, therefore, have an influence on the actions and affections, it follows, that they cannot be deriv'd from reason; and that because reason alone, as we have already prov'd, can never have any such influence. Morals excite passions, and produce or prevent actions. Reason of itself is utterly impotent in this particular. The rules of morality, therefore, are not conclusions of our reason.

No one, I believe, will deny the justness of this inference; nor is there any other means of evading it, than by denying that principle, on which it is founded. As long as it is allow'd, that reason has no influence on our passions and actions, 'tis in vain to pretend, that morality is discover'd only by a deduction of reason. An active principle can never be founded on an inactive; and if reason be inactive in itself, it must remain so in all its shapes and appearances, whether it exerts itself in natural or moral subjects, whether it considers the powers of external bodies, or the actions of rational beings.

[*A Treatise of Human Nature* by David Hume. Reprinted from the original edition in three volumes and edited, with an analytical index, by L. A. Selby-Bigge, M.A. Oxford: Clarendon, 1896.]

Kant, Immanuel (1724–1804) *Influential figure in deontology, the study of duty. Kant formulated the categorical imperative, a moral principle he believed applied universally. Kant thought that to be moral was rational and the only thing that is good without qualification is a good will. The following passages from Kant's* Grounding for the Metaphysics of Morals *illustrate Kant's view of morality as consisting of rational, universally binding rules, as well as his claim that only a good will is good without qualification.*

Everyone must admit that if a law is to be morally valid, i.e., is to be valid as a ground of obligation, then it must carry with it absolute necessity. He must admit that the command, 'Thou shalt not lie,' does not hold only for men, as if other rational beings had no need to abide by it, and so with all the other moral laws properly so called; and he must concede that the ground of obligation here must therefore be sought not in the nature of man or in the circumstances of the world . . . but must be sought a priori solely in the concepts of pure reason . . .

'There is no possibility of thinking of anything at all in the world, or even out of it, which can be regarded as good without qualification, except a good will. Intelligence, wit, judgment, and whatever talents of the mind one might want to name are doubtless in many respects good and desirable, as are such qualities of temperament as courage, resolution, perseverance. But they can also become extremely bad and harmful if the will, which is to make use of these gifts of nature and which in its special constitution is called character, is not good.

Hence there is only one categorical imperative, and it is this: Act only according to that maxim by which you can at the same time will that it should become a universal law.

[Kant, Immanuel. *Grounding for the Metaphysics of Morals*. 3rd ed. Translated by James Wesley Ellington. Indianapolis, Ind.: Hackett, 1981.]

Locke, John (1632–1704) *British philosopher influential in social contract theory. Locke thought that people would agree to form a government in order to better protect their natural rights and ensure the punishment of those who violated natural rights. Locke claims that government derives its legitimacy from the fact that people consent to be governed and that people consent to be governed for the sake of security and peace; in his view, when people agree to form a political community (a government), they agree to submit themselves to the will of the majority.*

Men being, as has been said, by nature, all free, equal, and independent, no one can be put out of this estate, and subjected to the political power of another, without his own consent. The only way, whereby any one divests himself of his natural liberty, and puts on the bonds of civil society, is by agreeing with other men to join and unite into a community, for their comfortable, safe, and peaceable living one amongst another, in a secure enjoyment of their properties, and a greater security against any, that are not of it. This any number of men may do, because it injures not the freedom of the rest; they are left as they were in the liberty of the state of nature. When any number of men have so consented to make one community or government, they are thereby presently incorporated, and make one body politic, wherein the majority have a right to act and conclude the rest.

For when any number of men have, by the consent of every individual, made a community, they have thereby made that community one body, with a power to act as one body, which is only by the will and determination of the majority: for that which acts any community, being only the consent of the individuals of it, and it being necessary to that which is one body to move one way; it is necessary the body should move that way whither the greater force carries it, which is the consent of the majority: or else it is impossible it should act or continue one body, one community, which the consent of every individual that united into it, agreed that it should; and so every one is bound by that consent to be concluded by the majority.

[*The Works of John Locke in Nine Volumes.* 12th ed. Vol. 4. London: Rivington, 1824.]

Marx, Karl (1818–1883) *German economic theorist who believed that the moral values and practices of a society are derived from the economic structures and conditions of that society. A short elaboration of Marx's views on moral and social values appeared in his preface to* A Contribution to the Critique of Political Economy *(1859).*

In the social production of their life, men enter into definite relations that are indispensable and independent of their will, relations of production which correspond to a definite stage of development of their material productive forces. The sum total of these relations of production constitutes the economic structure of society, the real foundation, on which rises a legal and political superstructure and to which correspond definite forms of social consciousness. The mode of production of material life conditions the social, political and intellectual life process in general. It is not the consciousness of men that determines their being, but, on the contrary, their social being that determines their consciousness. At a certain stage of their development, the material productive forces of society come in conflict with the existing relations of production, or . . . From forms of development of the productive forces these relations turn into their fetters. Then begins an epoch of social revolution. With the change of the economic foundation of the entire immense superstructure is more or less rapidly transformed. In considering such transformations, a distinction should always be made between the material transformation of the economic conditions of production, which can be determined with the precision of natural science, and the legal, political, religious, aesthetic or philosophic—in short, ideological forms in which men become conscious of this conflict and fight it out. Just as our opinion of an individual is not based on what he thinks of himself, so can we not judge of such a period of transformation by its own consciousness; on the contrary, this consciousness must be explained rather from the contradictions of material life, from the existing conflict between the social productive forces and the relations of production.

[Marx, Karl. *A Contribution to the Critique of Political Economy.* Translated by J. W. Ryazanskya. Moscow: Progress, 1977.]

Mill, John Stuart (1806–1873) *Classical utilitarian who distinguished between higher and lower pleasures, regarding pleasures of the intellect as superior in quality to pleasures of the body. In the following passage, Mill defends his view that some pleasures are superior to others.*

If I am asked, what I mean by difference of quality in pleasures, or what makes one pleasure more valuable than another, merely as a pleasure, except its being greater in amount, there is but one possible answer. Of two pleasures, if there be one to which all or almost all who have experience of both give a decided preference, irrespective of any feeling of moral obligation to prefer it, that is the more desirable pleasure. If one of the two is, by those who are competently acquainted with both, placed so far above the other that they prefer it, even though knowing it to be attended with a greater amount of discontent, and would not resign it for any quantity of the other pleasure which their nature is capable of, we are justified in ascribing to the preferred enjoyment a superiority in quality, so far outweighing quantity as to render it, in comparison, of small account.

Now it is an unquestionable fact that those who are equally acquainted with, and equally capable of appreciating and enjoying, both, do give a most marked preference to the manner of existence which employs their higher faculties. Few human creatures would consent to be changed into any of the lower animals, for a promise of the fullest allowance of a beast's pleasures; no intelligent human being would consent to be a fool, no instructed person would be an ignoramus, no person of feeling and conscience would be selfish and base, even though they should be persuaded that the fool, the dunce, or the rascal is better satisfied with his lot than they are with theirs.

[Mill, John Stuart. *Utilitarianism.* London: Penguin, 1987.]

Nietzsche, Friedrich (1844–1900) *German philosopher who, in opposition to views of ethics such as deontological ethics, distinguished between master morality and slave morality, describing the latter as an invention* *of the weak to oppose the strong. In the passage below, Nietzsche claims that what is good is power, as opposed to the qualities he negatively associated with Christianity. By power, Nietzsche did not mean power over others (such as political power) but rather the flourishing of oneself, such as creativity and maximizing one's potential.*

> What is good? Everything that heightens the feeling of power in man, the will to power, power itself.
>
> What is bad? Everything that is born of weakness.
>
> What is happiness? The feeling that power is growing, that resistance is overcome. Not contentedness but more power; not peace but war; not virtue but fitness (Renaissance virtue, *virtù*, virtue that is moraline-free).
>
> The weak and the failures shall perish: first principle of our love of man. And they shall even be given every possible assistance.
>
> What is more harmful than any vice? Active pity for all the failures and all the weak: Christianity.
>
> [Nietzsche, Friedrich. *The Antichrist*. Translated by H. L. Mencken. New York: A. A. Knopf, 1920.]

Plato (ca. 428–348 B.C.E.) *Greek philosopher who defended moral realism and wrote important dialogues in which Socrates was a key figure, asking questions such as the nature of piety and why one should be moral. In this passage, Plato describes justice as consisting of an appropriate harmony between the three parts of a person's soul (the appetitive element, spirit, and reason).*

> But in reality justice was such as we were describing, being concerned however, not with the outward man, but with the inward, which is the true self and concernment of man: for the just man does not permit the several elements within him to interfere with one another, or any of them to do the work of others,—he sets in order his own inner life, and is his own master and his own law, and at peace with himself; and when he has bound together the three principles within him, which may be compared to the higher, lower, and middle notes of the scale, and the intermediate intervals—when he has bound all these together, and is no longer many, but has

become one entirely temperate and perfectly adjusted nature, then he proceeds to act, if he has to act, whether in a matter of property, or in the treatment of the body, or in some affair of politics or private business; always thinking and calling that which preserves and co-operates with this harmonious condition, just and good action, and the knowledge which presides over it, wisdom, and that which at any time impairs this condition, he will call unjust action, and the opinion which presides over it ignorance.

[Plato. *The Republic*. Book IVersus Translated by Benjamin Jowett. New York: Macmillan, 1892.]

Rawls, John (1921–2002) *American philosopher who gave an account of justice as fairness, arguing within the overall context of social contract theory. Rawls described a formal procedure to determine what is just; he presents a form of social contract, based on the idea that rational, self-interested people would agree to a fundamental principle of justice.*

My aim is to present a conception of justice which generalizes and carries to a higher level of abstraction the familiar theory of the social contract as found, say, in Locke, Rousseau, or Kant . . . the guiding idea is that the principles of justice for the basic structure of society are the object of the original [contract]. I shall call [this] justice as fairness . . . All social values—liberty and opportunity, income and wealth, and the basis of self-respect—are to be distributed equally unless an unequal distribution of any, or all, of these values is to everyone's advantage.

[Rawls, John. *A Theory of Justice*. Cambridge: Harvard University Press, 1971.]

Rousseau, Jean-Jacques (1712–1778) *Influential French philosopher in social contract theory. Rousseau here notes that life without government (the state of nature) cannot go on forever and that people form a government (a "social contract") to ensure their own peace and survival.*

I assume that men have reached a point at which the obstacles that endanger their preservation in the state of nature overcome by their resistance the forces which each individual can exert with a view to maintaining himself in that state. Then this primitive condition cannot longer subsist, and the human race would perish unless it changed its mode of existence.

Now as men cannot create any new forces, but only combine and direct those that exist, they have no other means of self-preservation than to form by aggregation a sum of forces which may overcome the resistance, to put them in action by a single motive power, and to make them work in concert.

This sum of forces can be produced only by the combination of many; but the strength and freedom of each man being the chief instruments of his preservation, how can he pledge them without injuring himself, and without neglecting the cares which he owes to himself? This difficulty, applied to my subject, may be expressed in these terms:—

"To find a form of association which may defend and protect with the whole force of the community the person and property of every associate, and by means of which, coalescing with all, may nevertheless obey only himself, and remain as free as before." Such is the fundamental problem of which the social contract furnishes the solution.

[*Ideal Empires and Republics. Rousseau's Social Contract, More's Utopia, Bacon's New Atlantis, Campanella's City of the Sun.* With an Introduction by Charles M. Andrews. Washington, D.C.: M. Walter Dunne, 1901.]

Singer, Peter (1946–) *Important contemporary Australian ethicist whose philosophical work helped shape the recent growth and understanding of various issues in applied ethics, especially animal ethics. In this passage, Singer argues that beings capable of pleasure and pain deserve moral consideration, including nonhuman animals that are capable of pleasure and pain.*

If a being suffers there can be no moral justification for refusing to take that suffering into consideration. No matter what the nature of the being, the principle of equality requires that its suffering be counted equally with the like suffering . . . of any other being . . . So the limit of sentience . . . is the only defensible boundary of concern for the interests of others. To mark this boundary by some other characteristic like intelligence or rationality would be to mark it in an arbitrary manner. Why not choose some other characteristic, like skin color?

[Singer, Peter. *Animal Liberation*. New York: Avon Books, 1975.]

Socrates (469–399 B.C.E.) *Ancient Greek philosopher, teacher of Plato, and central figure in Plato's dialogues. Socrates asked philosophical questions such as what the nature of piety is and whether a person ever knowingly performs a morally bad action. Here Socrates questions Euthyphro about the nature of piety, suggesting that if what is good (or holy) is loved by God (or the gods) because it is good (or holy), then what is good (or holy) is good independent of being loved by God (or the gods).*

> But, friend Euthyphro, if that which is holy is the same with that which is dear to God, and is loved because it is holy, then that which is dear to God would have been loved as being dear to God; but if that which is dear to God is dear to him because loved by him, then that which is holy would have been holy because loved by him. But now you see that the reverse is the case, and that they are quite different from one another. For one *(theophiles)* is of a kind to be loved cause it is loved, and the other *(osion)* is loved because it is of a kind to be loved. Thus you appear to me, Euthyphro, when I ask you what is the essence of holiness, to offer an attribute only, and not the essence—the attribute of being loved by all the gods. But you still refuse to explain to me the nature of holiness. And therefore, if you please, I will ask you not to hide your treasure, but to tell me once more what holiness or piety really is, whether dear to the gods or not (for that is a matter about which we will not quarrel) and what is impiety?

[Plato. *Euthyphro*. Translated by Bejamin Jowett. New York: Macmillan, 1892.]

PART II
Political Philosophy

Introductory Discussion Questions

1. What rights do you have? Why do you have those rights (that is, what gives you those rights)?
2. Do you have any obligations to your local (or state or federal) government? Why or why not?
3. What is a (or the) government?
4. Do communities or governments, as opposed to the individuals who make up those communities or governments, have rights or responsibilities? For example, does the state of Nebraska have any rights or responsibilities? Why or why not?
5. Should there be a strong separation between church and state? Why or why not?
6. What purpose (or purposes) does law serve? When, if ever, is it appropriate to ignore or even violate a law?

What Is Political Philosophy?

Political philosophy is the study of fundamental aspects and concepts of human life in the context of communities. It involves the analysis and critique of collective human structures and organizations. The word *political* comes from the Greek word *polis,* meaning "nation" or "state." While some philosophical concerns focus on individuals—for example, what is the nature of mind or what is the nature of free will—and other philosophical concerns (such as metaphysics) focus on the nature of the world, political philosophy focuses on issues related to human social life, such as the nature of the state or the nature of rights or the nature of justice.

A primary concern of political philosophy is what exactly counts as a political unit. Today, most people would probably immediately think of nations as the typical "thing" that is a political unit. However, this was not always historically the case. A nation, in the sense we think of one today, is something that developed only in the past few hundred years, but people certainly had political structures and organizations long before then. In fact, very important and influential writings in political philosophy go as far back as Plato (ca. 428–348 B.C.E.), almost, 2,500 years ago. Even if one started with the concept of a nation as the basic and typical political unit, it is not exactly clear what a nation is. People use the concept of nation in ways that are not exactly the same as the concept of the state. For example, many Muslims speak of the nation of Islam, but they do not mean some specific state, such as Syria or Saudi Arabia. Also, many people living in the Canadian arctic refer to themselves as part of the First Nation living in what is now called

America, but they do not mean some specific state or province, such as Canada or British Columbia.

There are also aspects of human social life that have little, if anything, to do with what is usually considered to be political. For instance, there are cultural aspects of social life, such as the arts or sports that are not part of the meaning of *nation*. The Miss America pageant pertains only to the nation of the United States (that is, it does not include anyone outside of the United States), but it certainly is not part of the political structure or organization of the nation. In addition, there are many communities within a nation, yet many of these communities are not political (for instance, a community of Red Sox fans or Red Cross volunteers). Along with communities, there are a variety of ways that people live within and are part of groups and collectives. For example, when people are identified as employers (as opposed to employees), this is a group or collective, or when people are identified as having some ethnicity (such as being Hispanic American), or when people are identified together on the basis of some common feature (such as being senior citizens), these are all social groupings and collectives, but they are not part of the concept of nation.

At the same time, some people think of a nation as being the same as a state. However, again, this is not exactly correct. If by *state* one means the various structures and organizations that are used to regulate peoples' behavior in collective groups, then, once again, this is not obvious. There are structures and organizations that extend beyond individual states or nations, such as international pacts or organizations. The distinction between the state and government is also not sharp. The government is clearly only a part of what is the state, and any current regime, or group in power that runs the government, is certainly not the same thing as the state (when one regime is replaced that does not necessarily mean that the state has changed). One very basic issue in political philosophy, then, is about the very nature of what is a political unit (as opposed to some other social unit).

Another important issue within political philosophy is that of legitimacy and authority. That is, what makes a government legitimate (or not) and what gives it any appropriate authority over the citizens of the state? While today many people, especially those who live in Western nations, claim that what gives a government its legitimacy and proper authority is the "consent of the governed," this is not the view that is held worldwide, and it is not the view that had been held over history. Some people claim that individuals are primary, and all social collectives, including the state, are simply aggregates, or collections, of individuals. These collectives have no legitimacy or proper authority over individuals except and unless those individuals say so. Some other people disagree and claim that some collectives, at least, are not merely aggregates of individuals, but that communities have a status beyond the particular individuals within them. (For example, they say, it is teams that win games, not the individuals within those teams, so teams have a status beyond just being made up of individual players.)

Much of the debate over legitimacy and authority has to do with the concept and practice of representation. If a state is not legitimate, many philosophers argue, it is because it failed to become a state in an appropriate manner or because it does not act in an appropriate manner. That is, if the state does not represent the will of the people who are subject to the state, then, say these philosophers, it has no legitimacy or proper authority. However, the very issue of representation is complex. One sense of representation is that one thing is authorized to act for another thing. For instance, someone might have an agent or representative act for her when negotiating a contract. Another sense of representation that is similar to, but slightly different from, acting for someone is the sense of representation as symbolizing or standing for. For example, we might say that the flag represents the nation or that the eagle represents courage. Yet another sense of representation is that of being typical of. For example, we might say that a given person is representative of the dedicated average worker for some group.

These various senses of representation all relate to political contexts, especially with respect to representing the interests of those who are subject to the authority of the state. For instance, we say that elected officials, such as the president or a senator or even a local school board member, has legitimacy and authority to the extent that they in fact represent our interests. We might think that by representing us this means that they stand in for us and act for us (that is, the way we want them to act), but this is not necessarily the case. Because citizens (or whoever is subject to a state's authority) do not all agree on issues, representatives do not necessarily act for them in the sense of acting as citizens wish or in ways that citizens are interested. For instance, a state official might vote on some piece of legislation, making many citizens unhappy. In what sense, then, has this official represented those citizens?

This issue of representation is made even more complex by the fact that people have many different types of interests and are connected to many different types of groups. For instance, in some contexts age might be important, so that a citizen wants political representation with respect to health care for the elderly. In another context, race or ethnicity might matter, so that a citizen (perhaps even the same one who is elderly) wants political representation with respect to civil rights and protection against racial discrimination. In yet another context, a citizen's type of employment or where he lives (urban versus rural) might be relevant to wanting particular political representation. In a very broad way, these sorts of concerns are often spoken of as identity politics, that is, where one's identity—say, as being elderly or being Latino or being a farmer—are important for political representation. Many people have argued that such identity politics is important, while others have argued that it runs against the notion of all citizens being treated on a par with each other.

The issue of political representation is complex and not at all obvious, and it is one that political philosophers have wrestled with for centuries. As noted above, this issue directly relates to the issues of authority and legitimacy, since the state has these because of its representational nature—at least, so say many political philosophers.

While these topics such as the nature of the state and its proper role and function (say, to represent citizens) are very broad topics *about* politics, there are also many important topics *within* political structures and organizations that philosophers have focused on. One such topic is that of rights. Very broadly, rights are spoken of as either protections against others, including against the state, or as powers to act. In other words, we usually speak of our rights not to be harmed by others (that is, rights limit what others may legitimately do to us) or our rights to be able to do what we want (that is, rights empower or entitle us to act in certain ways). A very important issue within political philosophy is the nature of rights, including what justifies the rights that people have, what they have rights to, what limitations there are on people's rights, and even what kinds of things have rights. This is particularly important with respect to the relation between individuals and the state, that is, what rights people have within a state and also against a state. A flip side of this topic of rights is the nature of civil law. Laws are means of regulating people's behaviors and actions. An important issue within political philosophy, then, is the nature of law as well as how law relates to a state. (For example, do laws come from the state? Do they regulate not just people but the state itself? If laws have legitimacy and authority "over" the state in terms of regulating it, what is the relationship between laws and the state?)

Another important topic within the context of political structures and organizations is that of public versus private, that is, what aspects of people's lives are subject to public (i.e., state) regulation and what aspects are private and not subject to state regulation. What gives the state any legitimacy or proper authority to regulate private lives or behaviors of citizens? Even more, what aspects of people's lives are public and what aspects are private? For example, can the decisions of parents concerning the well-being of their children appropriately be regulated by the state? Can the state appropriately regulate people's interpersonal relationships (such as saying who may or may not get married or have sex)? Can the state appropriately censor information to individuals or require, say, schooling for children?

Yet another basic topic within political structures and organizations that political philosophy deals with is the topic of justice (and the closely related topic of equality). The notion of the state itself as being a just state is as old as the writings of Plato, who focused on this issue in *The Republic*. Beyond the question of what makes a state a just state—which is essentially the issue of the legitimacy and proper authority of the state—there is also the issue of justice within the state. One sense of justice has to do with distributive justice, or the appropriate distribution of things within the state or within society. For example, if a very small percentage of citizens are rich and the vast majority is poor, does the state have the legitimate authority to redistribute the wealth of the citizens in that state (for example, by taxing the wealthy and giving goods or services to the poor)? This speaks also to the issue of equality. Clearly, not everyone is identical with everyone else, so there is not perfect equality. What sorts of equality, then, are subject to appropriate state regulation? In what ways could or should citizens be considered equal to each other such that it is appropriate for the state to regulate people's lives? These sorts of topics—issues about rights and law and justice—are fundamental areas of concern within political philosophy, political because they involve collective human social life.

Normative Disciplines and Politics

One way of considering things, including politics, is to be descriptive. That is, one might simply want to describe some thing or event or situation. For instance, someone might describe the various features of dogs (say, their sizes, shapes, colors, perhaps various behavioral traits, such as barking or wagging their tails). Or when thinking about politics, someone might describe how a bill becomes law in Congress or what basic beliefs or attitudes are typically associated with some politician or political party or the different amendments that are part of the U.S. Constitution.

Besides describing things—that is, asking what is the case—someone might want to consider things prescriptively, or normatively. Being prescriptive has to do not with what *is* the case but what ought to be the case. Much like when a doctor gives someone a prescription, the point is that the doctor is not merely describing something but is telling the patient what to do (for instance, to take a certain dosage of medicine). To prescribe is not to describe; it is to speak of what should be the case or should take place. For example, if someone were to say that the U.S. Constitution does not explicitly address same-sex marriage, then that person is speaking descriptively. On the other hand, if that person were to say that the U.S. Constitution should (or should not) allow for same-sex marriage, then that person is speaking prescriptively.

Another term that is used with much the same meaning as prescriptive is the word *normative*. Like prescriptivity, the notion of normative (or normativity) has to do with more than simply describing things. The root for *normative* is "norm," that is, a standard or basic criterion for assessing things. (The word *normal* means what is standard.) When philosophers (and others) speak of something as normative, then, they mean norms or standards or criteria by which to assess and evaluate and judge something. Since political philosophy is not simply about describing politics but about analyzing and justifying basic political concepts and institutions and structures (for instance, asking: What is the proper function of the state?), political philosophy is said to be a normative discipline. When political philosophers ask, "What are rights?" or "What obligations do individuals have to the state and the state to individuals?" they are asking not descriptive questions but normative questions, because the answers they are looking for are not merely ones that describe how things happen to be but what does or can justify certain answers to those questions. Because political philosophy is a normative discipline, it is closely related to the other major normative philosophical discipline, namely, ethics.

There are many different views in normative ethics, with each attempting to say what is morally right. Of course, thinkers other than philosophers often make claims about what is moral and what is not. What is distinctive about the philosophical practice of normative ethics is the attempt to give good reasons for particular claims about what is morally right. Often normative theories give principles for right action, and often these principles are meant to apply universally, to all situations. Sometimes what philosophers consider is good shapes what they consider is morally right. For example, hedonism is the view that what is good is happiness, and according to one version of utilitarianism, right actions are those actions that produce the greatest happiness. One general approach to normative ethics is the approach of deontology. Deontological ethical theories, strongly associated with Immanuel Kant, give accounts of right action in terms of duties and rights.

A main alternative to deontological views are consequentialist views. According to consequentialism, what makes an action right is the value of its consequences. One version of consequentialism is utilitarianism. There are many versions of utilitarianism, in part because there are differing accounts of what consequences are morally relevant. For some versions of utilitarianism, for instance, right actions are those that produce the most happiness, or pleasure. That is, those are the kinds of consequences that are valuable, so right actions are those with those kind of consequences. For other versions of utilitarianism, the right kinds of consequences are those that satisfy the preferences of the beings affected. A third general approach to ethics is social contract theory, in which morality is seen as a kind of theoretical set of rules agreed on by rational people under a particular set of circumstances.

The two normative disciplines of political philosophy and ethics obviously overlap, but they are not identical. For example, the standards or criteria for what it is to be a good person might not be the same as those for what it is to be a good citizen. Likewise, what specific duties or obligations someone might have as a citizen (for instance, the duty to obey traffic laws) might not be the same as the specific duties or obligations that someone might have as a person (for instance, to be honest). In addition, there are questions that pertain to political philosophy that are not necessarily ethical questions (for example, What is the proper function of the state?). Nonetheless, both normative disciplines focus on how people ought to behave and what are appropriate standards and criteria for people's behavior. Still, the nature of the overlap between political philosophy and ethics is not one about which everyone agrees, because some people see communities and political groupings only as a matter of individuals who happen to get together, while others see communities and political groupings as more fundamental to human existence.

Rights

The concept of rights, and more specifically human rights, is a benchmark of modern political theory and policy. The philosophical analysis of rights begins with identifying rights as a feature of regulating behavior in social contexts. That is, rights function as a means of either protecting someone or empowering someone, but outside of the context of interacting with others, rights would have no function. As a form of regulating behavior, rights are often contrasted with goals and duties (or responsibilities). There might be a goal of protecting people against terrorist attacks, and this goal might lead to a conflict with people's rights to privacy. Or there might be a duty to keep one's promises, but this is different than claiming that someone has a right to be promised something. There are other means of regulating behavior, such as laws or force or persuasion. Rights, then, are one way of regulating behavior. Rights normally function to protect someone, such as a person's right to not be harmed, or to empower someone, such as a person's right to drive or vote. These are usually referred to as the functions of *immunity* or *empowerment*. The philosophical analysis of rights uses the following form:

S has a right to *X* against *Y* in virtue of *J*

In this form, *S* stands for the subject (or holder) of rights. Although individual humans are seen as typical holders of rights, other entities or agents are often also said to be rights holders: groups (such as women or children), future generations of humans (including unborn embryos), nation-states, corporations and other legal entities, some nonhuman animals, even the environment. One basic philosophical issue about rights is what counts as a legitimate rights holder?

One never simply has a right but always a right to *X*. There is always some content to a right. The content might be some specific goods or services, such as the right to an attorney, or the content might be the opportunity to obtain some goods or services, such as the right to employment. Different philosophical, social, and political views interpret the legitimate content of rights differently. One interpretation is referred to as negative rights, and a second interpretation is referred to as positive rights. Negative rights means that for one truly to exercise one's rights, then others have a duty or responsibility not to interfere with that rights holder. For example, if someone has a right to worship freely, then others have a duty simply to leave her alone and not interfere with or prevent her from worshipping. Positive rights mean that for one truly to exercise one's rights, then others have a duty or responsibility to provide some specific goods or services to the rights holder. For example, if someone has a right to health care, it is not enough for everyone else to simply leave him alone. Noninterference does not get him health care; rather something, such as medicine or treatment, must actually be provided to him. Some social and political views support both negative and positive rights, although some others hold that any positive right held by one person is necessarily a restriction on the liberties of others, because those others must provide some goods or services whether they want to or not.

Just as rights always have some content, they also always have some audience (the *Y* in the form above). That is, one always holds rights against someone or other. Some rights have a specific audience, while others have a general audience. If Al owes money to Betty, then Betty (not some other person) has a right to that money. However, some rights, such as someone's right to life, are held against all others; if Al has a right to life, then not only does Betty have a duty not to take Al's life, but so does everyone else have that same duty.

Finally, there is the issue of the justification of rights (the *J* in the form above). The issue of the justification of rights is not the same as the issue of the source of rights, although they are related. Or to phrase it differently, why someone has some right is not the same issue as where that right comes from. This is related to the issue of legal rights, which come from a given legal system, versus moral rights, which might not at all be recognized by a given legal system. For example, a legal system might permit slavery or some other flagrant form of oppression. Such legal permissions might not have a legitimate moral backing or justification. The concept of human rights derives largely from the moral rights perspective, supporting the view that individuals can and do have rights independent of, and often in opposition to, the legal system in which they live. The justification of rights, then, is not identical with the source of rights. Various claims have been made for the justification of rights in general as well as of specific rights. One claim is that rights are part of human nature, and without them people cannot function fully as moral agents or persons. Another view is that rights are the best means toward social stability, because people feel more secure believing that they have certain social immunities and powers.

Besides the conceptual aspects of rights that are highlighted in the form above, there are other philosophical and social issues related to rights. For example, there is the issue of the hierarchy of rights: Which particular rights outweigh or trump other rights, as well as other goals or duties, and why? The issue of abortion is often characterized as a conflict of rights: the right of a fetus to be born versus the right of the mother to self-determination. Likewise, the right of privacy for one person might conflict with the right of access to information of another person or agent. For example, a patient's right to privacy about medical status might conflict with an insurance company's right to information regarding what the company is paying for.

Freedom

There are various senses of freedom. In philosophy, one broad sense has to do with political freedom, that is, freedom with respect to the government or other people. For example, this sense is concerned with people having the right to free speech or free expression. A second broad sense has to do with metaphysical freedom, that is, free will, or people's ability to act on their own. For example, this sense is concerned with people being free to make some choice (say, choosing chocolate ice cream over vanilla ice cream), as opposed to that choice being determined by something outside that individual's control.

Within these two broad philosophical concerns (political and metaphysical), there are different senses of freedom. One sense is sometimes called negative freedom, meaning the absence of some imposed constraint. For example, we speak of someone as being (negatively) free to ride a bicycle if that person is not prevented from doing so by, say, being in jail. Another sense is sometimes called positive freedom, meaning having the conditions or ability to do something. So, we speak of someone being (positively) free to ride a bicycle if that person has a bicycle and knows how to ride it. Negative freedom is often referred to as "freedom from," meaning being free from constraints, while positive freedom is often referred to as "freedom to," meaning being free to do something (not merely being free from constraints).

With respect to constraints on freedom, some are said to be external, and some are said to be internal. For example, being locked in chains is an external constraint; the chains are external to the person himself. So, for example, being locked in chains is an external constraint to one's being free to ride a bicycle. On the other hand, being ignorant is an internal constraint; the ignorance is internal to the person himself. So, being ignorant of how to ride a bicycle is an internal constraint to one's being free to ride a bicycle. Generally speaking, things such as locked doors, barred windows, chains, etc., are external positive constraints, while obsessive thoughts, compulsive mental disorders, and perhaps even severe headaches are internal positive constraints. These are positive constraints because there is something that has a direct impact on one's freedom; there is something added, so to speak, to a person that constrains him. There are also negative constraints, which are cases in which the absence or lack of something is what constrains one's freedom. External negative constraints would be cases such as having a lack of money or lack of transportation. For instance, a person is not free to buy a book if that person does not have enough money to do so. In this case, it is the lack of something external to him that constrains him. Internal negative constraints would be cases such as having a lack of knowledge or strength or ability, etc. So, a person is not free to order food in a Swahili restaurant if that person does not speak Swahili (or cannot communicate effectively). The constraint is internal, because what is lacking is not some object or thing but some ability or capability.

The notions of freedom from and freedom to are important in political philosophy in terms of what kinds of freedom are relevant to people's social and political lives. For instance, some people argue that the government has a responsibility to provide people with certain external things (such as goods or services) in order for individuals to truly be free to live well. Others claim that for the government to provide these external things is a violation of their own freedom from being oppressed by the government. That is, for example, the government taxes people (an external constraint on them) in order to redistribute wealth in society (to relieve some constraint on others). The various notions of freedom and constraint are important with respect to responsibility, that is, how, if at all, we can hold people responsible for their actions if their actions are constrained internally and externally.

Classical Greeks: Plato and Aristotle

Plato

The most famous book written by the ancient Greek philosopher Plato (ca. 428–348 B.C.E.) is *The Republic,* about the nature of justice. In this book, Plato raised the question, what is justice? He argued that living well is the soul's function and that to fulfill this function requires justice. To live well, to do the right thing, he said, requires knowledge of what is true and real. Justice, however, is a matter both of the individual and of society in general (as Plato put it: the soul and the state). In each case, justice is a matter of balance and harmony among the parts of the soul or state. The soul, he said, was like a chariot driver trying to steer two horses. One horse is spirit, and the other horse is reason. So, our bodily senses (spirit) move us in one direction, while our reason moves us in another. The harmonious soul brings these into balance and steers the right course; this is what a just person is. With regard to the state, it, too, is a combination of different parts, not always in harmony with each other. A just state is one that is balanced and harmonious. For Plato, this meant that each part of society had its appropriate role and function. Those parts included the rulers, soldiers, and workers. The best state, then, is one in which each group performs its appropriate role (and does not try to do the job of another group), and those people who are best suited for the duties of a particular group are in fact part of that

Some of the philosophers depicted in Raphael's famous painting *The School of Athens* include Zeno of Citium, Epicurus, Pythagoras, Socrates, Heraclitus, Plato, and Aristotle. *(Painting by Raffaello Sanzio da Urbino [Raphael])*

group. For example, soldiers need to protect the state from those who might harm it, while workers need to provide the goods and services that are needed by people. Administrators, or rulers, need to govern well. He called these administrators "guardians," because they have the role of guarding the well-being of the state. The rulers, in a just society, acted like the chariot driver; they control the other parts of the state by making sure that they all operate in harmony. The rulers, for Plato, need to be the best and wisest people, the aristocrats. He even suggested that there should ultimately be a philosopher-king. (His trip to Sicily late in his life was an effort to train such a philosopher-king.) The reason for this, he said, is because philosophers seek wisdom and are the people who are most concerned with knowledge and with justice.

Who would be best at ruling? For Plato, it is philosophers. The reason for this is because philosophers are those who are concerned with true wisdom and with knowing what real justice is. Philosophers, he claimed, focus their lives not merely on the particular things and events of everyday experience but on the essence, or core nature, of things. Their concern is not simply about short-term personal benefit but truly living well. A philosopher-king, then, would focus on living well for the whole state, not just himself. While many people think of philosophers are being impractical and abstract, Plato thought that their devotion to the general, essential nature of things was, rather, what made them the most practical of guardians, because they would have both knowledge of what is good and right as well as the love and desire to be just.

Aristotle

Aristotle (384–322 B.C.E.), Plato's student, was also immensely influential in political philosophy. To understand his thoughts on politics, one must first understand something about his views on metaphysics (the study of reality) and ethics generally. This is because Aristotle claimed that to know what is good for people in a social and political context, one must know what is good for them, and to know that, one must know what kind of thing they are. For instance, what is good for a cat or a tree is, at least in part, different than what is good for a human, since cats and trees are different kinds of things than humans are. Of course, to the extent that they are all living beings, then they all need nutrients to live. However, the kinds of nutrients that trees need are not the same as what cats or humans need.

For Aristotle, the goal of human life is eudaemonia. The Greek term *eudaemonia* is usually translated as happiness, or flourishing. The term comes from the Greek word *eu*, meaning "good," and *daemon*, meaning "spirit." Literally, then, eudaemonia means the state of having a good spirit. Less literally, eudaemonia is the state of living or doing well: of flourishing or being happy. In ancient philosophy, eudaemonia was considered to be the ultimate goal and the ultimate good in human life. So eudaemonia is the state of living the good life for *humans* (it does not apply to nonhuman animals or inanimate things). Although eudaemonia involves happiness, here *happiness* does not mean a short-lived feeling (the way a person might feel, for instance, during a pleasant evening spent with friends). Rather, happiness has to do with the way one lives one's life as a whole. Moreover, eudaemonia is objective; it is not based on a person's individual preferences. Rather, the idea of eudaemonia is that there is a way of living that is the good for all humans. This does not mean that everyone must behave exactly the same way in order to live well and be happy—that everyone must pursue sports as a hobby, for instance. It does mean, however, that there are certain components of human flourishing and human happiness that are objective, that apply to every person's flourishing and happiness. Many ancient philosophers believed that living virtuously was one component of eudaemonia. On this view, it was not possible for a person to flourish and be happy unless she lived virtuously. It is usually thought that Socrates believed that living virtuously was sufficient for eudaemonia, that nothing else was needed. This was also the view of Plato and the Stoic philosophers. Aristotle, in contrast, claimed that although virtue was a necessary component of eudaemonia, it was not sufficient; that is, something more than virtue was required. In particular, Aristotle believed that some material goods were necessary to achieve eudaemonia. One could not, according to Aristotle, live a life of eudaemonia while living in abject poverty. Ancient philosophers also often connected eudaemonia with the use of reason. For instance, Plato and Aristotle argued that a life of eudaemonia is a life lived in accordance with reason. Because Aristotle believed that the function, or purpose, of humans is to reason, he regarded eudaemonia as fulfilling the human function in an excellent way. The Stoics, who believed that the universe was ordered in a rational way that is ultimately for the best, thought eudaemonia required living "in agreement with nature." In contemporary philosophy, eudaemonia has received renewed attention in virtue ethics.

In his writings on physics and metaphysics, Aristotle analyzed the concept of cause, and as noted below, he applied this even to looking at political systems. He argued that a full account of cause involved four components or, as some commentators on Aristotle say, four types of causes. They are: (1) material cause, (2) formal cause, (3) efficient cause, and (4) final cause. All four, for Aristotle, were necessary to fully understand cause, that is, how something (or some event or state of affairs) comes to be. For example, we see a tree (as a natural creation) or a statue (as a human creation) and wonder how it came to exist. The four causes were Aristotle's way of explaining how something comes to be. In effect, the four causes are answers to four separate but related questions. A material cause answers the question: *from* what does something come to be. A formal cause answers the question: *into* what does something come to be. An efficient cause answers the question: *by* what does something come to be. A final cause answers the question: *for* what does something come to be.

Starting with the example of a statue, the point of these four causes can be seen. First, a statue is made out of some material (for instance, bronze or stone). So, part of the explanation for how this statue came to be is the material from which it is made. If it had been made out of other material, it would be a different statue; much like a given person is made out of a particular grouping of DNA. What caused this statue, then, is explained in part by its material cause.

However, that very same material might have been shaped into a different statue. Any material thing, said Aristotle, always has some particular form or structure. That particular form or structure is part of the explanation for what that thing is. So, to explain this particular statue, it is not enough to only speak of the material cause; one must also speak of the formal cause, that is, the form into which those materials are.

An efficient cause is the notion that most people today think of as the (or a) cause of something. For Aristotle, an efficient cause is that by which something comes to be. In the case of a statue, it is by the work of the sculptor, who takes material and manipulates it into a particular form. The actions of the sculptor are the efficient cause of a given statue.

For Aristotle, there is also the final cause. The final cause is the purpose or end or goal that is met by the coming to be of something. In the case of a particular statue, the purpose might be to honor someone or some event. In the case of a tree or any natural thing (including any natural event or process), the purpose might be to promote the survival of some organism or the overall ecological balance of some natural system. The view that things are to be explained in terms of purposes or goals is called teleology (from the Greek word *telos*, meaning "end" or "purpose").

With respect to political systems, Aristotle noted that these four causes apply. That is, political systems have structure and form just as much as statues or trees do. Likewise, political systems have various functions and purposes (or final causes). The ultimate final cause of a political system, for Aristotle, is the good of its citizens, their eudaemonia. In particular, Aristotle thought that humans are political animals, meaning that humans are social and communal by nature. The polis, or community, is not something imposed on people but is natural. The lone individual is, for Aristotle, a much more unnatural notion. However, because a polis is made up of individuals, their good is the goal of the polis. Given this view, some later political philosophers have seen Aristotle's politics as modern, meaning that the good of the individual citizens is basic to any political community, while other political philosophers have seen his politics as more communal in nature, with the good of the individual being inherently tied up with the good of the whole community.

Divine Right: Thomas More

Theocracy

Most people understand theocracy as a form of government in which there is no official separation between the government and religion. More technically, however, a theocracy is a form of government in the sense that the structure of government is one in which religious officials are also governmental officials and religious doctrine forms at least part of the government. So, at the beginning of the 21st century, Iran is technically a theocracy, but Israel is not, even though Israel declares itself to be a Jewish state. Practically all of Israel's laws and governmental structures are secular, or nonreligious, as opposed to Iran, in which Islamic law, sharia, is also state law.

While the United States is a democracy (or, more technically, a republic), not a theocracy, the issue of the formal relationship between religion and government has been a part of American history from its beginning. The early colonies settled by European immigrants during the 1600s involved direct debate about the role of religion in the governments of these colonies. Some of the early colonies were, in fact, designed much along the lines of theocracies. For example, the Mayflower Compact that was adopted in 1620 by early English settlers spoke directly about forming a community ("a civil Body Politic") based on Christian scripture. Likewise, the Fundamental Orders of Connecticut from 1639 spoke of "an orderly and decent Government established according to God," with civil affairs to be "guided and governed" according to Christian laws.

On the other hand, Thomas Jefferson wrote explicitly of "building a wall of separation between Church and State," because, he wrote, religion is a private matter. In addition and for this reason, the U.S. Constitution included in the First Amendment of the Bill of Rights the phrase that "Congress shall make no law respecting the establishment of religion, or prohibiting the free exercise thereof." Although there are religious symbols connected to government (for example, coins in the United States include the phrase "In God We Trust"), most aspects of religion are not part of the very structure of the government nor are they state law (even if some civil laws are motivated by and consistent with certain religious doctrine).

While most people see the issue of the formal separation of religion and government as a difference between democracy and theocracy, not everyone agrees or sees such a distinction. For example, many Muslim officials (including philosophers, theologians, and government officials) claim that no human has legitimate authority over any other human. All authority comes from and belongs to God. The only legitimate civil laws and, indeed, the only legitimate governments are those that rule in accordance with God's laws. Along these lines, the Muslim philosopher Abu'l A'la Mawdudi claimed that the only real democracy is a theocracy, because no person, class, or group, not even the entire population of the state as a whole, can lay claim to sovereignty. God alone is the real sovereign; all others are merely His subjects. If God truly is the sovereign and lawgiver, then civil laws, those created and enforced by the state, need to be in accordance with the laws of God. Appropriate political power derives only from obedience to the laws of God, and people have an inherent right to overthrow inappropriate political systems just as much as they have an inherent duty to obey appropriate political systems. Nevertheless, most people (including many in Islamic countries) distinguish democracy and theocracy and advocate some separation between religion and government.

Divine Right of Kings and Thomas More

In the West, the most prominent version of theocracy was what came to be called the divine right of kings. This idea is associated primarily with political views during the late 1500s to the late 1700s. In the West, the relationship between the church and state was one that varied over time and was always complicated. On one hand, some of the earliest Christian teaching suggested a separation between religion and politics. For example, Jesus spoke of rendering unto Caesar what is Caesar's and rendering unto God what is God's. Many people understood this to mean that matters of this world, including politics and economics and social issues, are secular, while matters pertaining to one's soul and to the afterlife are religious. Likewise, many early Christians were persecuted by the states and communities in which they lived. Religion was seen as a personal relationship with God, not as a public, political one. On the other hand, from the beginning of Christianity the emphasis of living a good life was seen as inherently connected with communities. The doctrine of natural law—that is, moral laws that come from God—has a long tradition in Christian thought. The medieval philosopher and theologian Thomas Aquinas (1225–74) famously argued that secular civil laws (that is, laws coming from human lawgivers) have no binding force unless they are consistent with natural moral laws that come from God. Over time the Roman Catholic Church became the dominant political force in much of Europe, and this resulted at times in significant disputes with political rulers. By the middle 1500s, some political philosophers proclaimed the divine right of kings, the doctrine that certain kings ruled because they were chosen by God, and as a result they were accountable to no one but God.

One person who opposed, or at least challenged, this doctrine was the English statesman Thomas More (1478–1535). More came from a relatively wealthy and privileged family (his father was a judge) and was educated in classics (Greek and Latin culture). Early in life, he was torn between entering law as a profession and devoting his life to religion. At one point, he chose to join a monastery but later entered politics. While he rose in status to become a favored confidant of the English king Henry VIII, he fell into disfavor because he opposed Henry's antagonistic relations with the Church and especially Henry's plan to divorce his wife in order to marry another woman. As a result of his outspoken opposition to these actions of Henry VIII, More was found guilty of treason, imprisoned, and finally beheaded. Beyond this personal stand on moral principles, More is most known today as the author of *Utopia*. The word *utopia* is a play on two Greek words: *ou-topos* means "no place," and *eu-topos* means "good place." In More's book, Utopia was an island in the Atlantic in which he spelled out features of what he saw as

Seventeenth-century painting of Sir Thomas More and Bishop John Fisher

a better political and social system than those he saw in Europe. Among the features of his Utopia was communal property as opposed to private property. This is because in real life More saw great inequalities in people's lives, and he took these to be the result of some people having much property (and, hence, much wealth), while other people had no or almost no property (and, hence, lived in dire poverty). In addition, he saw communal property, as opposed to private property, as being more consistent with biblical teachings and with a religious life. In addition to communal property, there is public education for all and also religious toleration (except for atheists). For his personal actions and his writings, More is seen as an opponent of the divine right of kings and an influence on later liberal political thinkers such as John Locke.

Social Contract: Hobbes, Locke, and Rousseau

Social Contract Theory

Social contract theory covers political philosophy and ethics. In political philosophy, social contract theory is the view that a government somehow derives its legitimacy from the consent of the people it governs (it is as though there is a contract between a legitimate government and the people). In ethics, social contract theory is the view that morality consists of rules that rational, self-interested people would agree upon (it is as though people agree on a contract about how they can and cannot behave, in order best to promote their own interests). These two views are related but not the same. One could, for instance, take a social contract view about the legitimacy of governments without viewing all of morality in terms of a social contract, and vice versa.

A central idea of social contract theory is that individual people are better off cooperating than if they did not do so. Social contract theorists typically view humans as rational, self-interested beings who would, therefore, actually be motivated to cooperate with each other. To illustrate why cooperation is advantageous for everyone, philosophers such as Thomas Hobbes, John Locke, and Jean-Jacques Rousseau (each very influential in social contract theory) imagined humans living in a state in which people did not cooperate, a state without rules or government. This imaginary state is the state of nature, and philosophers described it in different ways, depending in part on their views of human nature. Hobbes, for example, described the state of nature as a state in which everyone was at war with everyone else. According to Hobbes, people tend to act only to further their own interests. The problem is that in the state of nature there are not enough resources to go around; people would selfishly compete for the same resources, attacking others to pursue their own ends. Yet no one could ever truly gain the upper hand, for the reason that people are roughly equal in their abilities (even the strongest person would not be safe from harmful attacks). Life in the state of nature, Hobbes famously said, would be "solitary, poor, nasty, brutish, and short." To escape the state of nature, people must agree to cooperate; they must agree to abide by certain rules. They must also agree on a way to enforce those rules, because otherwise people would break them to pursue their own self-interest. In Hobbes's view, a ruler must enforce those rules, and the ruler's political authority must be absolute, for only then could the ruler enforce the rules. Although granting absolute political power to a ruler might sound unattractive today, Hobbes believed that it would be rational: Only by doing so could one escape the state of nature and attain peace and security. So, as rational, self-interested beings, humans would agree to do so.

John Locke offered a more optimistic account of the state of nature. According to Locke, in the state of nature, people are equal and enjoy perfect freedom. Locke also believed that people have natural rights, even in the state of nature, such as the right to life, in addition to the moral duties not to attack others, restrict the freedom of others, or harm their property. Yet because people do not always abide by those rights (and because some people are less capable than others of defending their natural rights), people agree to abide by certain rules in order to better ensure the safety and security of each person. Like Hobbes, then, Locke thought of a social contract as an agreement made by rational people who seek to protect their own interests. Unlike Hobbes, however, Locke did not believe that the proper way out of the state of nature was through the establishment of a ruler with absolute political authority. Locke believed that a monarchy could be a legitimate form of government, provided that the monarch abided by a constitution and that the monarchy protected the people's natural rights. If a monarch violated those rights, however—such as by harming people or their property—then the monarch would have broken the social contract. In such a case people would no longer have a duty to obey the monarch. (These ideas were very influential on American revolutionaries during the 18th century.)

The best-known contemporary proponent of some version of social contract theory is John Rawls (1921–2002). Rawls used social contract theory to give an account of justice as fairness. He was specifically concerned with social institutions related to the distribution of wealth and opportunities in society (for example, Who should get to fill certain professions or hold political office? Who should be taxed, and how much?). Rawls proposed that just social institutions are those that abide by principles that free, rational people would agree on under certain conditions. In particular, they would agree on these principles when formulating them from behind a *veil of ignorance,* meaning that people would be ignorant of their own particular situations in life, such as of their race, sex, profession, talents, abilities, and so on. Rawls called the position behind the veil of ignorance the original position, and he thought that in the original position, people would not agree on principles or practices that would give an unfair advantage to one group of people (say, men) over another group of people (say, women). This is because they themselves would not want to be disadvantaged; ignorant of their own particular situations and status, people would be motivated to agree on the fairest principles possible. Rawls thought that one such principle was that each person should enjoy the most liberty possible that would be consistent with everyone having this same level of liberty. A second principle is that where there are unequal positions in society (such as positions with more wealth or more power than others), these inequalities must benefit those who are least well off in society. In addition, everyone must have the free, equal opportunity to fill those positions.

Social contract theorists disagree about the importance of whether people actually formed a social contract in the past. Those who believe that people did form such a contract face the question of why the contract would apply to the descendants of the people who initially made the contract (if the descendants never agreed to the contract, why should they be bound by its rules?). For other social contract theorists, the important point is that a social contract provides a good way of understanding what makes a government legitimate (or what morality consists of). In this view, the contract is hypothetical: Historically speaking, people never made such a social contract to escape the state of nature, but the notion of a social contract clarifies the issue of the legitimacy of government (or the nature of morality).

Social contract theory has been very influential in philosophical and political thought. Either as a way of accounting for the legitimacy (or lack thereof) in government or as a way of explaining morality, social contract theory enjoys certain attractions. First, people do commonly act in self-interested ways. A theory that takes that fact into account is a good theory in the sense that it does not make unrealistic demands (say, that people should often ignore their own interests). Second, it also provides a reason for why people ought to behave morally or (when a government, or social institutions, are legitimate) obey the laws and social institutions of one's nation: Doing so is ultimately in one's own best interests. Like other philosophical views, however, social contract theory has its detractors. One significant objection is that, as a theory of morality, social contract theory seems to leave out morally important beings. If morality is a set of rules agreed on between rational, self-interested beings, those rules would not seem to apply to beings who are incapable of forming an agreement in the first place. Nonhuman animals, infants, and severely brain-damaged people, for example, are not capable of agreeing to abide by rules in the way that normally functioning adult humans are. Yet many people believe we have moral obligations to those beings as well: It is not okay to torture animals or infants, for instance, even if they cannot come to an agreement about refraining from torture. Critics charge that insofar as social contract theory does not make room for such moral obligations, the theory is mistaken. Other criticisms of social contract theory come from feminist philosophers and philosophers focusing on race. Some argue that social contract theory is used not to advance just government or just institutions but to continue existing social inequalities (for example, inequalities between white people and black people). Another criticism is that the rational, self-interested individual so often described in social contract theory is described from a male perspective and therefore does not represent how humans in general actually are; it wrongly ignores qualities and experiences associated with women in particular.

Thomas Hobbes

Thomas Hobbes (1588–1679) was an English philosopher best known today as an important thinker in political philosophy. He was born prematurely when his mother feared that the Spanish Armada was coming, which Hobbes later humorously suggested explained his fearful nature. His father was a somewhat disreputable vicar. Hobbes studied at Oxford and later became a tutor for the aristocratic Cavendish family, with whom he remained connected throughout his life. He corresponded with René Descartes and other noted intellectuals of his time and famously tried to square the circle. Hobbes lived during the English civil war and was sometimes forced to leave the country for his own safety, as he acquired enemies with his political views. For example, after the English king lost power, Hobbes (a royalist) fled to France, where he lived for about 10 years. In addition to his strictly philosophical writings, Hobbes worked in mathematics and physics and published works of history and translations. Although in his own time he was sometimes called an atheist, whether Hobbes believed in God is controversial.

In metaphysics (the study of reality), Hobbes was a materialist: He believed that everything that existed was material. He argued that thought, dreams, the imagination, and indeed all mental activity can be explained in materialist terms, specifically in terms of mechanical matter in motion. That is, according to Hobbes, all mental activity is a matter of material stuff moving in a mechanical way. For instance, Hobbes claimed that sensations can be explained by external material objects somehow exerting pressure on the sensory organs—a person perceives a yellow banana, for example, when the photons bouncing off the banana exerts physical pressure on the eye, and this pressure causes physical pressure in the heart and brain. Hobbes was also an empiricist, believing that all knowledge depends on experience and on sensations in particular: Without sensations, we could not acquire knowledge, and indeed for Hobbes all knowledge is ultimately based on sensations.

Hobbes believed that human desires have physical causes. So, one has the desires one has because they are the result of a particular physical chain of events; in this way, one's desires are determined. No one chooses her desires because no one chooses the physical chain of events that cause them. Hobbes nonetheless believed it was possible for a person to be free. For Hobbes, freedom is not freedom to choose one's own desires but rather freedom from opposition; it is the ability to do what one wants. Suppose, for example, that a person wants to grow a garden. She does not freely choose to have that desire, which is just the result of a physical chain of events. However, she is free with respect to that desire as long as she is able to act on it. Hobbes thus offers a version of compatibilism, the view that it is possible both for humans to be free and for determinism to be true.

Hobbes is most famous for his work in political philosophy. In his most important work, *The Leviathan*, Hobbes gave an account of the nature and purpose of government, describing a version of social contract theory, according to which humans agree to give up their freedom to a ruler—a sovereign, to use Hobbes's term—in order to attain physical security. To illustrate, Hobbes imagined humans living without government, in what he called the state of nature. Hobbes thought life in such a state would be very bad, famously describing it as "solitary, poor, nasty, brutish, and short." The reason that life in the state of nature would be so bad is because, first, people would naturally be concerned mainly with their own interests. They would seek their own survival and their own advantage. Second, they would compete for the same resources—for example, the same especially desirable land or food. Third, Hobbes thought that in the state of nature no one could ever truly be safe from attack, because people are all about equal in their abilities (or equal enough such that each person would be vulnerable). Even a very strong person, for instance, could be attacked in her sleep. So, the state of nature would be a war of everyone against everyone else. There would be no cooperation, and people would constantly live in fear.

Hobbes thought that to escape the state of nature, people would need to agree to cede power to a sovereign. The sovereign would enforce laws and thus ensure the physical security of everyone under the sovereign. As Hobbes envisioned it, the sovereign would need absolute political authority. This was because, he believed, only a sovereign with absolute political authority would truly be able to enforce laws. If powers were divided between different branches of government, people would fight about the precise limits and scope of those powers. That in turn would lead to civil war, returning people to the state of nature. It was better to live under a ruler with absolute authority, Hobbes thought, than to return to a state of nature and live in constant fear of violence.

For Hobbes, then, rebellion against the sovereign is almost never justified. Yet Hobbes does seem to suggest it is justified if the sovereign no longer provides physical protection. Because the sovereign's subjects have ceded power to the sovereign for that purpose, one would seem to be justified in rebelling if the sovereign fails to protect. (One way of putting this is that it would be as if the sovereign had broken the social contract between herself and her subjects.) Hobbes wrote that people have a "right of nature" to protect themselves, a right they hold even in the state of nature, as well as under the sovereign.

John Locke

The English philosopher John Locke (1632–1704) was one of the most important and influential modern philosophers. The son of a lawyer, Locke studied at Westminster School and then at Christ Church, Oxford, where he was elected a studentship and received his degrees. He went on to study medicine and served as personal physician to the earl of Shaftesbury, while also becoming involved in the English government and helping to write a constitution for the colony of Carolina. Eventually Locke's connection to Shaftesbury, as well as his own views in favor of the English Parliament, entangled Locke in political controversies, and he moved to Holland for his own safety. There he became an adviser to William and Mary of Orange. When William and Mary became king and queen of England, Locke returned to England and served in various government positions. In addition to his strictly philosophical writings, Locke wrote on religious toleration, economics, education, religion, and other topics, achieving a reputation as one of the foremost English intellectuals of his time.

In political philosophy, Locke's views were very influential both inside philosophy and outside it; for example, the framers of the U.S. Constitution, such as Thomas Jefferson, based that document and the Declaration of Independence in part on Locke's ideas. Locke's ideas in political philosophy fall within the tradition of what has come to be known as social contract theory. In political philosophy, social contract theory is the view that a government somehow derives its legitimacy from the consent of the people it governs; it is as though there is a contract between a legitimate government and the people. A central idea of social contract theory is that individual people are all better off

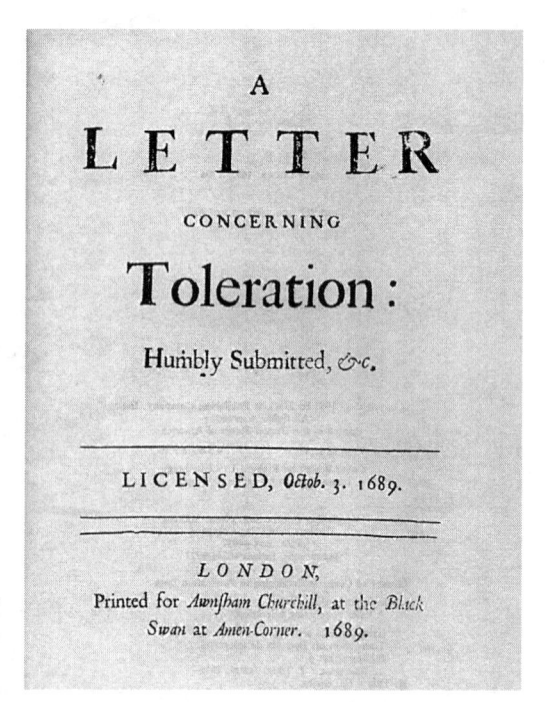

Title page of the 1689 edition of John Locke's *A Letter Concerning Toleration*

cooperating with each other than they would be if they did not do so. Social contract theorists typically view humans as rational, self-interested beings who would, therefore, actually be motivated to cooperate with each other. (The term *social contract theory* is also used in ethics for the view that morality consists of rules that rational, self-interested people would agree upon; it is as though people agree on a contract about how they can and cannot behave, in order best to promote their own interests. Here *social contract theory* refers to a view in political philosophy.)

Locke argued in favor of democratic government in which government is legitimate only if it rules with the consent of those who are governed. To illustrate the purpose of government and the legitimacy of government (or lack thereof), Locke imagined people living in a state of nature, a state without government. The idea was that by understanding what life is like without government, it would be possible to understand why people form governments, what government is for and, perhaps, when government is legitimate and when it is not. In his *Second Treatise of Government*, Locke suggested that humans did live in a state of nature at some point in the past, and that the heads of independent governments existed in a state of nature relative to each other (because they did not recognize a higher government ruling them all). However, the state of nature need not be understood as a description of a state in which humans actually existed in history and have since left. Rather, the state of nature is usually understood as an abstraction, an idea that is a useful tool for investigating the nature of government.

Locke saw the state of nature as a state in which everyone enjoys equality and freedom. In the state of nature, all are free to live life as they wish, within the limits of natural law. According to this natural law, which Locke wrote was the law of reason, "no one ought to harm another in his life, health, liberty, or possessions." Yet Locke thought that there were "inconveniences" associated with the state of nature. These inconveniences are due mainly to the fact that not everyone would follow the natural law. People tend to be biased in favor of themselves, Locke noted, and they are therefore likely not to view the natural law as applying to them. So, people's safety and the security of their property would be threatened. To escape the inconveniences of the state of nature, then, people agree to give up their perfect freedom and form a government. The purpose of the government is to keep people safe and their property secure, and the government does this by making laws and enforcing them (through punishment). Forming a government is in the best interests of those governed because the government protects the security of the people by making and enforcing law. The government derives its legitimacy from the consent of the governed, and the government should follow the will of the majority. According to Locke, even if in actual situations people have not explicitly consented to form a government or obey it, by living within a given state, they have given *tacit* consent to that government and are therefore obligated to obey the will of the majority (on which the government is based). When a government no longer protects the people's interests—when it violates a person's natural rights—then people are justified in rebelling against the government. Unlike Thomas Hobbes, Locke thought it was a mistake to give a ruler absolute power. This is because the purpose of forming a government is to attain security. But, according to Locke, to give a ruler absolute power would be to undermine one's security, placing a subject at the mercy of the ruler, and that would defeat the purpose of forming a government in the first place. It was better to remain in the state of nature, Locke thought, where at least one had perfect freedom, than to live under a ruler with absolute power.

Jean-Jacques Rousseau

Jean-Jacques Rousseau (1712–78) was an important French thinker best known today for his work in political philosophy. He was born in Geneva but spent a considerable part of his life in Paris. The son of a watchmaker, Rousseau was apprenticed to an engraver but abandoned the apprenticeship. His success as a writer was born when Rousseau wrote the winning essay in a contest that asked the question whether the arts and sciences had improved morality (Rousseau's answer was that they had not). He subsequently wrote various works on political philosophy, morality, society, education, and botany, in addition to writing operas, plays, a best-selling novel, and autobiographical works. Rousseau enjoyed friendships with important French thinkers such as Denis Diderot (1713–84) and maintained a longtime relationship with Thérèse Levasseur, whom he eventually married; prior to the marriage, she bore him several children whom Rousseau abandoned. He was forced to flee Paris in 1762 due to his controversial and unorthodox views about religion and lived for a time in Switzerland, as well as in Britain, where he quarreled with the Scottish philosopher David Hume. In 1767, Rousseau returned to France. He died in 1778.

In political philosophy, Rousseau is associated with social contract theory, according to which legitimate government is based on the agreement of the people governed (it is as if there is a contract between people and government). Other social contract theorists, such as Thomas Hobbes and John Locke, had described a theoretical state of nature, that is, a state of human existence in which people lived without government of any kind. Hobbes had described such a state of nature as "solitary, poor, nasty, brutish, and short," on the grounds that humans would constantly compete with each other for the same resources, warring against each other but able to gain no permanent advantage over each other. Rousseau's account of the state of nature differed markedly. For Rousseau, the state of nature is solitary, but it is happy. Although people in the state of nature cannot escape aging or the possibility of illness, there are plenty of resources to meet their basic needs, and people are well equipped to deal with dangers such as those posed by other ani-

Statue of Jean-Jacques Rousseau in Switzerland

mals. Moreover, humans in the state of nature are innocent, free from the corrupting influences of society. Such humans are noble savages. They are not exactly moral and nor are they immoral; rather, they are amoral, without morals altogether. Rousseau agreed with Hobbes that humans in the state of nature are self-interested in the sense that they are concerned with their own welfare. However, Rousseau also believed that humans naturally feel pity for the suffering of others. So, humans in the state of nature would act from an instinct for self-preservation, but their instinctive pity would prevent them from willfully and pointlessly harming others. Human capacities, according to Rousseau, are naturally good. Moreover, humans are perfectible. That is, they are not perfect now, but in principle it is possible for them to become perfect.

Of course, people do not always live in the state of nature. They begin to form communities at least in part because is it easier to accomplish some tasks in a group than individually; farming, for example, is easier if people divide the labor among themselves than if one person tries to complete all the necessary tasks herself. Yet it is society, Rousseau thought, that corrupts human beings. Living in communities with other people, people develop modern traits such as the tendency to want to be better than others. Civilization leads to hypocrisy, envy, and deceit. At the same time, Rousseau thought, it was only by forming civil society that people fully develop their reason, a sense of duty, and robust moral virtues.

A central concern of Rousseau's was freedom, and his most famous remark was "Man is born free; and everywhere he is in chains." He believed humans ought to retain their freedom even while living within political communities, under a government. For Rousseau, the way to preserve freedom while living under a government involves, first, the free and unanimous decision of every person within a political community to form that political community in the first place. All parties to a social contract, in other words, must actually and freely agree to that social contract. Second, in agreeing to form a government, Rousseau thought that each person must agree to submit to what he called the general will. The general will is a difficult concept in Rousseau's thought, and it has generated disagreement among Rousseau's interpreters. However, this much can be said: The general will is not just the collection of each person's individual will. Rather, the general will is the will of the entire political community as a whole. Whereas an individual might seek what benefits herself in particular, the general will seeks what will benefit the community as a whole. An individual might wish to make laws that will benefit herself, for example, such as tax laws that benefit her particular kind of business; the general will, however, makes laws to benefit the interests of the whole community rather than merely the interests of particular individuals (or even particular individual groups) within the community. Because the general will promotes the good of the entire community, by submitting to the general will, in Rousseau's view a person actually ensures her own freedom. This is so even if the general will causes some things to happen (such as certain laws to be passed) that an individual actually opposes.

Philosophy of Law

The philosophy of law, also called jurisprudence, is the philosophical analysis of concepts within and about the nature and practice of law. The focus is on civil laws, such as voting laws, as opposed to laws of nature, such as the law of gravity. The basic philosophical question that is usually asked about law is: What is (civil) law? Law is a means of regulating people's behavior, but there are also other means of regulating people's behavior, such as persuasion or peer pressure or even force. What is it, then, about law that distinguishes it from these other forms of regulating behavior and also account for the legitimate bindingness of law? The bindingness of law refers to the fact that laws bind us to behave in certain ways. If a robber threatens to harm me unless I hand over my money, I might feel bound to do so, but the bindingness in this case is not legitimate in the way that following a law is. What is it, then, about the nature of law that accounts for its legitimate bindingness in terms of regulating behavior?

There are several broad perspectives on answering this question about the nature of (the bindingness of) law. One perspective is called natural law theory. Natural law theory says that civil laws hold their legitimate function of regulating behavior because—and only because—such laws are in accordance with, or at least do not contradict, objective, natural, moral laws. By saying that there are objective moral laws that are natural, what is meant is that some actions are right and wrong, not because some individual or social group says so, but rather because there is an objective, nonsocial basis. Religious advocates of natural law theory say that this objective, nonsocial basis can be found in, say, divine commandments. For example, murder is wrong because God commands humans not to murder. Nonreligious advocates of natural law theory say that this objective, nonsocial basis can be found in certain features of human nature. For example, starving someone to death is wrong because humans need food to survive. A fundamental aspect of natural law theory is that there is a necessary and inseparable connection between morality and law. A common slogan of natural law theory is that an unjust law is no law at all. The point of this slogan is that a civil law—for instance, a statute that is enacted by some legislature—has no legitimate bindingness on people if that civil law is unjust (that is, if it violates some objective, natural, moral standard). People might comply with such a law, but according to natural law theory such compliance does not come from the legitimacy of the law but perhaps because people might feel threatened if they do not comply. A recent advocate of natural law theory was Martin Luther King, Jr.

Another perspective on the nature of law, and why it has any legitimate bindingness on people, is called legal positivism. Legal positivism says that what gives civil law its legitimacy is that it is the product of some recognized and accepted lawmaking body. For example, in the United States, laws are usually created by an elected body of legislators. There are specified rules and practices for how some bill that is introduced to legislators can become enacted as law. What makes something law, then, is that it has gone through some appropriate process. For legal positivism, there is no necessary connection between morality and law, even though we want and hope all of our civil laws in fact to be consistent with our moral views and standards. The point, however, is that what makes any law, even an unjust one, a legitimate law is that it was produced via an appropriate process. If, after having gone through that process, we think that the result is a bad result (that is, perhaps we think it is an unjust law or a bad law for some other reason), it is still law and can be undone by having the appropriate lawmaker(s) go through the process again and change the law.

A third perspective on the nature of law is called legal realism. Legal realism says that what makes something law is neither that it matches up with some objective, natural, moral law nor that it flows from some appropriate process. Rather, what really makes something law, is that the regulations of behavior contained in it are, in fact, enforced by the courts. It is actual judicial decisions, made by judges or juries that really determine what is law. If a legislature passed some bill and claimed it was now the law, but no judge or jury would convict anyone for violating that law, then, claim the advocates of legal realism, it is only a "paper law," not a real law. The reason it is not a real law is because it would not, in fact, actually regulate anyone's behavior and would not have any binding force on anyone. So, it is actual judicial decisions, not natural moral standards or appropriate legal processes, that determine and constitute what law really is, according to legal realism. The moral standards and appropriate processes might be relevant and important to the judicial decisions that actually get made, but for legal realism, those aspects, again, do not determine or constitute real law.

A fourth perspective on the nature of law is often called critical legal studies. Critical legal studies agrees with legal realism in that it is the actual judicial decisions that really matter with respect to what is law. In addition, however, advocates of critical legal studies also claim that law, as a social form of regulating behavior, is really about power and politics. Law is never, they say, merely a matter of some formal legislative process; nor is it a matter of complying with some objective, natural, moral standards. Rather, it is a means of promoting social, political agendas. This is obvious when we see how much attention is paid to who gets placed on the U.S. Supreme Court. In that case, say the advocates of critical legal studies, the politics of law is open and explicit.

Closely related to critical legal studies is what is called feminist jurisprudence. Feminist jurisprudence says that not only is law about power and politics but also, at least traditionally, it is male-oriented. With respect to the content and substance of specific laws, they claim, there has been and largely continues to be a male-oriented bias in many laws. With respect to process, they claim, there is also a male bias. For example, in the context of legal decision-making there is what is often called the "reasonable man" standard. This notion means that, while everyone might have particular values and perspectives on issues, in making legal decisions, judges and juries can rule according to what a reasonable man might do in a given situation. The problem, say the advocates of feminist jurisprudence, is that what a reasonable man might do in a given situation is not necessarily the same thing as what a reasonable woman might do. In certain legal contexts, then, there should be the appeal to a reasonable woman standard, just as, in other contexts, we might appeal to, say, a reasonable pilot standard (for instance, if the legal case involved the actions of some pilot) or we might think that an all-white jury would not be appropriate for trying an accused person who is not white. If civil laws are gender-blind, or if the legal system tries to be gender-blind, the result, according to some advocates of feminist jurisprudence, is not objective fair legal treatment but can well be unfair, since gender-blind actually results in male bias (even if unintentional).

Although the concern about the basic nature of law is fundamental to the philosophy of law, there are other issues that matter. One such issue concerns rights and justice. Both of these notions have to do with the appropriate limits of law, since these are both notions that involve the social regulation of behavior. Laws tell us often what we may and may not do, while, at the same time, rights are intended to limit how laws regulate us. Indeed, often rights are seen as being a protection against laws; for instance, preventing laws from being enacted or enforced that would violate some basic right to freedom of expression. On many occasions, there have been attempts to pass censorship laws, and the courts have rejected such attempts on the grounds of violating basic rights. Likewise, attitudes and views about social justice have resulted in the creation and enforcement of laws.

Two issues that philosophers have focused on that are more related to mundane legal practice are the issues of responsibility and punishment. What is legal responsibility? The philosophical concerns are not simply about describing what judges and legislators say but about analyzing the concept of responsibility. For example, we speak of someone as being causally responsible for some effect if that person caused that effect. We also speak of someone as being morally responsible if that person chose to act in some way and could be in the position of deciding whether or not such action was right or wrong. These two notions of causal responsibility and moral responsibility do not always overlap. For example, a small child might be causally responsible for some action, say breaking a lamp by knocking it over, but—being a small child—might not be morally responsible. From the philosophical point of view, then, there is the question of how legal responsibility relates to these other notions of responsibility. A typical philosophical approach to addressing this question is to ask what conditions would have to be met for someone to be held causally/morally/legally responsible and do those conditions match up with each other. A further issue here is the issue of omissions, that is, holding someone responsible—whether causally or morally or legally—not for what that person did, but for what that person did not do.

Punishment

Although most people use the concept of punishment quite broadly, the concept is a legal one, as distinguished from other forms of actions that harm or constrain people, such as acts of vengeance. That is, punishment can only be given for some offense against legal rules, and it must be intentionally administered by some recognized legal authority. So, where the legal system might imprison someone for having broken the law—and this is an act of punishment—an individual might confine someone for having done some action, but acting as an individual, this is not an act of punishment. There are many types of punishment, ranging from fines to some form of work or service to incarceration (such as detention or imprisonment) and even up to execution. There might be other forms of punishment, such as public exposure or humiliation, for example, in the case of publicly posting information on the Internet concerning convicted persons. Again, what makes such posting a case of punishment is that it is done by a recognized legal authority and in response to having been found guilty of violating some law. A private individual or group that posts the same information would not be a case of punishment but of private action, perhaps with the intent to cause humiliation or harm.

Besides the issue of how and how much to punish (for example, fines versus imprisonment versus community service), there is the even more basic issue of why people are or should be punished. It might be true that people are or should be punished always and only for breaking the law. This might seem obvious, but it is actually more complex than it appears at first. For instance, perhaps the harm caused by an action is the basis for punishment, rather than the simple fact that the action involves breaking the law. Some people argue that if there are victimless crimes (that is, actions that technically break a law but harm no one), then these should not be punished. The fact that there are different kinds and levels of punishment connected up to different kinds and levels of harm also seems to indicate that what is really being punished is the harm or wrongdoing of some action rather than the fact that it involves breaking the law. For example, intentionally murdering someone usually carries a stronger punishment than accidentally killing someone. Also, causing actual harm usually carries a stronger punishment than creating a potential harm, for example, injuring someone in a traffic accident versus speeding but not injuring someone. The fact that we usually think that the punishment should fit the crime points to the underlying sense that it is the harm or the wrong-doing that is done, more so than the mere fact of having broken the law, that is the basis for why people are and should be punished.

Given such issues as how to punish, how much to punish, and why punish, the concept of punishment is related both to the concept of justice and to the concept of responsibility. With respect to justice, punishment has to do with corrective justice, that is, correcting some previous act or case of injustice or unfairness. With respect to responsibility, punishment—as a legal concept—means legal responsibility (or liability), as opposed to moral responsibility or causal responsibility. That is, one might be held to be legally responsible, and therefore punishable, even if one is not morally or causally responsible.

There are two broad traditional philosophical perspectives on punishment. These perspectives address the issues noted above, such as why we punish, how and how much to punish, etc. The first perspective is utilitarianism. This view of punishment claims that the primary, and perhaps only, reason and justification for punishment is deterrence. In other words, by imposing punishments on people, we want to deter them from acting in ways that we do not endorse. Under this view, deterrence is supposed to be a necessary and sufficient condition for punishment. In a nutshell, why we punish someone is to prevent, or at least deter, both that person and others from engaging in certain actions. Under the utilitarian view, deterrence is also what appropriately determines how and how much to punish. So, if a small fine is sufficient to deter certain unwanted actions in the future, then that fine is the appropriate kind and level of punishment. However, if a stronger punishment is needed to deter those actions, then a stronger punishment is justified. The second broad traditional philosophical perspective on punishment is retributivism. This term is based on the notion of a "tribute" or offering in recognition of something and "re-," or giving back. So, retribution is the giving back to someone something in recognition of what they gave or did previously. This could be a positive, pleasant thing, such as rewarding someone for some previous good deed. However, almost always the notion of retribution is meant as something negative and unwanted; in the legal context, retribution is punishment. The view of retributivism is that we do and should punish someone for some previous criminal act simply because of desert; that is, they deserve punishment for what they did (or failed to do). Whether or not punishment actually is a deterrent for future criminal actions is not fundamental to retributivism. Although we hope that punishment does in fact deter future criminal acts, for a retributivist, deterrence is neither necessary nor sufficient for meting out punishment. Rather, it is guilt (and, hence, desert) that is necessary and sufficient. What determines how and whether a given punishment fits a given crime is whether it is deserved, not deterrence. Finally, a third alternative perspective is that therapy for offenders and/or restitution for victims is more important and more effective than punishment, both for the offenders and victims.

The Nineteenth Century: Socialism

Georg W. F. Hegel

Georg Wilhelm Friedrich Hegel (1770–1831) was born in Stuttgart, Germany. He was the son of a minor government official. Hegel studied theology at the seminary at Tübingen University, where he also became friends with the philosopher Friedrich Wilhelm Joseph von Schelling and Friedrich Holderlin (the German poet). Hegel earned a master's degree in theology but did not pursue the ministry. He worked as a private tutor and as a high school principal until inheriting some money from his father. He began to teach at the University of Jena, where he finished his dissertation and wrote *Phenomenology of Spirit*. Later, having lost this position in the wake of Napoléon's invasion of Prussia, he served as a newspaper editor. In 1816 he attained a position as a professor of philosophy at the University of Heidelberg and in 1819 accepted a position at the University of Berlin. By then he had become famous for his philosophical work. He died of cholera in 1831.

Hegel sought to construct a complete metaphysical system—that is, a system to explain all of reality. So, this system was to explain not only physical processes in the natural world but also human cultural activities, such as philosophy and religion. Of course, Hegel did not seek to give explanations in the same way that scientists today seek to give explanations, such as by identifying physical causes and mechanisms or

Portrait of Georg Wilhelm Friedrich Hegel (Painting by Ernst Hader)

conducting experiments. Rather, Hegel thought he could explain all of reality in broad terms, by explaining its overall structure.

What all of reality shares, Hegel believed, is rationality. Specifically, according to Hegel, reality is essentially rational. So, nothing that is real can be irrational (or nonrational). Reality is identical to rationality. If reality is rational, this implies that it can be understood, as indeed Hegel thought it could be; like other German idealists, then, Hegel broke from Immanuel Kant's claim that any aspect of reality is in principle unknowable. Hegel thought there is an Absolute, or Mind (sometimes translated as Spirit). Mind, as Hegel understood it, is not a person's own individual mind—it does not consist of a person's individual memories, desires, wishes, and so on. Mind is instead all-encompassing reality; it is this sense that Hegel's idealism is absolute, for it holds that everything real is essentially mind-dependent. Sometimes Hegel identified

Absolute Mind as God. Hegel himself was a Christian, specifically a Lutheran. However, Hegel also wrote critically of religion and even of Jesus, and to what extent Hegel's philosophical beliefs are consistent with traditional Christianity is controversial.

History itself is the unfolding of this Absolute. In particular, it is the process of Mind coming to self-consciousness and recognizing itself as the sole reality. Hegel, who regarded freedom as among the essential features of Mind, saw this process as culminating in freedom. Perhaps Hegel's thought is best illustrated through examining human history. In human history, there have been philosophical movements, political movements, movements in art, culture, and religion, and so on. For Hegel, these various movements have not come about randomly. As one would expect if reality is rational, there is an order to what happens in the world and what has already happened; moreover, there is a progression to the world's events. So, it is not as if one idea in human history is replaced by another idea that simply happens to be different than the old idea. Instead, the new idea is more complete and captures more of truth than the old idea. In particular, this is because the new idea incorporates aspects of one idea and its opposite to form a new idea that is superior to them both. This process of reconciling opposites to form a synthesis is called the Hegelian dialectic.

Hegel's own example of such a dialectic concerns the concepts of being, nothing, and becoming. Suppose we begin with the concept of being; as that is our starting point, we can call that the thesis. Now consider the opposite of being: nothing. Because it is the opposite of the thesis, nothing is the antithesis. The third movement in the dialectic is the synthesis, becoming. Becoming is a synthesis of being and nothing because it is neither being nor nothing, yet incorporates aspects of both. For example, a growing tadpole is in the process of becoming a frog. It is a tadpole, so it is something; that is to say, it exists or has being (or is an instance of being). However, it is not a frog (not yet), and in that sense it has an aspect of nothing (what does not exist). In the process of becoming a frog, it incorporates being (what exists).

Hegel thought that history progresses along such dialectical lines, by undergoing a thesis, an antithesis, and finally a synthesis—which itself forms a new thesis, to be opposed by an antithesis, until a new synthesis emerges. For example, in the history of ideas, suppose some people believed that having no government at all is the best form of human society, while others viewed an absolute dictatorship as the best form of human society. We can consider the first view the thesis and the second the antithesis. A synthesis might be the view that a form of democratic government is the best form of human society: It incorporates (to a degree) the aspect of freedom people might enjoy in a society without government while incorporating (to a degree) the order and stability of a society run by an absolute dictatorship. This is not Hegel's own example; it is just an illustration of how the progression of ideas in human history might work. Whatever ideas people do have, Hegel thought, and however those ideas might oppose each other, he believed it was possible for people to come to an agreement, an agreement that synthesized an original idea and its opposite.

Hegel believed that freedom was a fundamental feature of consciousness and that history unfolds with an endpoint of greater and greater freedom. For Hegel, such freedom exists within the context of the state, which he regarded as more important than individual people living within the state. Freedom does not consist simply of the ability to do what one wants without interference. Rather, freedom is the freedom to be rational.

Hegel is famous for his comments on consciousness and self-consciousness, which he illustrates through a story of the master and slave (sometimes Hegel's terms are translated as *lord* and *bondsman* instead of *master* and *slave*). According to Hegel, a person is conscious of herself only in opposition to something that is not herself. Put another way, self-consciousness arises only when one contrasts oneself with someone, or something, else. However, when two people meet, they each feel threatened by the other and therefore seek to dominate the other. Fearing death, one person eventually gives in to the other: The person who gives in is the slave, and the person who succeeds in dominating the other is the master. The slave works for the master, producing materials (food, for example). Yet a peculiar thing occurs in the master-slave relationship. The slave becomes independent in the sense that she learns to exercise control over her environment; it is she who produces material goods, and she attains self-consciousness through exercising control over the environment. At the same time, the master becomes dependent on the slave, for without the slave, the master would not survive. Moreover, the master's self-consciousness depends on the slave in the sense that the slave must recognize the master as master, whereas the slave's self-consciousness is not similarly dependent on the master.

Hegel's description of the master and slave suggests certain ideas about the nature of freedom and society. In a relationship where one person dominates the other, neither can truly be free: The person dominated is subject to the will of the person being dominated, but the person dominating depends on the act of dominating for her own status; in that way, far from being independent, the dominating person actually depends on the person dominated. What this shows is that true freedom is not to be found in dominator/dominated relationships and human society should not be based on such relationships.

Karl Marx

Karl Marx (1818–83) was one of the most influential thinkers of modern times. His writings were important not only during his lifetime; they also shaped much of Western culture throughout the 20th century. His impact was vast in the areas of philosophy, economics, sociology, and politics. Marx was born in Trier, Prussia (now western Germany). His family background was Jewish, but his father converted to Christianity shortly before Marx was born. As a student, Marx studied philosophy and law at the University of Berlin and then at the University of Jena. For years he worked as a journalist and newspaper editor, frequently criticizing his own government and other governments. In 1848 he published *The Manifesto of the Communist Party*, one of the most influential books of the modern era. After being banished from several European countries, he moved to Britain, where he lived in poverty but wrote hundreds of political and social articles and editorials. In 1867 he published *Das Kapital*, an analysis of economic systems and a critique of capitalism. He continued to live in Britain until his death in 1883.

With respect to philosophy, Marx was heavily influenced by the German philosopher Georg F. W. Hegel. Hegel emphasized the view that the world, including both the natural world and the social world, must be understood as developing systems, not merely as a collection of things and facts. For Hegel, events in the world, and indeed the world itself, went through stages of development, and this development was inevitable. This development was a movement toward what Hegel called consciousness. By this he did not mean just an everyday sense of being aware of something but that greater and greater possibilities were becoming realized. For example, in the natural world, new species and life forms evolved, while in the social world, new forms of government and social institutions were created. Marx took this notion of development and applied it especially to human experience within society.

Marx spoke of humans as having species-being. He meant that there is something unique about humans that distinguishes them from other species. What is unique about humans is that humans produce and create the conditions of their lives. That is, humans do not simply hunt and gather things; rather, humans manufacture and produce things. We are communal beings, said Marx, meaning that we are by our nature social beings, not hermits. As a result, there are social structures and institutions that shape how we produce and create the conditions of our lives. For example, in a rural, preindustrial culture, people lived on farms and spent most of their lives doing tasks just to stay alive, while in an urban, industrial culture, people live (largely) in cities and produce by going to work away from their homes, creating small units of some larger product. (Almost no one today grows all his own food or weaves his own clothes or builds his own home from basic materials.) As he put it, who and what we are (as people) coincides with what and how we produce. In his words, "The nature of individuals thus depends on the material conditions determining their production." By this he meant that people live in very different economic situations and economic structures. For instance, again, in a rural, farming culture, what and how people produce will be different than what and how they produce in an urban, industrialized culture. How we understand the world and how we understand even ourselves is shaped by these economic conditions and structures.

He spoke of economic conditions of life as the forces of production. Forces of production involve two related aspects. The first he called the materials of production, and the second he called the relations of production. The materials of production are the actual materials that go into what and how we produce. Again, in a hunting or gathering culture, those materials might be simple tools or implements to help hunt or gather or cultivate crops. In an urban, industrial culture, those materials might be factories or technological equipment. In a very modern context, such as the 21st century, important basic materials might be information technology, such as computers. Different materials of production can and will create different conditions for people's lives. For example, with the creation of cars and a highway system (or some form of mass transportation), workers can travel away from their homes and go to work away from their homes. As a result, factories and businesses can be located, say, in a city, away from people's homes, and work schedules can be set up so that workers meet together at the factory at certain times (quite different than, say, living on a farm or in a hunting/gathering community). Likewise, with modern information technology, people can telecommute and still get work done collectively without having to leave their homes.

The relations of production are the ways in which the materials of production are structured. For instance, in a capitalist economic system, the materials of production (that is, the factories and technologies) are owned by private individuals or private groups, while in a socialist economic system, the materials of production might be owned by the government. So, the materials of production are related to each other and to people in different ways in different economic systems.

Marx claimed that the forces of production (that is, the materials and relations of production) are the economic base of our lives and that they significantly shape how we see the world and how we see ourselves (or, as he put it, they shape our consciousness and our experience). According to Marx, for any economic base, there is an ideological superstructure built upon it. By this he meant that people come to have beliefs and values that they hold, but those beliefs and values are a result of living within certain economic structures. For example, a capitalist economic structure has relations of production that are private (that is, individuals own the factories and the businesses). As a result, Marx claimed, certain beliefs and values arise that reflect this economic structure and that promote this economic structure. So, he said, within a capitalist system, there arises an emphasis on individual priority and privacy, with the result that people value individualism and a political, legal system that protects individual rights and limited government (and downplays community or responsibility to others). Briefly, then, Marx's view is that people must produce in order to survive; in order to produce, there must be some mode of production (that is, means and organization, or materials and relations of production); social relations and patterns result from the mode of production, resulting in political

THE NINETEENTH CENTURY: SOCIALISM 171

Karl Marx monument in Chemnitz, Germany (Sculpture by Lev Efimovich Kerbel; photograph by Reinhard Höll)

and social and philosophical beliefs and values that reflect and promote that mode of production.

Even within a given economic system, Marx said, different people have different views because they experience different economic conditions in their everyday lives. So, the owners of the forces of production (the bourgeoisie) are wealthy, while many workers (the proletariat) are not wealthy but often struggle to get by. Indeed, workers become alienated from their lives in the sense that they must produce to survive, but what and how they produce is determined by others. The consequence is that owners and workers are different classes and they have, in his words, different class consciousness. Marx thought that there is inevitable conflict between different economic classes and that this conflict leads to social turmoil and even revolution. In some of his writings, Marx seemed to call for people to openly challenge the capitalist system and try to alter it, while in other writings Marx seemed to say that there is an inevitable series of stages of social and historical development that will result in a transformation from capitalism to socialism and finally communism.

Not only was Marx seen as radical in his own time (although not by everyone), but also even during the 20th century, when his influence was the greatest, he was seen by many critics as mistaken or dangerous. He was seen by many as being mistaken because, in spite of his predictions, workers have not suffered within capitalism; indeed, these critics argue, people's standards of living are the highest in capitalist societies. He was seen as dangerous by many because he was said to have led to a lot of social unrest and rebellion, as well as to the oppression of many people in those political systems (such as the Soviet Union and China) that claimed to follow his teachings. Nevertheless, many of the particular social policies and practices that Marx fought for, and were seen as radical, have been adopted and even embraced throughout the world: free public education, child labor laws, standardized working days with an emphasis on worker safety, universal voting rights, etc.

Communitarianism

Communitarianism is the name of a particular political philosophy. The root of the name is *community,* and a fundamental focus of this political philosophy is the importance and centrality of community. It is not the same thing as communism, the political philosophy that is usually associated with the writings of Karl Marx. For one thing, communitarianism does not reject the notion or practice of private property. The basic assumption of communitarianism is that individuals live *within* communities, not that communities just happen to be a collection of individuals. An important aspect of our social lives is that both individuals and communities must be respected and valued. As a political philosophy, communitarianism includes both a negative, critical part and a positive, constructive part. The negative part focuses on criticisms of other political philosophies, especially libertarianism and liberalism. The positive part focuses on advocating certain social and political policies and practices, namely, ones that value communities as well as the individuals within them.

For communitarians, liberalism (and the particular version of it called libertarianism) sees individuals as the primary, and perhaps only, things that matter for social and political concerns. Liberalism, they say, sees groups of people—including whole communities and societies and cultures—as just collections of individuals. Individuals are the things that have value and rights; groups have value and rights only to the extent that they derive them from individuals. For example, the government has the power to create traffic laws or to tax people, but only because individuals grant those powers to the government. A majority of individuals might have the power and right to establish laws that say what people may or may not do, but this majority really is just the collection of most individuals, so it is still the individual that is the central figure.

Communitarians claim that, of course, individuals are important and the powers and rights of individuals are very important. However, they claim that the view of liberalism is mistaken about the very nature of individuals. A phrase that communitarians use when they criticize liberalism is "the unencumbered self." By this phrase they mean that liberalism sees individuals as separate, unique, and fundamentally isolated entities who just happen to be part of communities. Communitarians disagree. They say that people are inherently, and always, members within communities. Communities are not merely add-ons, they say; rather, people are at their core communal, social beings.

A consequence of this view that we are not unencumbered selves is, for communitarians, the recognition of a balance between rights and responsibilities. They claim that liberalism only speaks of the rights of individuals, not of their responsibilities—other than not to infringe on the rights of other individuals. There is an overemphasis on individual rights, say communitarians, which is based on this view of the unencumbered self, and the result is that this leads to the neglect of care for others or for the common good. But, they argue, we need to balance the rights and freedoms of individuals with the rights and care of communities. Liberalism focuses on individuals' rights *against* communities. This might include, for example, an individual's right to distribute certain offensive material (such as racist or sexist literature) or say offensive things (such as racist or sexist slurs). Communitarians claim that these rights and freedoms must be balanced with the rights *of* communities and understood always as rights *within* communities.

In addition to claiming that people are not unencumbered selves, communitarians also say that liberalism's emphasis on individual rights and freedoms misses the point of why rights and freedoms matter. Communitarians say that what is important about having rights and freedoms is not simply that other people do not get to tell you what to do (or not do). The real importance of rights and freedoms, they say, is that rights and freedoms help people to fulfill their possibilities and potentials. In other words, what is important about rights and freedoms is not merely being free from the constraints and dictates of others; instead, the importance is that we are free to do and accomplish things. For communitarians, the freedom to simply sit around and watch television or play video games is a freedom that has little purpose or value. Rights and freedoms, they say, should be a basic part of living well, of the quality of life, in other words, of a good life. But a good life, they say, necessarily includes concern for community, because who we are as individuals is not isolated from who we are within communities.

This emphasis on balancing rights and responsibilities, of the good of individuals and the good of communities, is one way that communitarians stress the need to be concerned with what is *good* as much as with what is *right*. These two terms—*good* and *right*—do not mean the same thing, although they are related. Good involves content; that is, some things are good for people, and other things are not, they are bad for people. For example, smoking is bad for people. Right, on the other hand, does not necessarily involve content (or goods). Some actions or decisions are right, while others are wrong. For example, we might say that fulfilling one's duties is the right thing to do, whatever the content of those duties are. Communitarians claim that some actions and decisions are bad, even if they might be right, right in the sense that people are free to perform those actions or make those decisions. Communitarians, then, have often favored certain limitations on freedoms of speech or expression, when such speech or expression is (what they take to be) bad, such as racist or sexist cases. At the same time, many communitarians have favored stronger gun control laws, because they believe that the availability of guns has been more bad than good in American society. So, some of the policies they favor, such as restrictions on pornography, are ones that political conservatives like, while other policies they favor, such as greater gun control, are ones that political liberals like. For this reason, communitarians say that their political philosophy is neither conservative nor liberal. They advocate the importance of both individuals and of communities and strive for a balance between them. A common phrase they use is that they support a "responsive community," that is, an emphasis on community, but one that responds to the rights and needs of those individuals within it. At the heart of their view, they claim, is social justice, meaning, for them, that each member of a community owes something to all the rest and the community owes something to each of its members (dignity and respect for each and for all). Libertarians and other supporters of liberalism, however, claim that communitarianism, in spite of sounding like a reasonable philosophy of balancing rights and responsibilities, is actually a political philosophy that restricts people's freedoms.

The Nineteenth Century: Utilitarianism

Jeremy Bentham and John Stuart Mill are usually credited with formulating classical utilitarianism, the idea that whatever brings about the greatest good is the right thing to do. They applied this moral view not only to individuals and their actions but also to political philosophy.

Jeremy Bentham

The English philosopher Jeremy Bentham (1748–1832) was born in London and entered Oxford at just 12 years of age. The son of an attorney, he studied law after graduating, but he so disapproved of the British law system that he never practiced law, devoting his time to studying and writing instead. Although he wrote thousands of pages, Bentham published little during his lifetime; much of his work was published by followers. He spent a considerable amount of time and money in efforts to persuade the British government to award him a contract to build and manage a model prison, the *panopticon*. Bentham envisioned that prisoners within in it would be watched by prison guards at all times; however, the prison was never built. After his death, upon his request, Bentham's body was embalmed and kept in University College in London, where it is sometimes taken out to attend meetings by Bentham's modern-day followers.

Bentham's central project was to develop principles for a clear and just system of law. He based this project largely on two related views.

In his words, "Nature has placed mankind under the governance of two sovereign masters, *pain* and *pleasure*. It is for them alone to point out what we ought to do, as well as to determine what we shall do." So, first, Bentham believed that as a matter of fact people do seek their own pleasure or happiness and try to avoid pain. Second, he believed that people *ought* to act in ways that produce the greatest happiness for the greatest number of people affected. He called this the principle of utility, or the greatest happiness principle. (By *utility*, Bentham meant pleasure or happiness, terms he used interchangeably.) On this principle, everyone's happiness is equal; no one's happiness is more important than anyone else's. To decide the morally right thing to do, a person should calculate how much pleasure and pain an action is likely to produce and choose the action that will produce the greatest happiness for the greatest number. If, for instance, a person must decide whether to donate a sum to charity or spend it on coffee for herself, and donating the sum to charity would produce more happiness for the people affected than spending it on coffee, the right thing to do is donate the money to charity.

Similarly—crucially for Bentham—legislators should base laws on the principle of utility, enacting laws that maximize happiness for the greatest number of people. Bentham believed that the principle of utility provided a basis for clear, just, and humane legal and social reform. First, the principle of utility would provide an objective foundation for law. This is just because whether a law does or does not promote the greatest happiness is a matter of objective fact, as opposed to laws based just on legislators' private religious beliefs or personal prejudices. Second, laws based on the principle of utility would be clear, because they could be explained in terms of pleasure and pain, concepts just about everyone understands. Because Bentham believed that people act to maximize their own happiness, he believed that the way to ensure that laws follow the principle of utility is to formulate them so that people maximize happiness for the greatest number just by acting to maximize their own happiness. For example, suppose a law forbids people to steal from others and threatens thieves with punishment. Because punishment is painful, people would naturally be inclined to avoid it and therefore refrain from stealing. The law would thus help keep everyone's property safe and secure, and in this way it would promote the greatest happiness for the greatest number, in spite of the fact that individuals obey the law just to promote their own happiness.

For Bentham, the purpose of government itself is to promote the greatest happiness for the greatest number, and he specifically came to advocate representative democracy. His reasoning was as follows: People are naturally inclined to seek their own happiness, not necessarily the happiness of others; a king, for instance, is likely to seek his own happiness and not necessarily the happiness of all his subjects. But the purpose of government is to maximize happiness for the greatest number. So, to ensure that a government seeks to maximize the happiness for as many people under the government as possible, the government should be run by the people themselves—that is, a government should be democratic. To the question of why people should obey the government, Bentham believed that the principle of utility again provided the answer: People should obey the government insofar as doing so maximizes happiness. When people disobey the law and face punishment, Bentham believed that the appropriate role of punishment was just to deter crime; so, a punishment should be severe only to the point at which it deters crime, not any more severe.

Bentham was famously critical of the concept of natural rights. Rights, he believed, were best understood only as legal rights: People do not have rights independent of a legal system that grants them. He charged that the Declaration of Rights issued during the French Revolution confused the issue of what rights people wanted to have with what rights they actually have (for instance, desiring the right to own property, people assumed they actually had that right). Bentham called the concept of natural rights nonsense, and the notion that natural rights were unchangeable "nonsense upon stilts." Rights, he believed, should maximize happiness. But what maximizes happiness varies according to circumstances. So, it is a mistake to suppose that one's rights could never change.

John Stuart Mill

John Stuart Mill (1806–73) was the most important British philosopher of the 19th century. His influential writings covered such diverse topics as ethics, political philosophy, economics, logic, mathematics, and epistemology. His father, a friend of Jeremy Bentham, gave him a rigorous education at home, for example teaching him Greek when he was just three and Latin when he was eight. In 1826 Mill fell into a deep depression and came to believe that his upbringing had stunted his capacity for feelings; he emerged from his depression partly by reading poetry, particularly William Wordsworth. In 1830 Mill met Harriet Taylor, a married woman. He maintained a close, nonphysical relationship with her until marrying her in 1851, following her husband's death in 1849. Mill credited Taylor with being a major influence on his thought. In addition to his philosophical writing and pro-reform political activities, Mill worked for the East India Company for most of his professional life. He also briefly served in Parliament, where he advocated reforms such as granting women the right to vote.

One of Mill's best-known contributions to philosophy is as a defender of utilitarianism. Influenced by Bentham, Mill claimed that "actions are right in proportion as they tend to promote happiness; wrong as they tend to produce the reverse of happiness." Put another way, moral actions are those that promote happiness, and immoral actions are those that produce the opposite of happiness. By happiness, Mill meant pleasure, and he took pain and the absence of pleasure to be the opposite of happiness. So, Mill advocated hedonism, the view that what is good is happiness or pleasure. He also believed that people do in fact seek happiness. Mill's views differed from Bentham's in that while Bentham viewed all pleasures as equal (as long as the quantity of pleasure was the same), Mill distinguished between higher and lower pleasures. There were some pleasures, Mill thought, that were more valuable than other pleasures; for instance, the pleasure of viewing fine art is a superior pleasure to the pleasure of taking a hot bath, and in general, intellectual and aesthetic pleasures are superior to bodily pleasures. In a famous phrase, Mill wrote that it was better to be a dissatisfied Socrates than a satisfied pig. Mill based the distinction between higher and lower pleasures in part on the claim that people who had experienced both sorts of pleasures regarded high pleasures as superior. Mill also acknowledged that sometimes people act, not for pleasure or happiness itself, but rather for the sake of something else: For example, a person might work to become an accomplished pianist for its own sake rather than for the sake of being happy. In such a case, being an accomplished pianist is desired as a *part* of happiness, not as a means for happiness. For Mill, then, people do desire happiness and act to attain happiness, but they desire some things as part of happiness (and they do not desire those things for themselves unless they also desire them as part of happiness).

In addition to his ethics, Mill was an important defender of liberalism. Regarding political philosophy, Mill's book *On Liberty* was particularly influential. In that work, Mill defended individual liberty such as the freedom of thought and discussion. He also singled out for criticism the social pressure to conform, or the "tyranny of the majority." Against the tendency to insist that everyone conform to the same social customs, for instance, Mill defended individuality as a component to human well-being, arguing for the ability to make decisions according to one's own judgment and choose one's own plan of life. He also argued that society may exercise power over an individual against her will only insofar as it was necessary to do so to prevent her from harming others. It is not legitimate, then, to exercise power over a person only to prevent her from harming herself. For example, if a person's use of drugs harms herself, it is not acceptable to force her to stop using those drugs. (Of course, there might be times when drug use harms the drug user *and* other people; Mill recognized that it is a complex issue when behavior harms only an individual and when it harms others as well.) In addition to Mill's advocacy of this harm principle, Mill also argued for political and social equality between men and women. His book *The Subjection of Women* is a noteworthy instance of a feminist work—feminist insofar as it promotes the liberation of women—written by a male during the 19th century. Mill's views on the equality of men and women were out of step with the customs and beliefs of his time and were opposed by many people.

Harm Principle

A basic social, political, and legal concern is when, if ever, it is appropriate to limit people's liberty. We want to respect and uphold people's rights and freedoms, but we also recognize that there must be limits to them; people do not have the right to do anything they might want to do, such as taking someone else's life or property. What, then, are legitimate reasons for limiting someone's liberty? The British philosopher John Stuart Mill gave one answer to this question. His answer has been called the harm principle. The harm principle states that the only justification for limiting someone's liberty is to prevent that person from harming someone else. People should be free to do whatever they want as long as what they do does not harm someone else.

Although the harm principle seems straightforward and reasonable, there are a number of problems with it. First, there is the question of what *harm* means. There is the obvious sense that harm means physical harm. So, people do not get to kill or beat or in some other way physically harm another. However, what about other forms of harm? Is psychological harm covered by the harm principle? For example, if one person stalks or verbally harasses or abuses another person but never physically touches that person, is that behavior covered under the harm principle? It is not enough to simply say that there are laws in place to prevent or restrict harassing behavior, because the issue is whether there is a justification for limiting such behavior (and for having such laws). Pointing to laws that exist only moves the question back, because then the question becomes whether or not those laws are justified in limiting someone's liberty. Beyond psychological harm, what about economic harm? Is that meant to be included in the harm principle, so that one person's liberty can legitimately be limited if that person economically harms another person? Intuitively, we think that if such economic harm is the result of fraud and deception, then, yes, that kind of behavior may be limited. However, we think that if such economic harm is the result of simple competition in the marketplace—that is, one person economically harms another person by being more competitive and driving the second person out of business—then that kind of behavior should not necessarily be limited. So, the first question about the harm principle is what exactly does *harm* mean (and what cases of people's behavior would come under its label).

Another concern with the harm principle is whether it is meant to cover only *actual* harm that is caused or if it is also meant to prevent *potential* harm. For example, speed limit laws that regulate driving are set up not simply to limit actual harm that happens but in order to prevent such harm ahead of time. That is, a person can have his liberty limited—for instance, by getting a fine or a ticket or losing his driver's license, etc.—not because that person actually harmed someone by speeding or driving recklessly, but because that person was being potentially harmful. The point of such laws as speed limit laws is to prevent actual harm before it happens, and people's liberty is limited on the basis of merely potential harm. The problem here is that it is extremely difficult to identify potential harm and what potential harms may be appropriately limited, since just about anything could be potentially harmful or used in a potentially harmful way. There is the potential for harm any time that a person gets in a car, not just when speeding.

A third concern about the harm principle has to do with harm that results not because someone does something (such as hitting someone) but because someone does *not* do something. These are said to be cases of omission. For example, if one person sees a second person who is drowning, and the first person could easily help or rescue that drowning person, but simply chooses not to, has that first person harmed the second one?

These various questions about the harm principle focus on whether or not it is a good basis for legitimately limiting the liberty of persons. Many people have claimed that even if these questions can be acceptably answered, there are other concerns and other principles that should be used to limit liberty. One such principle is called the offense principle. This principle states that there are some situations in which offending others is enough to say that someone's liberty should be limited. For example, if a man stalking a woman is not literally harming her, at the minimum it is annoying and offensive (and perhaps even threatening). Likewise, people being extremely loud or shrill in some situations should have their liberty limited.

Another principle that has been claimed as a legitimate basis for limiting people's liberty is called the paternalism principle. This principle states that there are situations in which it is appropriate to limit a person's liberty so that he does not harm himself. The harm principle speaks only about not harming others, and it leaves open the issue of people harming themselves. The paternalism principle, however, says that there are conditions in which it is appropriate and right to prevent people from harming themselves. Such conditions would be in cases where the person does not know or appreciate the risks or dangers involved in some behavior. Also, such conditions would be in cases where the person is not acting in a thoughtful, deliberate way, perhaps because he is under extreme stress or in an emergency situation.

Finally, another principle for limiting people's liberty is what is called the welfare principle. This principle states that it is sometimes legitimate to limit people's liberty in order to benefit other people. For example, a tax structure that redistributes money to less privileged people is an example, or taxes on products such as cigarettes and alcohol, in which the money goes to support treatment programs for other people.

Inequality, Justice, and Liberty

Liberalism

Liberalism is a political philosophy. It is a view that puts primary emphasis on individual liberty and personal freedoms (the word *liberalism* comes from the Latin word *liber,* meaning "free"). The fundamental purpose and role for any government, or state, is to protect and preserve the liberty and freedoms of individuals. As a serious and important political philosophy, liberalism emerged during the early modern era in the West (the 17th and 18th centuries). It was this view that underlay both the American Revolution of 1776 and the French Revolution of 1789. Today, political philosophers and commentators usually speak of two broad forms or versions of liberalism: classical liberalism and modern liberalism. Classical liberalism emphasized political liberty and freedoms, focusing on limitations put on the state, while modern liberalism emphasized civil rights, focusing on responsibilities of the state. The philosophers John Locke and John Stuart Mill are commonly cited as prominent advocates of liberalism prior to the 20th century and John Rawls as a significant advocate during the 20th century.

Broadly speaking, liberalism places primary emphasis on individuals, as opposed to groups or societies as a whole. Groups, societies, cultures, etc., are all made up of individuals and are simply collections of individuals. Without those individuals, groups, societies, cultures, etc., would not exist. Individuals come together to form these larger groupings, but these groupings have no status or legitimacy beyond what they derive from the individuals that make them up. A common term for this is social contract theory. This is the notion that individuals form a society by, in effect, agreeing to a contract with each other in order to get along and live more easily. That is, two individuals agree to limit their actions and to regulate their behavior in certain ways; they agree not to kill each other or take each other's property, etc. They might even agree to give some other individuals (i.e., the police) the authority to enforce their agreement to behave in certain ways. For liberalism, this is the basic nature of groupings and of the state.

The proper function of the government is to protect the liberty of individuals, so, for liberalism there is a strong emphasis on individual rights, especially rights that are held against the government. The proper regulations of people's behavior—that is to say, the proper laws within a social context—are only ones that protect individuals from the aggressiveness of other individuals. This is often called the harm principle, and it says that individuals are free to do whatever they want as long as they do not harm other individuals (or individuals have the right to do whatever they want as long as they do not infringe on the same rights of others).

Along with this notion of the harm principle as the only legitimate limitation on people's liberty is a view that is often called neutralism. This is the notion that the government (and, broadly speaking, people) must be neutral with respect to what people decide for themselves is the good life. That is, the government (and other people) must remain neutral about how people choose to live their lives, as long as they do not violate the harm principle. For example, if someone wants to smoke and harm herself, that is no one else's business, and it is not a proper function of the state to restrict her. On the other hand, if secondhand smoke harms other people, then it is proper for the state to restrict that. (So, regulating smoking in certain public places is fine, for liberalism, but regulating smoking in one's private life is not.) For liberalism, one aspect of this view is that there is a strong separation between what is private and what is public.

With its emphasis on individuals and their liberty, liberalism puts a great focus on private property and a free-market economy. The proper role of the state is to protect the liberty of individuals, so the government should not take on the role of regulating or conducting economic matters, except to the extent of protecting individuals from being harmed by other individuals.

As already noted, there are two broad versions of liberalism: classical liberalism and modern liberalism. Both emphasize the primary importance of individuals and their liberty and rights. Classical liberalism stresses what are called negative rights, meaning rights that require people to leave others alone and not interfere with them. For example, for one person to exercise the right to free speech or free expression simply means that others must not interfere with that person speaking or expressing herself. Individuals are equal in the sense that they have equal rights and equality of opportunity. For instance, for classical liberalism, there should not be laws that restrict people's opportunities to get an education or start a business or run for public office, etc.

Modern liberalism, on the other hand, stresses what are called positive rights, meaning rights that require people to do something more than simply not interfere. For example, for one person to exercise the right to free speech or free expression means that she must be able to speak and express herself. But this ability presupposes that she has had certain things available to her. Or if someone has the right to education, it is not enough to simply leave her alone; being left alone does not provide anyone with an education. Instead, to truly get an education, one must have some things provided, such as teachers, books, etc. Modern liberalism, then, says that to have true equality of opportunity, there must also be equality of possibility. That is, people must have the possibility of having access to opportunities. Civil liberties are not enough, meaning liberties or freedoms from government regulation and constraints. In addition, says modern liberalism, there must be civil rights, that is, rights to goods and services in order for people to have true equal opportunity. For instance, modern liberalism—but not classical liberalism—would favor laws that require businesses and public buildings to provide handicap access (that is, access to those buildings for people with physical disabilities). The reason that classical liberalism opposes such laws is that they violate the negative rights of business owners, while the reason that modern liberalism favors such laws is that they ensure that disabled people have equal opportunity of access.

Today those people who tend to identify with classical liberalism more often are called libertarians. Those people who tend to identify with modern liberalism are called progressives. Within American political culture, those people who are labeled as liberals normally tend to favor modern liberalism. Many of today's political conservatives identify with much of classical liberalism; however, they do not embrace the moral neutralism of classical liberalism. Another contemporary political philosophy that often criticizes both versions of liberalism is communitarianism.

Justice

The concept of justice is fundamental to people's interactions and to social and political philosophy as well as to ethics. It is such a basic concept that it is difficult to define, and indeed, philosophers (and others) do not all agree on exactly what justice is. From the beginnings of philosophy, many conceptions of justice have been proposed and argued for, with perhaps the most famous being Plato's analysis of it in his book *The Republic*. One difficulty with discussing justice is that it is closely related to other important notions that are also hard to define, such as equality and the concept of deserving something.

Today, philosophers speak of two broad senses of justice: procedural justice and substantive justice. Procedural justice has to do with just process. We think that a process is unjust if it is biased or skewed in some way or on some basis that we think is inappropriate or irrelevant. A just process is one that is not unjust. For example, if we are playing some game and the referees or umpires seem to be favoring one team over another (say, by calling fouls on only one team even when both teams perform the same actions), then we think that this is unjust; that is, we think the rules of the game are not being applied to both teams justly. Or in an election, if we think that some ballots or voters are being excluded for inappropriate or irrelevant reasons, we think that there is an injustice happening. (Not all exclusions would necessarily be unjust; if a particular person has failed to register to vote, then that person's ballot might be excluded, but this would not necessarily be an injustice.) As another example, if some law were applied differently to different persons for what seem to be inappropriate or irrelevant reasons, then, again, we would say that there is an injustice with the legal process (the law is not being applied in a just way). Over the years, much of the focus of constitutional law has been over issues of procedural justice, that is, making sure that inappropriate and irrelevant factors (such as, perhaps, issues of race or gender) are not built into the law or the application of the law. (This issue is often spoken of as due process.) While procedural justice often involves upholding some sense of equality—for instance, treating like cases alike or weeding out irrelevant biases—equality of outcomes is not necessary for justice. For example, in a sporting event, one team wins and another loses; this is an unequal outcome. However, as long as we believe that the rules of the game were followed equally, we do not think that the outcome was unjust. Likewise, as long as we think that an election was fair and open, we do not think the outcome is unjust, even if our favored candidate loses.

Besides procedural justice, the other broad sense of justice is substantive justice. This has to do with the substance, or outcomes, of interactions. Within substantive justice, there are several forms of justice. One is called distributive justice. Distributive justice involves the just distribution of goods or services or other things of social value. Goods and services (say, money or objects or opportunities for education) can be distributed among people in many different ways. For instance, one person could own or possess all of them, or everyone could have exactly the same amount of each good or service, or there could be some other distribution. What would make the actual distribution just or unjust? What standards or criteria would determine whether a particular distribution of goods and services is just or unjust? Philosophers and others have given many different answers to these questions. One criterion that has been suggested is merit. As long as you deserve what is distributed to you, then the distribution is just. This, of course, depends on what counts as merit. Another criterion that has been suggested is luck. For instance, if two people play the lottery, and one of them wins, it is not because that person deserves to win, but because he is lucky; however, since the process was fair and equal (it was a random drawing of numbers), then the outcome is just, at least not unjust. Another criterion that has been suggested is utility. This view is that whatever distribution of goods and services leads to the greatest happiness of the greatest number of people is the just distribution. Yet another criterion that has been suggested is need. This is the view that goods and services should be distributed in order to meet the needs of people. Of course, what those needs are would have to be made clear, as well as why some things are legitimate needs (as opposed to wishes or luxuries). In addition, there is the issue of how to justly distribute goods and services if there are not enough to meet everyone's needs (so that, by itself, need would not suffice). Among many nonphilosophers (and some philosophers) another suggested criterion is God. That is, some people have argued that standards and criteria for justice are given divinely; they are laid out in, say, divine commandments.

Among philosophical claims about distributive justice, probably the most famous and influential have been the views of Plato, utilitarianism, and John Rawls. Plato's view was that justice is a balance or harmony of people (or groups) performing their proper role in society, and thus everyone gets his due. Utilitarianism, as noted above, holds that justice is a matter of whatever outcome actually brings about the greatest happiness. So, if it turned out that a famous celebrity or athlete is distributed much more than a nurse or a teacher (that is, received much more money, and, so, more goods and services), then this is a just distribution, as long as this makes more people happy. (So, more people are willing to pay money to see a famous celebrity or athlete work than they are to see a nurse or teacher work. For utilitarianism, this must be an indication that they are happier with this distribution than otherwise.) Rawls proposed the view that justice is fairness, meaning that as long as a system of distribution is set up to exclude built-in biases—that is, as long as the system is fair—then the outcome is just. Each of these views has been challenged and critiqued by many other philosophers, and there is not a generally accepted standard or criteria for distributive justice today.

The other major form of substantive justice is called corrective justice (sometimes called retributive justice). This form of justice has to do with what happens once an injustice has occurred. While distributive justice is focused on what we consider to be a fair distribution of goods and services, corrective justice is focused on what to do when an injustice has taken place. For example, the issue of legal punishment is a significant part of corrective justice. If we think that someone has acted in ways that violate accepted rules, then we might think of that as an injustice, either in terms of procedural justice or in terms of distributive justice. For instance, if someone commits a crime, we might think of that as a violation of social rules (hence, a violation of procedural justice), and as a result of that crime there is an unjust distribution of goods or services (such as stealing someone else's money, resulting in a redistribution of goods). Other people claim that the criminal must be brought to justice and be given some form of punishment so that justice can be served. This sense of justice, again, is corrective justice (or correcting an injustice that has happened).

There are two basic philosophical perspectives on corrective justice (or punishment): utilitarianism (or deterrence) and retributive justice (or desert). Utilitarianism holds that the reason people should be punished as a means of corrective justice is that punishment will deter people from acting unjustly in the future. In addition, the amount of punishment (or corrective justice) is determined by what will in fact deter people from acting unjustly in the future. So, if a small fine suffices to deter people from speeding, then that is what is a just corrective. If a heavy fine or perhaps imprisonment is needed to deter, then that is what is a just corrective. The retributive view holds that the reason people should be punished, as a means of corrective justice, is that they simply deserve it; they have disrupted the just balance or have violated the just system of rules. Even if punishing a criminal did not deter that person or others, the criminal would still deserve punishment, under the retributive view. For example, if someone accidentally caused some damage to another person's property, the retributive view would say that the person needs to be punished (perhaps by repaying the victim or restoring the victim's property), whether or not the person is deterred in the future from acting in certain ways. Justice, in this view, is not about utility but about what is deserved.

The two broad forms of substantive justice (distributive and corrective) often overlap. For instance, issues of reparation or affirmative action involve both forms. In the case of past discrimination against minorities, there was an unjust distribution of goods and services (minorities were unfairly discriminated against). Now, acts of reparation or of practices of affirmative action are intended as steps toward corrective justice. There remain unresolved issues about justice, beyond those noted above concerning acceptable standards and criteria of justice. There are issues of what count as relevant agents of justice and injustice. For instance, many people claim that a whole social system can be unjust, that injustice can happen even if no particular individuals are trying to act unjustly (for example, that discrimination can occur even unintentionally).

John Rawls

The American philosopher John Rawls (1921–2002) is often credited with reviving serious attention to political philosophy in general and with social contract theory in the late 20th century. During the first half of the century, academic philosophers largely ignored social and political philosophy. This was due mostly to the influence of logical positivism, a school of thought that focused on the analysis of language and insisted that questions about values, including moral and political values, were best left to social scientists. At the same time, the social and political philosophy that was being done tended to emphasize either utilitarian or Marxist thought. The publication in 1971 of Rawls's first and most famous book, *A Theory of Justice*, changed that. He brought back to the forefront the notion of rigorous normative political philosophy from a social contract perspective.

Rawls was born in Baltimore, Maryland. He attended Princeton University, where he received his undergraduate education in the early 1940s, as well as earning his Ph.D. there in 1950. In the interim, during World War II, he served in the U.S. Army. After receiving his Ph.D., he taught at several prestigious schools (including Princeton, Cornell, and MIT) before joining the faculty at Harvard University in 1962, where he remained for the rest of his career. During his lifetime he published several important books, but *A Theory of Justice* remained his lasting legacy.

Throughout his works, Rawls was concerned with matters of social justice. He was noted for advocating the view of "justice as fairness." Rawls's concern was with establishing conditions for social justice. He was concerned to rule out built-in biases that make society unjust, for instance, racism, sexism, etc.

In an effort to weed out such biases from being built in to social structures and laws, Rawls suggested a hypothetical situation, which he referred to as the original position. In the original position, people are assumed to be self-interested and rational. That is, they are concerned about their own well-being and interests (not necessarily at the expense of others) and are usually quite clever about how to advance their own well-being and interests (that is, they are rational).

Rawls asked what sorts of principles of justice rational, self-interested people would adopt and accept if they knew nothing about themselves other than that they will live under these principles. That is, they would not know if they were male or female, young or old, white or black (or some other race), gay or straight, etc. He referred to this as being behind a veil of ignorance, meaning ignorance concerning these details about themselves. For example, if someone suggested that only whites could hold elected offices, would a rational, self-interested person agree to this—not knowing whether or not he or she was white? Rawls thought that, no, a rational, self-interested person would not accept such a suggestion. After all, once the veil of ignorance is lifted, if that person turned out not to be white, he would be barred from holding political office.

Rawls claimed that from behind such a veil of ignorance, rational, self-interested people would come up with two fundamental principles of justice. The first he called the equality principle. This principle states that each person is to have an equal right to the most extensive basic liberty compatible with a similar liberty for others. This simply means that everyone is socially and politically equal with respect to what rights and liberties they have. However, people are different and unequal in various ways. A rational, self-interested person would want to acknowledge and accept many of those differences and would not consider some differences to be the cause of injustice. For example, one person might not care to make a lot of money, while another person might be very interested in making money. If so, there is nothing inherently unjust about one person working hard to make a lot of money while another person spent time relaxing and not making a lot of money. There would result an unequal distribution of wealth, but in itself that would not be unfair or unjust. So, Rawls said that behind the veil of ignorance, rational, self-interested people would come up with a second principle of justice, which he called the difference principle. This principle states that social and economic inequalities are to be arranged so that they are both (a) reasonably expected to be to everyone's advantage, and (b) attached to positions and offices open to all. This simply means that rational self-interested people would accept differences in terms of having social goods as long as those differences served their self-interest. A later formulation of these principles was as follows: The liberty principle states that "Each person has an equal right to the most extensive total system of equal basic liberties compatible with a similar system of liberty for all," while the second fundamental principle, "If there are inequalities in liberty or income," contains two parts; the first being the difference principle (those inequalities "work out to the advantage of the least well-off"), and the second being the equal opportunity principle ("the positions that are better off are open to all qualified people").

Finally, Rawls suggested that people who are behind a veil of ignorance—and, so, cannot build in biases to the basic social systems—would agree to a single, basic principle of justice: All social values—liberty and opportunity, income and wealth, and the bases of self-respect—are to be distributed equally unless an unequal distribution of any, or all, of these values is to everyone's advantage.

Equality

There are various concepts of equality, but for most people the importance of equality arises in moral and social contexts. For example, there is the concept of numeric equality, meaning simply the same number. Where numeric equality matters to people might be in cases when something is to be distributed among a group and we believe that everyone should get the same as everyone else; that is, an equal distribution is a fair distribution. However, numeric equality is not always what we believe is fair, or a sense of equality that is important to us. In this context, philosophers speak of the difference between treating equally and equal treatment. For instance, suppose there are three children in a family. The parents want to be sure not to show favoritism, so for every child they give the same birthday present, say, a basketball. One of the children loves to play basketball, one is neutral about it, and one hates playing basketball. Now, there is a sense in which all three children are treated equally by the parents; they all receive the same thing, a basketball. However, from the perspective of the children, there is not equal treatment; the gift of a basketball has very different meaning for each of them. In such a case, treating equally—that is, numeric equality—is not the same thing as equal treatment. It is not received as being equal (whether or not it is intended as being equal).

Related to the distinction between treating equally and equal treatment (and simple numeric equality) is the issue of equal in what respect. Two people might be equal in various ways and unequal in various ways. It is not simple equality or inequality that matters, but equality that is relevant to certain concerns. For example, in both moral and legal contexts, we believe that people should have equal rights or equal opportunities. However, even this notion is not uncontroversial. For instance, some rights apply to only some people, not to all people. As an example, there are special legal benefits set aside for veterans, such as special low-interest loans from the government. Or there are parking spaces that are reserved only for handicapped people; in effect, they have the right to park in them, but no one else has that right. This case points to the fact that equality is one moral and social value, but it is one that we balance along with other moral and social values.

Equality is closely connected with justice, though not identical with it. As the examples above show, there are cases in which we believe that inequality, or at least unequal treatment, is just and fair—as with providing special parking spaces for some individuals or special low-interest loans for some individuals. In particular, we relate equality both to procedural justice (that is, having fair procedures) and substantive justice (that is, fair outcomes of those procedures). For instance, if two teams receive equal treatment by the referees or umpires in a game, then whatever the outcome is (that is, whoever wins the game) is seen as just—because there was equal treatment in terms of process, although there was an unequal outcome (one team won and one team lost).

Libertarianism and Robert Nozick

Libertarianism is a political philosophy. The term *libertarianism* is also used in the context of debates about free will and determinism, but this is a different meaning of the word. Political libertarianism is a view that puts primary interest in individual liberty and personal freedoms. Because of this emphasis on individual liberty and person freedoms, libertarians claim that they are neither liberals, in the sense of modern American politics, nor conservatives. They are not liberals, they say, because today's political liberals (usually Democrats) often turn to the government to solve social problems or make social policies, frequently at the expense of individual liberty and personal freedoms. They are not conservatives, they say, because today's political conservatives (usually Republicans) often turn to the government to enforce their own moral and social values on others; again, frequently at the expense of individual liberty and personal freedoms.

Libertarianism is a version of the larger political philosophy of liberalism. Broadly speaking, liberalism focuses on the political liberty of individuals against constraints and restrictions by the government. Historically, liberalism is associated with the political revolutions of the 1700s, including the American Revolution and the French Revolution, against what people saw as repressive governments. Today, commentators often speak of classical liberalism and modern liberalism, with classical liberalism emphasizing the political rights of individuals and the limitation on government power over individuals, and modern liberalism emphasizing the economic rights of people to have access to goods and services. Libertarians identify themselves with classical liberalism and distance themselves from much of modern liberalism (which they associate with today's political liberals).

Libertarians argue that every person is the owner of his own life and no one is the owner of anyone else's life. Therefore, every person has the right to act according to his own choices, as long as those choices and actions do not infringe on the right of others to act according to their own choices. Governments, and all social groups, are only collections of individuals. Any value or powers or rights—that is, any authority—that governments (or other groups) have are derived from individuals and is legitimate only to the extent that it does not violate the rights and freedoms of individuals. The sole function of government, for libertarians, is to protect the rights of individuals. For instance, libertarians point, with approval, to the words of the U.S. Declaration of Independence, which include the claim that "all men are created equal . . . with certain unalienable rights; that among these are life, liberty, and the pursuit of happiness. That, to secure these rights, governments are instituted among men, deriving their just powers from the consent of the governed." Governments do not grant or create rights and freedoms, say libertarians; rather, they secure and protect them (if they are functioning appropriately).

For libertarians, along with the emphasis on the rights to life, liberty, and the pursuit of happiness is the right to property. People's property is the outward sign of their rights to life and liberty. For libertarians, if some individual took your property without your consent, that would be considered theft and would be wrong. The same, they say, is true if the government took your property without your consent. It is theft and a violation of your right to life and liberty, because your property is the result of your choices and actions. If anyone, including the government, can legitimately take your property without your consent, then, in effect, say libertarians, they own your actions; they may control your life. Much of modern social and political practice, say libertarians, violates the proper role of government. For example, for libertarians, the government should not be requiring mandatory education or providing health care or regulating business (except to punish those whose business practices violate the rights of individuals). The only legitimate laws are ones that protect individuals from others. So-called paternalistic laws, that is, laws that "protect people from themselves and their own bad choices," are, to libertarians, violations of individual rights and freedoms. For instance, laws that require people to wear seat belts in cars or helmets while riding motorcycles are improper constraints by the government. Wearing seat belts or helmets are good things, say libertarians, but it is not the proper role of the government to force people to do such things if they do not want to. Besides so-called paternalistic laws, other laws that require people to help other people—so-called welfare laws—are also ones that libertarians oppose. Although it would be good to help others (at least, some others in some contexts), it is not the proper role of the government, or anyone else, to force people to do so. Some libertarians have argued in favor of anarchy, that is, that there is no legitimate role for government at all, but most libertarians claim that government is necessary, but only to protect individuals and their property.

Critics of libertarianism include the supporters of communitarianism, a political philosophy that emphasizes a balance between individuals and communities, claiming both that communities are not simply collections of individuals, and also that individuals' lives and liberties are only possible in the context of communities. Critics also include the modern liberals, who argue that people's liberty and freedoms require some basic goods and services in order for political freedoms to be possible. They argue that political freedoms have little meaning if someone has inadequate shelter or food, so they have a right to have basic needs met; furthermore, meeting those needs is a proper function of government. Libertarians reject both of these sorts of criticisms. They claim that communities are not possible without individuals, so any value or status that a community might have is derived from the value or status of individuals that make up that community. Also, although people have basic needs for goods and services, those goods and services must come from someone. So, if people have a right to them, then that means that someone else must provide them, whether or not they want to. To force someone to provide for another person is, in effect, for libertarians, to enslave them, to make them act, without their consent, on behalf of others.

Among modern philosophers, Robert Nozick (1938–2002) embraced libertarianism, while Ayn Rand was associated with it but did not embrace it (although libertarians embrace much of her political philosophy). In 1974, Robert Nozick published his most famous work, *Anarchy, State, and Utopia,* in which he argued for libertarianism. This book was seen as a response to the modern liberalism of John Rawls's book *A Theory of Justice.* Certainly many people prior to Nozick had defended libertarianism, but his work was taken more seriously by political philosophers, as it was seen to be more than simply a political tract, but as a reply and challenge to the work of Rawls. In his book, Nozick claimed that people are entitled to what they have as long as they acquired it in a just manner, either by creating it or having it appropriately transferred to them. For example, if a person works and is paid for that work, the person is entitled to her pay. With that pay, she can purchase goods (that is, they are appropriately transferred to her), to which she is now entitled. As long as there is no coercion or fraud going on, the person is entitled to what she possesses. If there are social inequalities, such as Bill Gates having much more money than, say, his gardener, that is not unjust (as long as there was no coercion or fraud in how either of them acquired their possessions). Furthermore, for Nozick, it would be unjust if the political and legal system forced Bill Gates to redistribute his possessions to his gardener (that is, if Bill Gates was taxed so that some of his wealth was given to others). While this view was not new or unique to Nozick, he explicitly responded to the renewed interest and defense of modern liberalism that was reflected in the work of Rawls and, for this reason, was treated more seriously by other political philosophers than were and are other libertarian supporters.

Ayn Rand

Ayn Rand (1905–82) was a popular and influential philosopher who founded a school of thought that she called objectivism. Her real name was Alisa Rosenbaum. She was born in St. Petersburg, Russia, to a middle class family. As a young woman, she witnessed the Russian Revolution of 1917 that led to the creation of the Soviet Union. She left the Soviet Union at the age of 21, immigrating to the United States, and she never returned. She made a career writing, first as a screenwriter in Hollywood and later as a novelist. Her two most famous novels, *The Fountainhead* and *Atlas Shrugged,* remained best sellers decades after they were first published. She also wrote numerous philosophical nonfiction works and, late in life, edited the *Objectivist Newsletter.*

Rand called her philosophical system objectivism because she argued that the world is objective, that is, independent of anyone's beliefs or interests. In addition, this objective world implies that there are both means and standards of knowledge that are also objective. Those means and standards are reason and rationality, which Rand claimed were humans' only source of knowledge. Likewise, there are objective standards of ethics and moral behavior.

Rand claimed that because humans do not have inborn instincts that allow them to survive in the world, they must rely on what is distinctive about them, namely, their capacity to reason. Furthermore, because humans must make choices in order to survive (that is, they must make choices about what to eat, for example), they must be allowed to make such choices. That is to say, they must be free to be able to choose. As she often phrased this, "man is an end in himself" and each individual must live by his own mind for his own sake. The ethical view that follows from these facts, she said, is that of rational self-interest. By this she meant that people must use reason to survive, and acting in one's own self-interest is the appropriate goal of action. She entitled one of her most influential books *The Virtue of Selfishness,* emphasizing her view that being selfish—that is, caring for oneself—is not bad (as most ethical doctrines claimed, she said), but good. Given rational self-interest as the appropriate means and standards of moral behavior, she argued for capitalism as the only morally appropriate economic system and for the role of government to be limited only to the protection of the rights of individuals.

Rand claimed to be heavily influenced by the writings of Aristotle and to be particularly opposed to the views of Immanuel Kant and Plato. Kant, she claimed, tried to undermine any sense of an objective world along with any sense of reason as the means for people to engage with that world. Plato, she said, advocated a false reality of ideal Ideas and also a nondemocratic form of government. Both, she said, had harmed all later philosophy. She also argued repeatedly against Christianity and religion in general. Her writings were very influential for the political view of libertarianism, although she was quite critical of what she said was the anarchy and nihilism in that view.

Concluding Thoughts

Tragedy of the Commons

In 1968, the American philosopher Garret Hardin (1915–2003) described the tragedy of the commons, a scenario in which unrestricted use of a shared resource leads to the ruin of that same resource. Suppose there is a shared pasture, called the commons because it is owned by no one and common to all. On this pasture, herdsmen graze their cattle as they wish. At first all is well: The herdsmen get to feed their cattle, the cattle are fed, and the pasture is healthy. Eventually, however, each grazer adds another steer to the pasture, and then another, and then another. With the addition of each new steer, the herdsman who owns the steer benefits: He gets to feed his steer at no additional cost. It is true that with many more cattle grazing, the quality of the land begins to suffer, the soil is less productive, and there is less grass. But no single herdsmen suffers this consequence alone; it is shared by all. So, by adding additional cattle, each herdsman benefits rather a lot and is hurt only a little. Reasoning this way, the herdsmen continue to add more cattle to the pasture, with the eventual result that overgrazing ruins the pasture altogether: This is the tragedy of the commons.

The significance of the story is less that such events actually occurred in history than that it illustrates certain interesting points. Hardin himself connected the story to overpopulation: Unrestrained reproduction, he believed, would lead to there being too many people for the natural resources to support. The tragedy of the commons relates to other environmental concerns. For example, the world's oceans and the animals within it belong to no one, and it is in the individual interests of each commercial fisherman to catch as many fish as would be profitable. But if everyone who fishes commercially behaves this way, eventually there are likely to be no more fish, a bad situation for everyone.

Philosophically, the tragedy of the commons illustrates that it is possible for people to become worse off just by rationally pursuing their own self-interest. Given this fact, a second issue is how best to prevent scenarios like the tragedy of the commons. One answer is that common resources ought to be placed into the hands of private property owners, who would have an incentive to care for those resources properly. It is not obvious, however, how resources such as the air, rivers, and the oceans can be privatized. Another option is to regulate shared resources while keeping them in common (belonging to no individual person or organization).

Concluding Discussion Questions

1. What aspects of modern democracy would Plato and Aristotle criticize and why? Are their criticisms legitimate?
2. Hobbes thought that people living in a state of nature would have miserable lives, while Rousseau thought that it is the modern state of society that makes people miserable. Which view seems more correct? Why do they both see governments as a matter of social contract?
3. If politics is about how people should behave collectively and ethics and religion are also about how people should behave, then should there be a separation of ethics/religion and politics? What, if anything, is wrong with a theocracy?
4. Karl Marx claimed that political and legal systems were really reflections of underlying economic systems. Is he right; do economic forces drive politics and law?
5. Utilitarianism focuses on the greatest good for the greatest number. Is this consistent with democracy? Is it always consistent with democracy? Does utilitarianism result in a tyranny of the majority over the rights of the minority?
6. John Rawls's liberal view emphasizes equality and social justice, while Robert Nozick's libertarian view emphasizes personal liberty. How, specifically, does each criticize the other? Is there conflict or tension between equality/social justice on the one hand and personal liberty on the other?

Further Reading

Aristotle. *The Politics and the Constitution of Athens.* Translated by Stephen Everson. Cambridge: Cambridge University Press, 1996.

Avineri, Shlomo, and Avner de-Shalit, eds. *Communitarianism and Individualism.* Oxford: Oxford University Press, 1992.

Ishay, Micheline, ed. *The Human Rights Reader: Major Political Essays, Speeches and Documents from Ancient Times to the Present.* 2nd ed. New York: Routledge, 2007.

Miller, David. *Political Philosophy: A Very Short Introduction.* Oxford: Oxford University Press, 2003.

Nozick, Robert. *Anarchy, State, and Utopia.* New York: Basic Books, 1974.

Plato. *The Republic.* Translated by Alan Bloom. New York: Basic Books, 1991.

Rawls, John. *A Theory of Justice.* Cambridge, Mass.: Harvard University Press, 1971.

Simmons, A. John. *Political Philosophy.* Oxford: Oxford University Press, 2007.

Stewart, Richard M., ed. *Readings in Social and Political Philosophy.* 2nd ed. Oxford: Oxford University Press, 1996.

Straus, Leo, and Joseph Cropsey, eds. *History of Political Philosophy.* 3rd ed. Chicago: University of Chicago Press, 1987.

Swift, Adam. *Political Philosophy: A Beginner's Guide for Students and Politicians.* Malden, Mass.: Polity Press, 2006.

Wolff, Jonathan. *An Introduction to Political Philosophy.* Oxford: Oxford University Press, 2006.

Glossary

civil disobedience acts of protest against what are seen as unjust laws or social practices and policies; they are actions directed against a legal or political system, not against individuals.

communitarianism a political philosophy that emphasizes a balance between personal liberties of individuals and their responsibilities to their communities; communitarians criticize liberalism and libertarianism as failing to appreciate the importance of community.

dialectical materialism the view that human history is shaped by material, economic forces that undergo predictable stages of development; usually associated with Marxism, it was seen as an account for the inevitable emergence of communism.

equality a state of sameness or relevant similarity; in political philosophy, it is usually seen as a value related to social justice in the sense that people are treated in fair and just ways (for instance, that all people have equal rights or opportunities).

harm principle the view that the only justification for limiting the freedoms of individuals is to prevent harm to other individuals.

identity politics the notion that specific categories of how people are identified (or how they see their identity) are relevant for social and legal purposes; supporters claim that such identities (for instance, being African American or being handicapped) are important to ensure justice, while opponents claim such identities are embraced in order to receive special treatment.

justice the social and political value of what is right and appropriate; in terms of procedure, it means treating like cases alike (that is, in a nonbiased way), while in terms of content, it means right and appropriate treatment (such as principles for distributing goods in society).

legal positivism the view that what makes something a law, and therefore has legitimate force to regulate people's behaviors, is that it is created by a recognized and appropriate lawmaking body; usually seen in opposition to natural law theory.

legitimacy the notion that a legal and political system is appropriate and its existence is acceptable to its citizens.

liberalism a political philosophy that emphasizes personal liberties of individuals; classical liberalism, which focuses on minimizing the power of the state over individuals, is often called libertarianism, while modern liberalism, which focuses on conditions for social equality, places a more active role for governments to provide social welfare.

libertarianism a more recent term for classical liberalism, which emphasizes personal liberties of individuals, particularly by minimizing the power of the state over individuals.

Marxism the political philosophy associated with the writings of Karl Marx, which emphasized the economic underpinnings of legal and political systems as well as the social and ethical values associated with them; a view that embraces social equality via governmental regulations.

natural law theory the view that what makes something a law, and therefore has legitimate force to regulate people's behaviors, is that the law is consistent with objective (natural) morality; unjust laws, say supporters, are not legitimate laws; usually seen in opposition to legal positivism.

normativity the approach to considering something in terms of standards (or norms); usually distinguished from considering something only in descriptive terms; a normative approach to something often is said to focus on what ought to be the case, rather than only on what is the case.

rights a social relation that regulates behavior, either in terms of how moral agents are empowered (that is, what they may do) or in terms of how moral agents are protected (that is, what others may not do).

social contract the view that social collectives, especially states, are the result of (and derive their legitimacy from) individuals choosing to come together to form social bonds and relations; in effect, individuals sign a contract to regulate their behaviors in certain ways and to establish social institutions, such as police or courts, to ensure such regulation.

state of nature the view that social collectives, especially states, are artificial, that is, created by individuals choosing to come together to form them; the view that in nature humans do not live within political systems any more than do any other organisms.

theocracy a form of government such that the structure of government is one in which religious officials are also governmental officials and religious doctrine forms at least part of the government.

tragedy of the commons the view that the unregulated use of what is common, or publicly shared rather than privately owned, inevitably results in people being worse off and that policies and practices that are good for individuals in the short run will not necessarily be good for them in the long run.

utilitarianism the ethical view that what makes an action right is that it leads to good consequences; in the context of politics, it is usually formulated as the principle of the greatest good for the greatest number is the right action or policy.

utopianism a view, derived from the fictional place of Utopia, in which proposed social policies and programs that are intended to be beneficial are in fact harmful or impractical.

veil of ignorance a hypothetical notion, associated with the writings of John Rawls, in which principles of justice are formulated by rational, self-interested persons who are ignorant of their identity (so as to eliminate inappropriate biases being built in to basic principles of justice).

Key People

Aristotle (384–322 B.C.E.) *Greek philosopher who is today considered probably one of the two most influential Western philosophers of all time, along with his teacher, Plato. Aristotle saw communities and governments as natural and necessary for people to live truly good and happy lives. The following selection is from his work* Politics, *in which he states the proper function of a government.*

> Every state is a community of some kind, and every community is established with a view to some good; for mankind always act in order to obtain that which they think good. But, if all communities aim at some good, the state or political community, which is the highest of all, and which embraces all the rest, aims, and in a greater degree than any other, at the highest good . . .
>
> When several villages are united in a single community, perfect and large enough to be nearly or quite self-sufficing, the state comes into existence, originating in the bare needs of life, and continuing in existence for the sake of a good life. And therefore, if the earlier forms of society are natural, so is the state, for it is the end of them, and the [completed] nature is the end. For what each thing is when fully developed, we call its nature, whether we are speaking of a man, a horse, or a family. Besides, the final cause and end of a thing is the best, and to be self-sufficing is the end and the best.
>
> Hence it is evident that the state is a creation of nature, and that man is by nature a political animal. And he who by nature and not by mere accident is without a state, is either above humanity, or below . . .
>
> The proof that the state is a creation of nature and prior to the individual is that the individual, when isolated, is not self-sufficing; and therefore he is like a part in relation to the whole. But he who is unable to live in society, or who has no need because he is sufficient for himself, must be either a beast or a god: he is no part of a state. A social instinct is implanted in all men by nature, and yet he who first founded the state was the greatest of benefactors. For man, when perfected, is the best of animals, but, when separated from law and

justice, he is the worst of all; since armed injustice is the more dangerous, and he is equipped at birth with the arms of intelligence and with moral qualities which he may use for the worst ends. Wherefore, if he have not virtue, he is the most unholy and the most savage of animals, and the most full of lust and gluttony. But justice is the bond of men in states, and the administration of justice, which is the determination of what is just, is the principle of order in political society.

[Aristotle. *The Politics of Aristotle.* 2 vols. Vol. 1. Translated into English with introduction, marginal analysis, essays, notes, and indices by B. Jowett. Oxford: Clarendon, 1885. Available online. URL: http://oll.libertyfund.org/title/579/75395. Accessed July 28, 2011.]

Bentham, Jeremy (1748–1832) *British philosopher and social reformer who was important in classical utilitarianism. He thought that morally right action is action that produces the greatest good for the greatest number. His most important writing on political philosophy was* An Introduction to the Principles of Morals and Legislation. *The following selection is taken from this work.*

Nature has placed mankind under the governance of two sovereign masters, *pain* and *pleasure*. It is for them alone to point out what we ought to do, as well as to determine what we shall do. On the one hand the standard of right and wrong, on the other the chain of causes and effects, are fastened to their throne. They govern us in all we do, in all we say, in all we think: every effort we can make to throw off our subjection, will serve but to demonstrate and confirm it. In words a man may pretend to abjure their empire: but in reality he will remain subject to it all the while. The *principle of utility* recognizes this subjection, and assumes it for the foundation of that system, the object of which is to rear the fabric of felicity by the hands of reason and of law . . .

The principle of utility is the foundation of the present work: it will be proper therefore at the outset to give an explicit and determinate account of what is meant by it. By the principle of utility is meant that principle which approves or disapproves of every action whatsoever, according to the tendency which it appears to have to augment or diminish the happiness of the party whose interest is in question: or, what is the same thing in other words, to promote or to oppose that happiness. I say of every action whatsoever; and therefore not only of every action of a private individual, but of every measure of government.

. . . The community is a fictitious *body,* composed of the individual persons who are considered as constituting as it were its *members.* The interest of the community then is—what? The sum of the interests of the several members who compose it . . . A measure of government . . . may be said to be conformable to or dictated by the principle of utility. . . .

[*The Works of Jeremy Bentham.* 11 vols. Vol. 1. Published under the superintendence of his executor, John Bowring. Edinburgh: William Tait, 1838–43.]

Hegel, Georg W. F. (1770–1831) *German philosopher who shaped much of Western philosophy especially during the early 1800s. He proposed a dynamic system of thought in which all of history, including human social and political systems, were evolving toward a complete and perfect union. His views on political philosophy were most fully spelled out in his work* Philosophy of Right, *from which the following selection is taken.*

The state is the actuality of concrete freedom. But concrete freedom consists in this, that personal individuality and its particular interests not only achieve their complete development and gain explicit recognition for their right . . . they also pass over of their own accord into the interest of the universal; they even recognize it as their own substantive mind; they take it as their end and aim and are active in its pursuit. The result is that the universal does not prevail or achieve completion except along with particular interests and through the cooperation of particular knowing and willing; and individuals likewise do not live as private persons for their own ends along, but in the very act of willing these they will the universal in the light of the universal. . . .

[Hegel, Georg. *The Philosophy of Right.* Translated by T. M. Knox. Oxford: Clarendon, 1952.]

Hobbes, Thomas (1588–1679) *English political philosopher. In his most important work,* The Leviathan, *Hobbes gave an account of the nature and purpose of government, describing a version of social contract theory, according to which humans agree to give up their freedom to a* *ruler, or sovereign, in order to attain physical security. The following selection is from this work.*

The final cause, end, or design of men, who naturally love liberty, and dominion over others, in the introduction of that restraint upon themselves, in which we see them live in commonwealths, is the foresight of their own preservation, and of a more contented life thereby; that is to say, of getting themselves out from that miserable condition of war, which is necessarily consequent . . . to the natural passions of men, when there is no visible power to keep them in awe, and tie them by fear of punishment to the performance of their covenants, and observation of those laws of nature . . .

The only way to erect such a common power, as may be able to defend them from the invasion of foreigners, and the injuries of one another, and thereby to secure them in such sort, as that by their own industry, and by the fruits of the earth, they may nourish themselves and live contentedly; is, to confer all their power and strength upon one man, or upon one assembly of men, that may reduce all their wills, by plurality of voices, unto one will: which is as much as to say, to appoint one man, or assembly of men, to bear their person; and every one to own, and acknowledge himself to be author of whatsoever he that so beareth their person, shall act, or cause to be acted, in those things which concern the common peace and safety; and therein to submit their wills, every one to his will, and their judgments, to his judgment. This is more than consent, or concord; it is a real unity of them all, in one and the same person, made by covenant of every man with every man, in such manner, as if every man should say to every man, *I authorize and give up my right of governing myself, to this man, or to this assembly of men, on this condition, that thou give up thy right to him, and authorize all his actions in like manner.* This done, the multitude so united in one person, is called a *commonwealth*, in Latin *civitas*. This is the generation of that great *leviathan*, or rather, to speak more reverently, of that mortal god, to which we owe under the immortal God, our peace and defense. For by this authority, given him by every particular man in the commonwealth, he hath the use of so much power and strength conferred on him, that by terror thereof, he is enabled to perform the wills of them all, to peace at home, and mutual aid against their enemies abroad. And in him consists the essence of the commonwealth; which, to define it, is one person, of whose acts a great multitude, by mutual covenants one with another, have made themselves every one the author, to the end he may use the strength and means of them all, as he shall think expedient, for their peace and common defense.

[Hobbes, Thomas. *The English Works of Thomas Hobbes of Malmesbury; Now First Collected and Edited by Sir William Molesworth, Bart.* 11 vols. Vol. 3. London: Bohn, 1839–45. Available online. URL: http://oll.libertyfund.org/title/585/89852. Accessed July 28, 2011.]

Locke, John (1632–1704) *English philosopher who advocated a social contract theory and argued for limited government. His writings were influential on both philosophers and politicians. Thomas Jefferson included much of Locke's political philosophy in his own framing of the U.S. Declaration of Independence. Locke's most famous work in political philosophy was his* Second Treatise of Government, *from which the following selection is taken.*

If man in the state of nature be so free, as has been said; if he be absolute lord of his own person and possessions, equal to the greatest, and subject to nobody, why will he part with his freedom? Why will he give up his empire, and subject himself to the dominion and control of any other power? To which it is obvious to answer, that though in the state of nature he hath such a right, yet the enjoyment of it is very uncertain, and constantly exposed to the invasion of others; for all being kings as much as he, every man his equal, and the greater part no strict observers of equity and justice, the enjoyment of the property he has in this state is very unsafe, very unsecure. This makes him willing to quit a condition, which, however free, is full of fears and continual dangers: and it is not without reason, that he seeks out, and is willing to join in society with others, who are already united, or have a mind to unite, for the mutual preservation of their lives, liberties, and estates, which I call by the general name, property . . .

The great and chief end, therefore, of men's uniting into commonwealths, and putting themselves under government, is the preservation of their property . . .

Thus mankind, notwithstanding all the privileges of the state of nature, being but in an ill condition, while they remain in it, are quickly driven into society. Hence it comes to pass that we seldom find any number of men live any time together in this state. The inconveniencies that they are therein exposed to, by the irregular and uncertain exercise of the power every man has of punishing the transgressions of others, make them take sanctuary under the established laws of government, and therein seek the preservation of their property. It is this makes them so willingly give up every one his single power of punishing, to be exercised by such alone, as shall be appointed to it amongst them; and by such rules as the community, or those authorized by them to that purpose, shall agree on. And in this we have the original right of both the legislative and executive power, as well as of the governments and societies themselves.

[Locke, John. *The Works of John Locke in Nine Volumes*. 12th ed. Vol. 4. London: Rivington, 1824. Available online. URL: http://oll.libertyfund.org/title/763/65388. Accessed July 28, 2011.]

Marx, Karl (1818–1883) *German social philosopher who believed that the moral and political values and practices of a society are derived from the economic structures and conditions of that society. His writings became very influential in the late 1800s and throughout the 20th century, especially his short tract* A Communist Manifesto *and his longer work* Das Kapital. *The following selection is from his work* A Contribution to the Critique of Political Economy.

In the social production of their life, men enter into definite relations that are indispensable and independent of their will, relations of production which correspond to a definite stage of development of their material productive forces. The sum total of these relations of production constitutes the economic structure of society, the real foundation, on which rises a legal and political superstructure and to which correspond definite forms of social consciousness. The mode of production of material life conditions the social, political and intellectual life process in general. It is not the consciousness of men that determines their being, but, on the contrary, their social being that determines their consciousness. At a certain stage of their development, the material productive forces of society come in conflict with the existing relations of production, or . . . From forms of development of the productive forces these relations turn into their fetters. Then begins an epoch of social revolution. With the change of the economic foundation of the entire immense superstructure is more or less rapidly transformed. In considering such transformations, a distinction should always be made between the material transformation of the economic conditions of production, which can be determined with the precision of natural science, and the legal, political, religious, aesthetic or philosophic—in short, ideological forms in which men become conscious of this conflict and fight it out. Just as our opinion of an individual is not based on what he thinks of himself, so can we not judge of such a period of transformation by its own consciousness; on the contrary, this consciousness must be explained rather from the contradictions of material life, from the existing conflict between the social productive forces and the relations of production.

[Mark, Karl. *A Contribution to the Critique of Political Economy*. Translated by S. W. Ryazanskya. Moscow: Progress, 1977.]

Mill, John Stuart (1806–1873) *British philosopher and social reformer, who was an important advocate of utilitarianism. He argued that the greatest good for individuals as well as for society generally was attained by allowing personal liberties. The only restriction on those liberties is the harm principle, that is, that one could not harm other people. His most famous work in political philosophy was* On Liberty, *from which the following selection is taken.*

The object of this essay is to assert one very simple principle, as entitled to govern absolutely the dealings of society with the individual in the way of compulsion and control, whether the means used by physical force in the form of legal penalties, or the moral coercion of public opinion. That principle is, that the sole end for which mankind are warranted, individually or collectively, in interfering with the liberty of action of any of their number, is self-protection. That the only purpose for which power can be rightfully exercised over any member of a civilized community, against his will, is to prevent harm to others. His own good, either physical or moral, is not a sufficient warrant. He cannot rightfully be compelled to do or forbear because it will be better for him to do so, because it will make him happier, because, in the opinion of others, to do so would be wise, or even right. These are good reasons for remonstrating with him, or reasoning with him, or persuading him, or entreating him, but not for compelling him, or visiting him with any evil in case he do otherwise. To justify that, the conduct from which it is desired to deter him must be calculated to produce evil to some one else. The only part of the conduct of any one, for which he is amenable to society, is that which concerns others. In the part which merely concerns himself, his independence is, of right, absolute. Over himself, over his own body and mind, the individual is sovereign.

[Mill, J. S. *On Liberty*. London: Longmans, Green, and Co., 1913.]

More, Thomas (1478–1535) *English statesman who challenged the concept of the divine right of kings, both in his professional activities as well as in his writings. Today he is best known as the author of* Utopia, *a book that describes a fictional land and political system. The following selection is taken from a book by Jean-Jacques Rousseau about ideal empires.*

In all other places it is visible, that while people talk of a commonwealth, every man only seeks his own wealth; but there, where no man has any property, all men zealously pursue the good of the public; and, indeed, it is no wonder to see men act so differently; for in other commonwealths, every man knows that unless he provides for himself, how flourishing soever the commonwealth may be, he must die of hunger; so that he sees the necessity of preferring his own concerns to the public; but in Utopia, where every man has a right to everything, they all know that if care is taken to keep the public stores full, no private man can want anything; for among them there is no unequal distribution, so that no man is poor, none in necessity; and though no man has anything, yet they are all rich; for what can make a man so rich as to lead a serene and cheerful life, free from anxieties . . .

Is not that government both unjust and ungrateful, that is so prodigal of its favors to those that are called gentlemen, or goldsmiths, or such others who are idle, or live either by flattery or by contriving the arts of vain pleasure; and on the other hand, takes no care of those of a meaner sort, such as plowmen, colliers, and smiths, without whom it could not subsist? But after the public has reaped all the advantage of their service, and they come to be oppressed with

Sir Thomas More and his family in 1592 *(Painting by Hans Holbein the Younger)*

age, sickness, and want, all their labors and the good they have done is forgotten; and all the recompense given them is that they are left to die in great misery. The richer sort are often endeavoring to bring the hire of laborers lower, not only by their fraudulent practices, but by the laws which they procure to be made to that effect; so that though it is a thing most unjust in itself, to give such small rewards to those who deserve so well of the public, yet they have given those hardships the name and color of justice, by procuring laws to be made for regulating them.

[Rousseau, Jean-Jacques. *Ideal Empires and Republics. Rousseau's Social Contract, More's Utopia, Bacon's New Atlantis, Campanella's City of the Sun.* Introduction by Charles M. Andrews. Washington, D.C.: M. Walter Dunne, 1901. Available online. URL: http://oll.libertyfund.org/title/2039/145520. Accessed July 28, 2011.]

Nozick, Robert (1938–2002) *American philosopher who argued in favor of libertarianism, the view that the only proper role of government is to protect the rights of individuals. His most famous work was* Anarchy, State, and Utopia, *from which the following selection is taken.*

The minimal state is the most extensive state that can be justified. Any state more extensive violates people's rights . . . [Here] we consider the claim that a more extensive state is justified, because necessary (or the best instrument) to achieve distributive justice . . .

The term 'distributive justice' is not a neutral one . . . we are not in the position of children who have been given portions of pie by someone who now makes last minute adjustments to rectify careless cutting. There is no *central* distribution, no person or group entitled to control all the resources, jointly deciding how they are to be doled out. What each person gets, he gets from others who give to him in exchange for something, or as a gift. In a free society, diverse persons control different resources, and new holdings arise out of the voluntary exchanges and actions of persons.

[Nozick, Robert. *Anarchy, State, and Utopia.* New York: Basic Books, 1974.]

Plato (ca. 428–348 B.C.E.) *Greek philosopher who today is considered probably one of the two most influential Western philosophers of all time, along with his student Aristotle. When his mentor, Socrates, was put on trial by the citizens of Athens and then executed, Plato saw this as a sign of a weakness of democracy and his later writings on political philosophy reflect his concerns about the best form of government, which he saw as aristocracy (or rule of the best, from the Greek word aristos, meaning "best"). The following selection is from his work* The Republic, *in which he claims that philosophers would be the best guardians (rulers) because they alone care about justice and the Good and not merely about their own welfare.*

But in reality justice was such as we were describing, being concerned however, not with the outward man, but with the inward, which is the true self and concernment of man: for the just man does not permit the several elements within him to interfere with one another, or any of them to do the work of others,—he sets in order his own inner life, and is his own master and his own law, and at peace with himself; and when he has bound together the three principles within him, which may be compared to the higher, lower, and middle notes of the scale, and the intermediate intervals—when he has bound all these together, and is no longer many, but has become one entirely temperate and perfectly adjusted nature, then he proceeds to act, if he has to act, whether in a matter of property, or in the treatment of the body, or in some affair of politics or private business; always thinking and calling that which preserves and co-operates with this harmonious condition, just and good action, and the knowledge which presides over it, wisdom, and that which at anytime impairs this condition, he will call unjust action, and the opinion which presides over it ignorance...

Well, I said, and you would agree (would you not?) that what has been said about the State and the government is not a mere dream, and although difficult not impossible, but only possible in the way which has been supposed; that is to say, when the true philosopher kings are born in a State, one or more of them, despising the honors of this present world which they deem mean and worthless, esteeming above all things right and the honor that springs from right, and regarding justice as the greatest and most necessary of all things, whose ministers they are, and whose principles will be exalted by them when they set in order their own city?

[Plato. *The Dialogues of Plato*. Translated into English with analyses and introductions by B. Jowett, M. A. in 5 Vols., 3rd edition revised and corrected. Oxford: Oxford University Press, 1892. Available online. URL: http://oll.libertyfund.org/title/767. Accessed July 28, 2011.]

Rawls, John (1921–2002) *American philosopher who gave an account of justice as fairness, arguing within the overall context of social contract theory. Rawls described a formal procedure to determine what is just; he presents a form of social contract, based on the idea that rational, self-interested people would agree to a fundamental principle of justice.*

My aim is to present a conception of justice which generalizes and carries to a higher level of abstraction the familiar theory of the social contract as found, say, in Locke, Rousseau, or Kant... the guiding idea is that the principles of justice for the basic structure of society are the object of the original [contract]. I shall call [this] justice as fairness... All social values—liberty and opportunity, income and wealth, and the basis of self-respect—are to be distributed equally unless an unequal distribution of any, or all, of these values is to everyone's advantage.

[Rawls, John. *A Theory of Justice*. Cambridge, Mass.: Harvard University Press, 1971.]

Rousseau, Jean-Jacques (1712–1778) *French thinker best known for his work in social and political philosophy. He claimed that it is modern society that makes people miserable and unhappy. However, because we have formed social and political communities, we now blend our own personal wills to a general will. The following selection is from his work,* Social Contract.

Man is born free, and everywhere he is in chains. Many a one believes himself the master of others, and yet he is a greater slave than they. How has this change come about? I do not know. What can render it legitimate? I believe that I can settle this question.

If I considered only force and the results that proceed from it, I should say that so long as a people is compelled to obey and does obey, it does well; but that, so soon as it can shake off the yoke and does shake it off, it does better; for, if men recover their freedom by virtue of the same right by which it was taken away, either they are justified in resuming it, or there was no justification for depriving them of it. But the social order is a sacred right which serves as a foundation for all others. This right, however, does not come from nature. It is therefore based on conventions.

If, then, we set aside what is not of the essence of the social contract, we shall find that it is reducible to the following terms: 'Each of us puts in common his person and his whole power under the supreme direction of the general will; and in return we receive every member as an indivisible part of the whole.'

Forthwith, instead of the individual personalities of all the contracting parties, this act of association produces a moral and collective body, which is composed of as many members as the assembly has voices, and which receives from this same act its unity, its common self (moi), its life, and its will. This public person, which is thus formed by the union of all the individual members, formerly took the name of city, and now takes that of republic or body politic, which is called by its members State when it is passive, sovereign when it is active, power when it is compared to similar bodies. With regard to the associates, they take collectively the name of people, and are called individually citizens, as participating in the sovereign power, and subjects, as subjected to the laws of the State. But these terms are often confused and are mistaken one for another; it is sufficient to know how to distinguish them when they are used with complete precision.

[Rousseau, Jean-Jacques. *Ideal Empires and Republics. Rousseau's Social Contract, More's Utopia, Bacon's New Atlantis, Campanella's City of the Sun.* Introduction by Charles M. Andrews. Washington, D.C.: M. Walter Dunne, 1901. Available online. URL: http://oll.libertyfund.org/title/2039/145417. Accessed July 28, 2011.]

PART III
Philosophy of Art

Introductory Discussion Questions

1. What is art? Is it a product or a process (or both)? What is an artwork? Can anything be an artwork? Can anything not be an artwork?
2. What distinguishes good art and bad art? What can count as a standard or criterion of good art?
3. What makes an experience an aesthetic experience (as opposed to some other kind of experience)?
4. What is beauty? Is beauty necessary for art? Is beauty even relevant to something being good art?
5. What is the relationship between art and morality? Can good art depict something that is immoral? Can art influence people in bad (or good) ways?
6. What is the role of art in society? How does art influence people? Is censorship of art ever acceptable or appropriate?

Aesthetics: Philosophy of the Arts

Aesthetics is the branch of philosophy that is concerned with the study of beauty and matters that are related to beauty. It is closely connected with the broader topic of the philosophy of art. However, the philosophy of art covers topics that extend beyond beauty, such as the social and moral aspects of art (for example, under what conditions, if any, it is appropriate to censor art in public settings) and the relationship between art and language, since both involve meaning and representation (for example, how works of art can have or convey meaning about something). Some philosophers, however, say that there is no important difference between aesthetics and the philosophy of art, but rather that the term *aesthetics* is merely an older word that has been replaced by the term *philosophy of art*. The reason, they say, for the newer term is that *philosophy of art* parallels other more recent areas in philosophy, such as philosophy of science, philosophy of religion, philosophy of education, etc. In addition, they say, the focus of philosophy itself has shifted over the years away from making claims directly about art and instead, like philosophy of science and other areas, analyzes the concept of art and related concepts (such as expression and meaning).

The word *aesthetics* comes from the Greek term *aistheta*, meaning "things that are perceptible by the senses." This word was used to distinguish those things that could be known by the senses from those immaterial things that could be known only by reason or imagination; they were called *noeta*. So, the original meaning of aesthetics was not simply about beauty or beautiful things but a broader sense of knowledge. Nonetheless, early on, this type of knowledge became connected to beauty. For instance, in the writings of Plato, a distinction was made between knowledge of physical, material things and knowledge of nonphysical, immaterial things. We can know particular objects, such as dogs or trees, by encountering them with our senses (we see and hear and touch them), but that kind of knowledge is different than our knowledge of the concept of Dog or Tree (which involves no particular dogs or trees, but instead the ideal concept of them). For Plato, there is a progression of knowledge from particular things to their Ideas (or ideal Forms). Likewise, there is a progression from knowing the beauty of material things to knowing the essence of Beauty itself. Eventually, the term *aesthetics* was used not as a general sense of knowing but only in relation to beauty. Also, while today most people think of aesthetics and beauty in relation to art, the term actually includes the notion of beauty in other things, such as nature and even in, say, mathematical patterns.

One philosophical issue connected to beauty and aesthetics is the very nature of beauty (and also the lack of, or opposite of, beauty, ugliness). The first distinction about the nature of beauty is that it is sometimes taken in a descriptive way and other times taken in an evaluative way. The descriptive way simply means that something is described as being beautiful. The evaluative way means that beauty is not merely some feature of a thing, like its size or weight, but involves some value. So, given two things, if one is said to weigh 10 pounds and the other is said to weigh 20 pounds, that is quite different than if one is said to be beautiful and the other is said to be ugly (or plain).

This distinction between descriptive and evaluative ways of speaking of things points to another fundamental issue connected to the nature of beauty. That issue is about the nature of aesthetic objects. In other words, what kinds of things, or objects, can properly be described or evaluated as being aesthetic at all, and why? What kinds of things are even within the realm of aesthetics? This relates to what philosophers sometimes call a category mistake. For example, the notion of weight is relevant to some things but not others; dogs and trees are properly said to have some weight or other (that is, a given dog weighs a certain amount), but ideas or colors are not properly said to have any weight (that is, it simply makes no sense to ask how much red weighs and if red is heavier than yellow). The concept of weight applies to some things, but not all things. So, the question is: To what things does the concept beauty apply?

Yet another issue related to the very nature of beauty and aesthetics is what are called aesthetic properties, or features. Even among those things that are properly said to be within the realm of beauty, is beauty *in* those things? That is, is beauty something that is part of those things and something that we can discover in them (just as having a certain size or weight is something we can discover in them)? Or is the beauty in things not a property of the things themselves but rather a feature that we impose on them? The philosophical term for this is that beauty is a relation, not a property. In other words, nothing is beautiful in itself, but beauty is a relation between something and us. An analogy is that nothing is food in and of itself but is food only to the extent that it is related to something that eats it. An apple is just an apple, according to this view, but what makes an apple food is that something (say, humans) consumes it, and it is food only in relation to being consumed as food. There are features about apples and about humans that makes apples food for humans (and there are features about poisonous things and about humans that makes those things not food for humans), but the concept of food is a relational concept. Likewise, this view says, beauty is also a relation. This is not exactly the same thing as saying that beauty is in the eye of the beholder, or that beauty is subjective. Something being food is not "in the eye (or mouth) of the beholder." That is, there are facts about some objects and facts about humans that account for why some things are food for humans and some things are poisons for humans. So, being a relation is not the same thing as being subjective.

One more issue about the very nature of beauty and aesthetics is the nature of an aesthetic experience. This is the issue of what makes a certain experience one that is aesthetic rather than, say, one that is ethical or political. Two people might encounter the same thing, perhaps a work of art or some natural landscape, but have very different experiences. One might look at a painting or a sunset over the mountains and have the experience of having seen something beautiful and moving; the other person might look at them and have the experience of thinking of how those things might be made profitable, that is, be sold so that he could receive money for them. The first person has an aesthetic experience, but the second person does not. The issue, then, is what is the nature of an aesthetic experience; what makes that experience aesthetic?

All of the issues above are said to be metaphysical issues about aesthetics. That is, they are about the nature of beauty and aesthetics. There are also epistemological issues about beauty and aesthetics. These are issues about how beauty is known. One view is that beauty is known by having a certain kind of aesthetic sense. Just as people can know, say, colors by having a sense of sight or can know sounds by having a sense of hearing, so, too, people can know beauty by having a sense of aesthetics. This is sometimes referred to as *taste*, not in the sense of tasting things with one's mouth, but of having "good taste" or being refined. Some philosophers claimed that taste is something that is inborn (or not) and cannot be learned. For them, a blind person cannot learn to see colors (even if they learn facts about colors or how to speak about them), and a deaf person cannot learn to actually hear sounds (again, even if they learn facts about sounds or how to speak about them). In the same way, they say, aesthetic taste, or an aesthetic sense, cannot be learned (even if people learn facts about beauty or how to speak about it). Other philosophers, however, claim that taste can be learned, much like a wine tasting expert can learn to make very fine distinctions about different wines.

Another view about how beauty can be known is not by having some aesthetic sense or taste but by knowing facts that relate to beauty and aesthetics. For example, two people might hear a particular song, but one of them knows nothing about musical theory or musical structure, while the other is very knowledgeable about those things. The first person might not think that the song is beautiful, but the second person (the expert) might understand the very complex patterns and time signatures that have been blended together in the song, and that second person might claim to see beauty in that song because of knowing these facts. For that person, the ability to see and appreciate the beauty is a matter of knowing and understanding the complex arrangements that are contained in the song.

While this appreciation by the expert might well be the result of greater understanding and awareness, there is also the view that knowing beauty is not a matter of knowledge of facts but of emotional feeling. That is, a different view of what it is to know beauty is that such knowledge is not so much a matter of cognitive awareness of facts but instead is a matter of a type and level of feeling. Knowing beauty and having an aesthetic experience, they say, is less like knowing facts about the complexity and structure of something and more like having an intense emotional response. The knowledge, or perhaps recognition and appreciation, of the beauty of a song or a sunset, they say, is more like the joy that a young child feels when she is playing than it is like an engineer solving some problem. A child can know the beauty of a flower, they say, as much as or more than a botanist, even if the botanist knows much more about the flower.

This last view points toward the issue of what philosophers have called the sublime. There is something, say some philosophers, that is awe-inspiring or lofty about real beauty. There is sublimity relating to something that is overwhelming and has grandeur. Some philosophers have argued that an encounter with genuine beauty—perhaps a stunning landscape—makes one speechless at that moment. It makes a person feel reverent and spiritual, but it is not because of knowing lots of facts. Few people are geologists, but many people have encountered some natural beauty and felt awe. The question for many philosophers is: What is the nature of that (feeling of) awe and how does it relate to other things that we feel and know? This feeling is not the same as pleasure. While such a feeling can be pleasurable and make us feel very good—perhaps because we feel connected to other things—it can also make us feel overwhelmed and even unimportant in the grand scheme of things. Recognizing that the feeling of awe and sublimity is so dramatic and perhaps even indescribable, nonetheless it leads to the question of the nature of that feeling: Is it the result of some feature of beauty in things or the features of things or, like food, is it the result of being a relation to other things? For example, does—or could—a wild animal have a sublime experience? Even if only humans could have such an experience, is that because the thing that is experienced is itself sublime?

Plato

The ancient Greek philosopher Plato (ca. 428–348 B.C.E.) is renowned for his criticism of art and artists. For the most part, Plato saw art as a particular form of what the Greeks called *techné,* or knowledge related to doing or making something. Arts, in effect, were a form of craft, so Plato (and others) spoke of the art of horsemanship or the art of political statesmanship. The arts—that is, poetry, drama, etc.—were seen as a kind of craft. However, to the extent that art was a matter not of production (such as the art of horsemanship, in which someone produced a good rider or a tame horse), but rather of imitation (such as writing a poem or a play about horses), then art was imitation (the Greek term was *mimesis,* from which English gets the word *mimic*). Art as imitation was, for Plato, a matter of representing something. For instance, a painting of a horse represents a horse (or perhaps, horses generally); it imitates them in the sense of being an image of them. Obviously, a painting of a horse is only like a real horse in the sense of looking like one. Just as a shadow of a person is real, but a lower level of reality than a real person, for Plato, so, too, a painting of a horse is less real than an actual, physical horse. In addition, as noted earlier in the discussion about Ideas, for Plato, an actual, physical horse is real, but less real than the Idea of Horse. In a sense, an actual, physical horse is just a copy or representation of the more real Idea of Horse. Likewise, a painting of a horse is a copy of a copy! It is even more removed from Ideas than the physical object it represents. Art, then, for Plato, is akin to shadows and images; it is a low level of reality. To the extent that people might experience art as representing reality, then, it can be deceptive and, hence, bad. Whether intended or not, art can lead people away from seeking and knowing what is truly real (Ideas).

In addition to art as being a low level of reality and as being a distraction from seeking or knowing truth, Plato also claimed that art is passionate, and this was of concern to him for two reasons. One reason was that art arose from passion, rather than from reason or rationality. Artists are inspired; they are enthusiastic (literally, "filled with gods"), so even if they manage to produce a work of beauty (meaning that they produce an artwork that is merely a shadow of the Idea of Beauty), they do so not from knowledge but from passion. The second reason this was a concern to Plato is that art can also evoke or provoke passion—as opposed to reason—in the person who encounters the art. Art can stir people up! For Plato, this feature of art can be dangerous, because it is passionate and not reasoned.

A final concern for Plato about art, and a concern that is related to its nature as being both imitative and passionate, is that art can (and, he said, often does) portray things and people that are bad in ways that make them appear not so bad. (This is probably even truer today than during Plato's time; it is not at all uncommon that the hero of a movie is someone who tricks and deceives others for purely selfish gain.) Quite simply, for Plato, art can make what is bad appear to be good, and a possible result of this is that art can lead people to confuse the bad with the good and to pursue what is bad.

Despite the concerns that Plato had about art—that it is at best a shadow of reality, that it derives from passion rather than reason, that it can mislead people—he nonetheless recognized and appreciated the power of art. Also, he acknowledged that art was a basic human way of approaching Beauty and, as such, could be important and (morally) valuable. Indeed, the power of art, why it can be so moving, stems from its relation to Beauty and to Goodness.

Aristotle

Aristotle's Poetics

Aristotle (384–322 B.C.E.), Plato's student, also wrote about art, primarily poetry, which, for him, included drama and epic poetry. The word *poetry* comes from the Greek term *poiesis,* meaning a form of "making." Poetry (that is, art in general) was, for Aristotle, a form of mimesis, or imitation. It was a form of making something by imitating, or representing, something. In particular, for Aristotle, art imitated life, meaning that, just like things in nature, poetry involved the unfolding of something from its potentiality to its actuality according to the four causes. His famous book on the nature of art, *Poetics,* is essentially a description of the structure of poetry and its function. For example, the material cause of poetry includes things such as rhythm and harmony and language (or for music, rather than language, it might include tone). But just as a group of bricks by themselves do not make a house, so, too, a group of words or tones do not make a work of art. Rather, there must also be a formal cause, for Aristotle. That is, those materials must be structured in some way. The structural (formal cause) of poetry, for Aristotle, consisted in components such as plot and character and setting of, say, a tragic drama. In addition, they consisted of unities of action, time, and place (so, the events that unfold in the story take place within a specific time period and locale). The efficient cause of poetry is, of course, the poet or playwright or composer. Finally, for Aristotle, art has a function or purpose (or a final cause), which is to provide what he called proper pleasure through catharsis.

Catharsis

Catharsis is a Greek term meaning "purging or purification." In philosophy, the term is most often associated with Aristotle, who linked catharsis with tragic drama (plays that are tragedies). By the very concept of tragedies in the literary sense, terrible things happen in tragedies. People commit horrific acts, such as murder and incest. People suffer, sometimes unjustly. People die, often innocent people. Yet in Aristotle's time, as well as in our own, people choose to watch tragic dramas (of course, today we are likely to watch tragic movies in addition to tragic plays). It seems we choose to watch them because we enjoy them. But how can there be enjoyment in watching terrible—even though fictional—things unfold? In his book *Poetics*, Aristotle suggests that one reason that tragic drama appeals to us is that by watching tragedies, we can undergo a catharsis of negative emotions such as fear and pity. That is, viewing tragedies allows us to rid ourselves of these emotions, and in this way viewing tragedies brings a certain relief and cleansing. On another interpretation, viewing tragedies allows emotions such as fear and pity to be purified; on this reading of Aristotle, tragedy does not allow us to rid ourselves of these emotions, but it makes these emotions purer than they were. In either case, according to Aristotle, viewing tragedies is beneficial; it has a positive effect.

As it is controversial how Aristotle thought catharsis actually worked, it is also controversial whether Aristotle believed that catharsis was the main purpose of tragedy. However, Aristotle's comments on tragedy and catharsis are often considered in contrast with (and perhaps as a reply to) Plato's view of drama. Plato criticized drama for inciting negative emotions and thereby having a bad effect on society; Aristotle's comments on tragedy run counter to this view.

Aristotle's remarks about catharsis and about the (possible) positive aspects of art were not the only differences he had with Plato about art. In addition, he claimed that while art is indeed mimesis, this is not a bad thing. Whereas Plato thought that art was a low level of reality because it was an imitation of things, Aristotle claimed that imitation was natural and useful. After all, he said, humans are naturally drawn to imitation; it is largely how babies learn. Mimesis, then, can be useful and not necessarily a mere poor reflection of some higher realm of reality. Furthermore, art can be a means of discovery, both for the artist and for the audience. By creating or encountering a work of art, one might very well come to discover and learn something that will in fact make her a better person. Finally, Aristotle differed from Plato by saying that poetry (art) is a skill that can be learned, so it does not arise simply by inspiration or emotion. Art is a craft, one that involves tools and techniques and results in a product that can be evaluated. There are reasons, Aristotle said, that some plays are better than others, so art is not merely about passion and emotion (even if those are parts of the creation and experience of art).

The Emergence of Modern Aesthetic Theory

Enlightenment

The Enlightenment, also sometimes called the Age of Reason, corresponds basically with the 17th and 18th centuries. It is a term that is used to speak of the general intellectual and cultural climate, primarily in Europe, during those two centuries. Historians often speak of the scientific revolution and the rise of modern political philosophy as major aspects of the Enlightenment. Many enduring names of Western culture are from this time: in science, Isaac Newton (1642–1727); in literature, John Milton (1608–74); in economics, Adam Smith (1723–90); in social commentary, Jean-Jacques Rousseau (1712–78); in theology, Jonathan Edwards (1703–58); in American politics, Thomas Jefferson (1743–1826); in philosophy, René Descartes (1596–1650), John Locke (1632–1704), Immanuel Kant (1724–1804), and a group of French philosophers known as Les Philosophes.

During this time, new views about the nature of art and aesthetics emerged. Overwhelmingly, the dominant shift in aesthetics was the emergence of the notion of an aesthetic sense, or taste. There are various meanings of the term *taste*. The most familiar is the one related to food, namely, taste as one of the physical senses (along with touch, sight, smell, and hearing). This conception of taste is different than, but related to, art and aesthetics. In aesthetics, taste is the notion that is associated with the term *good taste,* meaning a refined sense of aesthetic and artistic value. This conception of taste involves the notion of aesthetic experience. For example, when someone encounters a work of art, she can have a variety of experiences related to that encounter. Someone might watch a film or listen to a musical composition and be moved by it. This would be an aesthetic experience; it is an experience that has to do with the artistic nature of the encounter. On the other hand, someone might watch a film or listen to a musical composition and have no response to it or, perhaps, think of it only in terms of how much money it might make. This would not be an aesthetic experience but some other kind of experience related to that encounter. A question in the philosophy of art and aesthetics is: What accounts for the nature of an aesthetic experience (as opposed to some other kind of experience)? One answer to this question is that people have a special faculty, or sense. That is, just as people have physical senses (such as sight and hearing), they also have aesthetic senses, namely, taste. It is, in effect, an aesthetic perception.

Although this notion of taste was common for most philosophers of art at this time, the philosopher who most people today associate with supporting this view was the 18th-century British philosopher David Hume. For Hume, we "perceive" beauty or other aesthetic features in art (and in nature) because we have the sense of taste. Just as some people have better or worse senses of smell or sight or hearing than other people, so, too, Hume said, some people have better senses of aesthetic taste than others. Those people with the better aesthetic sense—or, better taste—are the ones who can appreciate art better than others. Although aesthetic sense, or taste, might be inborn (just as some people are born with better hearing or sight), taste can be trained and improved (or diminished). For instance, someone can be taught to distinguish various features of fine wines and come to be a sophisticated wine taster. So, too, with exposure to fine arts one can develop one's aesthetic sense.

Hume, however, was not the first or the only philosopher to advocate this view of taste as a fundamental concept of aesthetics. His predecessor Joseph Addison (1672–1719) is often credited with being the first philosopher to emphasize this notion. Addison spoke of senses as being associated with pleasure and pain. For example, a light that is too bright can be painful to look at or a sound that is too loud can be painful to hear. On the other hand, some light and some sounds produce pleasur-

Portrait of Joseph Addison from 1719 *(Painting by Michael Dahl)*

able sensations for us. Aesthetic sensation, or taste, he thought, was associated with the imagination (not direct perception). Imagination comes from images, of course, that are supplied by our usual five senses (so, for example, we can imagine a purple cow, even though we have never seen one, because we have seen patches of purple and we have seen cows). Art, he said, is a matter of imagination; we do not go out into the world and just bump into works of art, rather we create them.

Addison claimed that with respect to art, there are three basic pleasures of the imagination: sublimity, novelty, and beauty. That is, when we find a work of art pleasurable, it is because of one or more of these three qualities. Aesthetic sense, or taste, is our capacity to discern these.

Another philosopher of the time who was (and remains) famous for his writings on art and aesthetics was Francis Hutcheson (1694–1746). Much like Addison before him and Hume after him, he claimed that we have an aesthetic sense (taste). He referred to it as an inner sense of beauty. Actually, Hutcheson claimed that people have many different senses, including the "usual" five senses (sight, hearing, touch, smell, taste) but also including a moral sense and an empathetic sense. That is, he thought that people have an inner moral sense of right and wrong. He thought that no one needed to be taught, for instance, that murder is wrong or that being kind is good. Likewise, he thought that people have an inner sense of empathy toward others. We simply know when someone else is suffering or is joyous.

In addition to these moral senses, Hutcheson claimed that we have an inner aesthetic sense. He spoke of this sense (along with the other senses) as being immediate and innate, meaning that they do not have to be learned or taught. Just as we have the sense of sight that is immediate and innate (that is, when we look at something, we see it right away whether we like it or not), so, too, our aesthetic sense is immediate and innate (again, we directly perceive beauty or lack of it). A phrase that is sometimes used to refer to this is aesthetic disinterestedness. This simply means that our aesthetic sense, or taste, is indifferent to our interests, much as our usual five senses are indifferent to our interests. For example, if I hear a loud crash in the next room, when I enter that room I might not want to see a broken lamp on the floor, but if there is one there I will see it whether I like it or not! My sense of sight is disinterested; what I see is not determined by what I am interested in seeing. Likewise, Hutcheson thought, our aesthetic sense is also disinterested. He claimed that our capacity to perceive (directly and immediately) beauty, or the lack of it, in something was not a matter of our interests and choices. This is why we are sometimes struck by how beautiful (or perhaps, ugly) something is. Of course, we can later analyze and debate and perhaps even reject that immediate sensation, but we experience it nonetheless, for Hutcheson. (By insisting that we have an inner sense of beauty, Hutcheson did not mean that the standards or criteria of beauty

Portrait of Anthony Ashley Cooper, third earl of Shaftesbury, in the 1732 edition of *Characteristicks of Men, Manners, Opinions, Times*. (Painting by J. Closterman Pinx; engraving by Gribelin Sculp)

are within us, any more than the standards or criteria of, say, loudness, are within us.)

Yet another important philosopher of the time who wrote about art and aesthetics was Anthony Ashley Copper, third earl of Shaftesbury (1671–1713). Although he, too, believed that we had an inner aesthetic sense, unlike most of his contemporaries, Shaftesbury was influenced more by Plato than by the new empiricist philosophy. Shaftesbury claimed that Beauty and Goodness (or the Good) are one and the same. This is because both are reflections of, even components of, a natural, divine order of things. For Shaftesbury, nature, as the creation of God, is orderly; it is both beautiful and good (since the creation of God could not be bad or ugly, traits so different from God). It is no wonder that we find nature beautiful and even awesome (in the sense of inspiring awe), for Shaftesbury. This beauty and awesomeness he referred to as sublimity; we find nature to be sublime, or great. Because of this natural and sublime orderliness, Shaftesbury saw harmony as a basic value. In addition, it is through art primarily that humans can (attempt to) mirror or capture these features and, so, come to experience Beauty and Goodness. It is through artistic creation—that is, by the creation of order and harmony out of disorder—that we can most closely approximate nature (and, hence, Beauty and Goodness). In this way, then, art is an imitation of nature; not in the sense of the content of art being, say, landscapes, but in the sense that, for Shaftesbury, art, like nature, is symbolic and requires interpretation and understanding but is still based on an inner sense.

Kant and Schiller

Immanuel Kant (1724–1804) was one of the greatest Enlightenment philosophers. Having looked at the determinism of natural laws (in *The Critique of Pure Reason*) and the necessity of assuming human freedom (in *The Critique of Practical Reason*), Kant wrote a third major work *(The Critique of Judgment)* in which he addressed, among other things, art and aesthetics. Art was, in effect, a third domain or kingdom that bridges the other two kingdoms of nature and freedom. It is the imaginative quality of art that bridges these other two kingdoms. This is because, on the one hand, like freedom imagination goes beyond what is present (for example, we can imagine a mountain of fudge chocolate even though we have never actually encountered one), while, on the other hand, imagination is built on images, on what we have encountered in the world (again, the image of a mountain of fudge chocolate depends on the image of a mountain and of fudge chocolate, both of which we have encountered). Imagination, then, is both in the world and yet beyond the world, so to speak; it reflects both nature and freedom but is not the same as either.

Where the fundamental principle of nature is conformity to law (for instance, all physical objects being subject to the law of gravity) and the fundamental principle of freedom is what he called final purpose (moral action), the fundamental principle of art is purposiveness. Art is always purposive activity, for Kant. We create or produce something, but the end of that activity is not to create or produce some practical device but rather something that is purely for pleasure. Art, as art, does not have any practical purpose or value; its purpose and value is in the pleasure it brings. Of course, there are different kinds and levels of pleasure, said Kant, and the fine arts are those that have the capacity to stimulate the imagination, to enlighten us, and to make/allow us to go beyond everyday sensory experience and to have sublime experiences.

Kant recognized that judgment of the beautiful is based on feeling, so to that extent it is subjective. At the same time, however, he claimed that it is not merely subjective; this is because it is a feeling that is connected to something outside itself. Those things that gratify us, he said, may be only subjective, but those things that truly please us (the things that we find beautiful) go beyond only subjective feeling. For example, for Kant if someone asked why you like vanilla ice cream better than chocolate, probably the only thing you could say is that you just do; it just tastes better to you. However, if someone asked you why you found one poem beautiful but not another poem, there are some things about the poems that you could point to. Kant was not saying that there are absolute, objective features about one poem that makes it beautiful and other absolute, objective features about another poem that make it not beautiful; instead, the point is that the pleasure derived from beauty is not simply the gratification derived from things.

In addition, Kant claimed that an artist is not merely someone who is skilled in some craft, but rather is a particularly sensitive individual, a genius. There is a view that if, say, Einstein had not come up with the theory of relativity, someone else would have (because it describes how the world is, so the data is "out there" for anyone clever enough to see it), but that if Beethoven had not composed his Fifth Symphony, it might never have been composed (because it is a creation of human freedom, not a collection of data "out there" waiting to be discovered). Although Kant did not give this example, it reflects his view of artistic genius. Artistic genius is more than inspiration, but it is a matter of inspiration nonetheless.

Friedrich Schiller

Friedrich Schiller (1759–1805) was a German intellectual who was influenced by Kant's writings and who argued for the importance of aesthetic education. Schiller was the son of a military doctor and studied at a military academy for his formal schooling, ultimately studying medicine, which he later abandoned. While he was a student, he

Portrait of Friedrich Schiller from 1785 *(Painting by Anton Graff)*

became acquainted with the arts and wrote a play (*The Robbers*). The play was critical of contemporary society and was seen as being pro-revolutionary, with the result that he was arrested and warned to cease such work. He did, turning instead to history and philosophy, finally securing a teaching position at Jena University. In his professional life he befriended the famous intellectual Johann Wolfgang von Goethe (1749–1832).

With respect to art and aesthetics, Schiller is best known for his book *On the Aesthetic Education of Man in a Series of Letters,* published in 1794. In these letters, Schiller claimed that people act on the basis of three impulses: material, formal, and aesthetic. The material impulse has to do with our physical nature, the formal impulse with our moral nature, and the aesthetic impulse with our artistic nature. (These three impulses reflect the influence of Kant's notions of nature, human moral freedom, and artistic purposiveness.) When Schiller published this book in 1794 two events were fresh in his mind, the publication of Kant's *Critique of Judgment* (in 1790) and the French Revolution (in

1789), followed by the Reign of Terror. These convinced Schiller that morality was dependent upon aesthetics, that without an appreciation and experience of art, moral sensibilities would not truly develop. People, he thought, needed aesthetic education as a necessary condition for true moral education; they needed to try to experience Beauty before they could genuinely experience Goodness and Truth. Aesthetic education, for Schiller, allows and promotes people to be capable of developing and fulfilling their moral potential.

Romanticism

Romanticism was a reaction against the emphasis on reason and science that was associated with the Enlightenment. The Romanticists saw the overall view of the Enlightenment as being too sterile and rational. They thought that this view basically portrayed and understood the world as a great, complex mechanism devoid of meaning. They rejected much of that view and, instead, said that the world was a great, complex organism, something that grows and develops and has meaning. People are agents in the world prior to being knowers of the world, they said, meaning that people are not just (or primarily) rational thinkers in a mechanical world but are living beings who experience things at an emotional and spiritual level at least as much as at a cognitive level. What really matters, they claimed, was our subjective, personal connection with the world. Along with that view was the notion, for many Romanticists, that people need to escape the trappings of modern urban society and get back to nature. In America, the most famous example was Henry David Thoreau (1817–62) and his stay at Walden Pond. Another example is a line from the poem of Ellen Hooper (1812–48): "I slept, and dreamed that life was Beauty; I woke, and found that life was Duty." Her point, of course, was that in typical modern social life, people miss what is truly important and meaningful and instead focus on mundane obligations that come from social duties. A catchword to express this view was to live passionately.

This focus on subjectivity and on things having meaning only because they are related to selves led to an emphasis on intuition, feeling, imagination, and creativity—not reason and science—as the major form of knowledge for the Romanticists. Intuition and the ability to "learn the lessons of Nature" (as opposed to civilized society) were considered to be fundamental to having real knowledge.

Another component of Romanticism was a sense of being connected with the world as a whole by living passionately in the moment. Margaret Fuller (1810–50), for example, wrote: "I am immortal! I know it! I feel it!" Ralph Waldo Emerson (1803–82) wrote about what he called the Oversoul, meaning a connection with all things, nature as well as other people. The Romanticist view of religion was one of personal spirituality and immediate subjective connection with all things (so, along with that, a rejection of organized religions). A famous essay at the time was written by William Ellery Channing (1780–1842), entitled, "Human Likeness to God." In this essay, Channing claimed that the features we say are in God, such as love and being sublime, are actually derived from features that we find in our own souls. The idea of God, he said, is the idea of our own spiritual nature, purified and enlarged.

The rise of Romanticism in European culture was prominent in the arts, for example, in literature (Goethe's *Faust*) and music (Beethoven's passionate symphonies), as well as among European philosophers at this time. One of the most famous was Søren Kierkegaard (1813–55), who wrote impassioned works on the importance of subjective, and even irrational, experience.

Among the philosophers who explicitly focused on the nature of art and aesthetics was the German thinker Friedrich Wilhelm Joseph von Schelling (1775–1854). The son of a Lutheran pastor, Schelling was born in Leonberg. At the young age of 15, he studied theology at the University of Tübingen, where he met and became friends with the poet Friedrich Hölderlin (1770–1843) as well as Georg Wilhelm Friedrich Hegel (1770–1831). Schelling earned his doctorate in philosophy and later studied at Leipzig University. He worked as a private tutor for a time before beginning his academic career at various universities and in academic organizations; he received his first academic appointment at the University of Jena when he was just 23. His friendship with Hegel ended over what Schelling saw as a criticism by Hegel of Schelling's ideas in one of Hegel's books. Following Hegel's death, Schelling ultimately replaced Hegel as a professor at the University of Berlin.

More so than some other philosophers of his time, Schelling is linked to Romanticism, and he counted among his friends the German writer Johann Wolfgang von Goethe (1749–1832). Schelling's thought underwent various changes throughout his long career. His early work was influenced by his contemporary Johann Gottlieb Fichte (1762–1814) in particular. Like Fichte, Schelling was concerned with human freedom and the self. However, in his philosophy of nature, Schelling sought to give nature an importance equal to that of the self. Rejecting the common Enlightenment view that the natural world consists of matter moving mechanically, Schelling instead regarded nature as an organic whole and as something that changes and develops in a purposeful way. As an analogy, Enlightenment thought viewed the natural world as rather like a complex clock, with many individual parts; Schelling regarded the natural world as something more like a tree, something alive and developing as a whole toward something in particular (as a sapling develops toward maturity). What nature develops toward, according to Schelling, is human beings; in this way, nature comes to consciousness. For Schelling, then, there is no sharp distinction between nature and mind. "Nature is to be invisible mind," Schelling wrote, "mind invisible nature."

With respect to art and aesthetics, Schelling thought that a universe governed by physical causes (nature) and a free person (the self) could be reconciled. He claimed that in the artistic intuition, the self is both conscious and unconscious at the same time, because the artist is both deliberate (conscious) yet also inspired (unconscious). By unconscious, Schelling, of course, did not mean asleep or knocked out; he meant not overtly aware and purposive. In a sense, then, in the creation of art, one acts out of necessity (in the sense of that person's actions being part of a causal world) and also free (in the sense of creatively going beyond what is the present state of affairs). Inspiration and feeling are the keystones of artistic creativity for Schelling; they are the expression of the unconscious freedom of the artistic genius. Schelling's work was soon picked up and expanded upon by the much more influential philosopher, Hegel.

Georg Wilhelm Friedrich Hegel

Georg Wilhelm Friedrich Hegel (1770–1831) developed what has been called the Hegelian dialectic, a process of reconciling opposites to form a synthesis. Truth, for Hegel, becomes realized and is expressed in a variety of ways and forms. One of those ways is through beauty, which, he claimed, is the aim of art. Hegel referred to beauty as the sensuous appearance, or show, of the Idea (or Truth). Aesthetics, then, is the science of the beautiful, at least in fine art. (Hegel distinguished beauty in fine art versus beauty in nature and his focus for aesthetics was beauty in fine art.) For Hegel, although art can be pleasurable and even lead to contemplation and moral improvement, those are (perhaps useful) by-products of art. But its ultimate nature is the expression of truth. Art, he said, originated in people as a means of creative growth and self-realization. By creatively expressing ourselves, we come to a greater realization of ourselves, and we also become freer, more complete as persons. This is the case not only when we create works of art, but also when we behold and contemplate works of art. For Hegel, art gives what he called "outer sensuous shape" to inner spiritual content, again a matter of dynamic, dialectical change and growth.

This dialectic growth, he said, was the case not only for individuals but also (perhaps even more importantly for Hegel) for humanity and history at large. Looking at the history of art, Hegel claimed that there were three ages (or stages) of art. These three ages displayed a dialectical growth. He called the first (and, for him, the simplest) stage *symbolic* art. In symbolic art, the form is related to its content, but in an inadequate way. Because art is the expression of truth via beauty, in symbolic art this expression is inadequate. Symbolic art is highly abstract, and form is what dominates (again, not adequately expressing its spiritual content). He cited architecture, especially non-Western architecture, such as the Egyptian pyramids, as an example. The second stage of art he called *classical* art. In classical art, he thought, the spiritual content reaches its highest level that can be expressed in a representational way. He associates this stage of art especially with classical Greek sculpture, in which beauty is expressed through the representation of the human body. In classical art, abstract form does not dominate, as in symbolic art. Classical art is still primarily sensuous and, so, is the antithesis of symbolic art. Both forms (and stages) are surpassed by the final stage of art, *romantic* (or romanticist) art. Romantic art is the freest form and expression of beauty, going beyond the concrete portrayal and depiction of classical art as well as beyond the concrete form and abstraction of symbolic art. Romantic art is the most fully spiritual stage of art. Among romantic arts Hegel includes painting, music, and (for him the highest form) poetry, as these arts involve (and demand) the freest form of creativity. With romantic art, Hegel said, art had reached its pinnacle.

Arthur Schopenhauer

Arthur Schopenhauer (1788–1860) was a Prussian philosopher who was well known in the middle of the 1800s but whose fame faded after he died. His reputation today (and even during his life) was that of being a pessimist, although he did not think of himself as such. Schopenhauer was born in Danzig (now Gdansk, in Poland) to a relatively wealthy family. His father was a successful businessman who wanted his son also to go into business when he grew older. This was not what Schopenhauer wanted, however and at the age of 17, when his father died, he was able to convince his mother to allow him to go to college instead. He wrote his most famous work, *World as Will and Idea,* in his late 20s. After completing his education, Schopenhauer taught at the University of Berlin, but was unhappy in an academic position, so he soon left the university and, because of his wealth, never again held a steady job.

Schopenhauer's views were heavily influenced by Plato (ca. 428–348 B.C.E.) and Immanuel Kant (1724–1804). From Plato, Schopenhauer came to believe that there are levels or grades of reality. For example, a person's shadow is real (on a sunny day there really is a shadow that is cast by someone), but that shadow is less real than the person herself (since the shadow will disappear if the light source is blocked, but the person does not disappear). Likewise, for Plato and for Schopenhauer, abstract concepts are even more real than individual, physical things. Even though there are no dinosaurs that exist, the concept of dinosaur does; it can continue on even after the last dinosaur stops existing, much like a person continues on even after her shadow goes out of existence. For Schopenhauer (as for Plato) there is reality above and beyond the "merely" physical, sensory objects of the everyday world. Ultimate reality is not what we perceive by our senses.

From Kant, Schopenhauer came to believe that the intellect comes between reality and us. For Schopenhauer, perception and experience never tells us what the world itself is like; all we can ever know is how things appear to us, how we experience them. In effect, the world that we (can) know is the world of representation or idea (that is, our ideas about the world). Furthermore, he claimed, scientific understanding

Portrait of Arthur Schopenhauer from 1815 *(Painting by Ludwig Sigismund Ruhl)*

of the world is even further removed from reality, because science is an abstraction of and from our experiences. Schopenhauer went even further, stating that scientific understanding of the world fails to match our experiences. For instance, science might tell us the nature of light as being certain wavelengths of electromagnetic radiation. This, he said, is empty; it tells us nothing about the experience of light. A blind person who could not see, say, red light would have no true knowledge of it by being told that it is a certain wavelength of electromagnetic radiation.

In a word, for Schopenhauer, the subjective experience can never be captured by any objective description.

Turning his back, then, on science as giving us any genuine understanding of the world, Schopenhauer claimed that the real basis of experience (and knowledge) is will. All things, for Schopenhauer, have a fundamental essence of longing or will. In particular, the will to live is what is first and foremost. Will is also everywhere (he remarked that will is the thing-in-itself). For example, people act, of course, because they choose (that is, they will). But, in addition, this drive to live is throughout nature, such as a bird instinctually building a nest or an acorn naturally developing into an oak tree. Given this fundamental and pervasive fact of will, the reason many people saw Schopenhauer as being pessimistic is because he claimed that will always outstrips satisfaction. That is, we never stop longing and desiring, even though those longings and desires might not be fulfilled. The result, he said, is inevitable unhappiness.

The "cure," so to speak, for Schopenhauer, was embracing and finding solace in art. Art, he said, provides one with a greater connection to what is real because art is basically subjective and personal. Again, the example of light is useful. In a painting we might experience light in a way that is more meaningful than in a scientific description of it. Art, for Schopenhauer, speaks more directly to our will than to our intellect and, for that reason, is more satisfying and meaningful. Through aesthetic experience and contemplation, we can become more connected to a level of abstract reality that goes beyond the immediate, physical everyday world.

For Schopenhauer, art had two primary functions, a cognitive function and a moral function. The cognitive function, as just noted, is that art provides a greater connection to reality than science does because the will is more real than intellect. The moral function is, as also noted above, that art gives meaning and solace; in a sense it tames the will by satisfying it (at least more than science does). Having an aesthetic attitude, for Schopenhauer, was basic to living a good life. By "aesthetic attitude" he meant approaching things in the world (that is, our experiences) from the perspective of feeling more than from intellect. He believed, for example, that looking at a portrait was a fuller experience than merely looking at a person's face because as a work of art the portrait both forces and allows us to contemplate and experience more than the immediate physical world. (Of course, one could look with an aesthetic attitude at a person's face, but, then, one would be treating it as a portrait, in effect.) Of all the arts, Schopenhauer thought that music, in particular, was the highest and most basic. This is because, by dealing purely with tones and sounds, music was the most directly connected to feeling and longing. Other arts, of course, engage people at the level of emotion and will, but they also have intellectual components to them. For example, poetry and literature involve words, for which we have intellectual associations. Sculpture and architecture involve three-dimensional objects, so we have cognitive, perceptual associations with them. Music, however, is truly abstract in the sense that it is non-perceptual. (Of course, we perceive the tones and sounds of music, but the content of what we hear does not correspond to things or objects.) Again, for Schopenhauer, music is the most abstract and the most emotional of the arts, the least connected to perception and intellect.

Friedrich Nietzsche

Friedrich Nietzsche (1844–1900) is usually associated with the 20th-century philosophical tradition of existentialism, but his work ranges far beyond that. He often wrote about art and aesthetics. His writing itself is unusually artful, by traditional philosophical standards. He often wrote in aphorisms, poetry, and even stories (as in his book *Thus Spoke Zarathustra*) rather than constructing lengthy, systematic arguments.

Nietzsche emphasized creativity as one aspect of an excellent, meaningful life, and in *Thus Spoke Zarathustra,* Nietzsche described the superman (sometimes translated as the overman). As he put it, man is something to be overcome, and the superman is the meaning of the Earth. Humanity is something to be overcome in the sense that humans can become something much better than what we are now—freer, stronger, more creative, more affirming of life. The superman is the meaning of the Earth in the sense that what can give meaning to our lives is a striving to overcome—or, in Nietzsche's phrase, a striving to *become* what we *are* in the sense of striving to realize one's potential. In addition, with the death of God, we are free to create our own values. To put the point another way, because God does not provide the basis for morality, we must decide for ourselves what is good and what is not, what is worth valuing and what is not. The superman, then, for Nietzsche, was the person who, as he phrased it, created himself. He even identified the great German thinker Johann Wolfgang von Goethe (1749–1832) as an example of such a person. Goethe, he said, was "an event," someone who not only mastered the science of his day but who also created great artistic works.

Although Nietzsche wrote about art and aesthetics throughout his works, most people focus on his first book, *The Birth of Tragedy*, when they speak of his views on these topics. In this book Nietzsche had contrasted what he called the Apollonian impulses toward logic, restraint, and aesthetic beauty (impulses he associated with the Greek god Apollo) with the Dionysian impulse toward joy, creativity, and reckless, even destructive energy (associated with Dionysus, the Greek god of wine). In particular, he said, Greek tragedy was the result of striking a dynamic balance between these two fundamental drives or forces. The tension between the Apollonian and the Dionysian is not quite that of logic versus emotion. Rather, the Apollonian represents both the source and aims of what he saw as plastic arts, such as sculpture and poetry, in which the art is associated with dreams and aspirations. The Dionysian represents (again both the source and aims of) what he called drunkenness or revelry and impulse. Each of these two drives or forces are fundamental to human life, and both are necessary for true creativity. We strive to achieve and overcome things in our lives, and at the same time, we are driven by inspiration and desire. What Nietzsche saw as the genius of Greek tragedy was that it saw creativity as a struggle, or contest, in which these two drives or forces were coupled together in a way that portrayed life as not discovering meaning but creating meaning. For Nietzsche, artistic creativity is the result of struggle and something that is won, so to speak; it is, in effect, an expression of power. Artistic creativity, of course, involves passion, but passion is only a necessary condition; that passion must be directed and harnessed. (As many artists would say, art is not just inspiration but also perspiration.)

Expressivism and Definability

Expressivism

The notion of expressivism applies to various areas in philosophy, but especially the philosophy of art. The root of the term *expressivism* is "express," which comes from the Latin words *ex* and *pressare,* meaning to "press out" or "squeeze out." To express oneself is, of course, to state or announce something. Expressivism is a view or position centered on the importance of a person expressing himself.

In the context of art, and the philosophy of art, expressivism is the view that art is the creative expression of oneself. Many people have argued that the basic and primary importance of art is that it is a form of creative self-expression. One of the most famous advocates of this view was the Russian novelist Leo Tolstoy (1828–1910). Tolstoy claimed that the defining aspect of art was the expression of emotion. Where, say, science expressed (or, to use his word, transmitted) thought, art expressed emotion. Good art is and should be something that moves us, not something that convinces us. Furthermore, good art should actually transmit the feelings of the artist through the artwork to the audience (or the person who experiences the artwork). A successful artist, he claimed, should be (and will be) able to make the audience feel what he (the artist) felt when creating the artwork. In addition, for Tolstoy, the value of art is that it involves the transmission of emotion. By doing this, people are more strongly connected to each other.

Portrait of the Russian novelist Leo Tolstoy from 1873 *(Painting by Ivan Nikolaevich Kramskoi)*

However, many philosophers of art, as well as artists, have questioned the view that art is essentially expression. For one thing, the simple fact of self-expression does not obviously constitute art. A young child in the midst of throwing a temper tantrum is engaged in (creative) self-expression, but it is not at all obvious that this is art! So, one question posed by philosophers is whether creative self-expression is by itself sufficient for something to be art (and the case of a screaming child suggests that it is not). Is creative self-expression even necessary for something to be art? There are cases where it, again, is not obvious. An artist might be given very specific instructions and guidelines for creating some artwork, and this might involve little or no self-expression. For example, an artist might be commissioned to paint someone's portrait in such-and-such a way. The result might be an artwork, but it is not necessarily a case of self-expression.

Even if self-expression is important in the creation of art, there are questions of *what* is expressed, *how* it is expressed, and *why* it is expressed. When an artist creates a work of art, it might be that the person's feelings are what are expressed or it might be the person's thoughts or beliefs that are expressed or perhaps it is something else that is being expressed. How an artist might express, say, her feelings or beliefs about personal betrayal or about innocence and redemption could be in very concrete ways (such as putting in specific content in her artwork) or in very abstract ways (such as using certain colors or shapes or tones in her artwork). In addition, there might be a variety of reasons or causes or motivations for this self-expression, such as personal therapy or purging of feelings or thoughts or, perhaps, to inform or entertain or even to shock others.

Many philosophers, as well as many artists, claim that self-expression is not what is important in the creation of art, but communication is. That is, self-expression is a one-way statement; it is an artist expressing herself, and that is all. Perhaps no one would ever encounter or experience the artwork. Communication, however, is a two-way statement; it involves an artist using art as a means of connecting to others, not merely stating or announcing her feelings or beliefs. This—that is, communication with others—is what many artists claim is valuable about art. Still others claim that the goal of creating art is not merely self-expression or merely communication but to have an impact on others. The goal is to evoke or even provoke feelings or thoughts or action in others as a result of the artist's artwork. Expressivism, that is, creative self-expression, then, is not what is important or valuable about art, but having an impact on others is.

Family Resemblance and Art

The notion of family resemblance points to the similarities, while at the same time the differences, between family members. That is, in some respects individuals share certain features with their family members, but only certain features. For example, an individual might look like his mother in the sense that they have similar colored eyes or similar colored hair or similarly shaped noses. On the other hand, that individual might look like his sister in various ways, say, similar colored eyes, similar basic face shape, etc. At the same time, that individual might not share other features with those family members. For instance, he might have different colored hair than his sister or different face shape than his mother. The fact is that people look like their fellow family members in some respects, but not necessarily in all respects. They resemble their family members, but are not carbon copies of them.

This simple observation relates to philosophy because a basic concern of philosophy, since its beginnings, has been to understand the nature of things. Traditionally, philosophers analyzed basic concepts by asking, "What is X?" where "X" might be truth or beauty or knowledge or friendship, etc. The typical process was to look for the essence of some concept or thing by seeking a set of necessary and sufficient conditions that would characterize that concept or thing. For example, if we wanted to know what is knowledge? we might look for the features or characteristics that something would have to possess in order for it to be a case of knowledge and also what features or characteristics something would have to lack for it not to be a case of knowledge. Only those things that had all and only those particular features would then be cases of knowledge. One might suggest, as many philosophers have, that there are defining, essential features of knowledge even if we do not yet know what they are. In addition, there are reasons why we rule out certain things from being cases of knowledge—for example, mere guesses—and that points to saying that guesses do not have the necessary or sufficient features of knowledge, whatever those features might be.

The philosopher Ludwig Wittgenstein (1889-1951) claimed that for many concepts there is no essence to them and, hence, no set of necessary and sufficient conditions that they satisfy. For example, he said, consider all of the things that we call games. Some games, such as Monopoly or Scrabble, involve a game board and various game pieces, but that is not true of all games (for instance, playing tag). Some games involve scoring points, but not all games do (for instance, tag, again). Some games involve multiple, competing players, but not all games do (for instance, playing solitaire). It might be the case that all games involve some set of rules in order to play the game (although that might not be true); but many things besides games also involve sets of rules, so having rules does not necessarily characterize or specify the unique essence of games. An analogy to help illustrate this point is to consider the nature of a rope. A rope is composed of many overlapping threads, but no single strand of thread runs through the entire length of the rope. So, there might be no single feature that runs through all cases of games, but, instead, a collection of overlapping features. That is to say, some—but not all—games involve multiple players, while other—but not all—games involve scoring points, etc.

Wittgenstein's point, then, was that it is philosophically a mistake to insist that concepts or things (or words) must have an essence. Rather than having an essence, many basic concepts might just have a family resemblance. So, knowledge—a typical concept that is important to philosophers—might not have an essence; there might very well be many kinds of things that we would appropriately call knowledge, even though they differ in some basic ways with other things we call knowledge. There might not be any single feature (or condition) in common among various cases of knowledge: knowing you have a headache, knowing your name, knowing how to ride a bike, knowing the square root of 25, knowing that George Washington was once the U.S. president, knowing that there are electrons, etc. It might turn out that there really is some essence to knowledge, but Wittgenstein claimed that we should not assume that there is and that philosophers should not assume that there must be.

A further point of Wittgenstein's in speaking about family resemblance is that, because many concepts or things or words do not necessarily have an essence, when it comes to following a rule, there might not be a single, essential form or structure to the rule or to the cases that are thought to illustrate a rule. For example, suppose you are given the following numbers—3, 5, 7—and you are asked what number comes next (that is, what rule would generate the next number). There are at least two reasonable answers. One answer is that 9 is the next number, because the sequence is odd numbers in succession (that is, 9 is the next odd number). On the other hand, another answer is that 11 is the next number, because the sequence is prime numbers in succession (that is, 11 is the next prime number). The original group of three numbers does not necessarily have an essence (of being odd or being prime). However, Wittgenstein said, we usually think of rules as, in effect, giving direction or guidance because there is some core essence to them. Just as with single concepts, though, rules—and how to follow rules—might not have an essence but only family resemblance.

This view of family resemblance was most famously applied to art by the American philosopher Morris Weitz (1916–81). Weitz argued that there is no definition of art, because art is an open concept. It is open in the sense that the concept is fluid and constantly changing, as well as simply having no set of defining conditions. Even if one considered traditional arts, such as painting, music, dance, architecture, etc., there simply are no set of features that all of these arts share and that nonart does not share. In addition, new activities and enterprises emerge that come to be called art. For example, historically there was great controversy and opposition to considering photography as an art, although today just about everyone accepts it as one. Other examples today might include activities such as juggling. For Weitz, we do not discover whether or not something is art, we decide whether or not it is, and we decide this for many different reasons and on the basis of many different criteria. Nonetheless, he said, there is an important function for trying to capture what sort of concept art is, but that function is not to describe facts about the world but rather to prescribe how we evaluate things. That is, so Weitz said, to say of something that it is art, is to evaluate it, particularly to praise it. *Art* is an honorific term, he said, not merely a descriptive one. Although this is not the same notion of expression as in the view of expressivism, it is a sense that to experience art is a matter of expressing an evaluation of something as being positive.

Challenges in the Twentieth Century

Although throughout history conceptions of art have changed, new lines of art and new lines of thought in the 20th century brought about significant revisioning and reimagining of art and aesthetics. Some of the most famous contemporary pieces of art led—indeed, forced—people to reconsider how they understood and experienced art. For example, in 1917, the French artist Marcel Duchamp (1887–1968) turned a common urinal upside down, labeled it "Fountain," and displayed it as a work of art. In the middle of the 1900s, the musician John Cage (1912–92) composed and performed his infamous piece "4'33," in which he sat on stage at a piano for four minutes and 33 seconds and did nothing (at least, he did not play any piano keys). Also, Andy Warhol (1928–87) displayed in an art gallery a collection of Brillo Soap Pad boxes. Each of these artworks, along with countless others, challenged basic conceptions of who the artist is, what exactly an artwork is, and what is the nature of aesthetic experience.

With respect to who the artist is, artists and philosophers began seriously to address this very issue. Traditionally, of course, everyone assumed that the artist is the person (or, sometimes, persons) who created or produced the artwork. Da Vinci was the artist who painted Mona Lisa; Beethoven was the artist who composed his Fifth Symphony, etc. However, by merely sitting at the piano and not playing any keys, what Cage did was to force his audience to listen to all of the other sounds that were around them in the auditorium, in a sense having them focus on what sounds they found to be worthy of attention. This sort of act led later thinkers to even declare "the death of the author," because they claimed that it is mistaken to think that art is a matter of something being created in the head of one person, then via sounds, gestures, words, etc., being transmitted to others (the beholders of the artwork), who then received the artwork and the meaning of it. The audience, in effect, they said, was also the artist. How one experienced the work was part of the creative artistic process. The audience did (does) not merely passively receive art or the meaning of what is intended; rather, the audience is part of the active process of creating the artwork and its various meanings. (In literature, this view is often called the reader response view, again, suggesting that how a reader responds to a work of literature is, at least in part, an active element of what the work is and means.)

With respect to what a work of art is—for example, is a stack of soap boxes in an art museum or in a grocery store a work of art?—this became an open and explicit emphasis for artists and philosophers more than it had in the past. In particular, the issue of the form of an artwork became of paramount importance. One way this issue was approached was to ask about context. How much of the context of a work of art is crucial, or even necessary, in order to understand or appreciate that work of art? Does one need to know biographical information about an artist in order to truly understand or appreciate a work of art? For example, if a person read a particular poem or novel without knowing that the author was, say, homosexual or had been a subject of child abuse, would that work of art be the same as if the reader knew those facts? Would knowing that the author lived in a certain century as opposed to another century matter? What kinds of context are relevant or important for grasping and experiencing a work of art; for that matter, for determining what the work of art is?

Besides asking about context, others have also asked about form versus content. That is, what makes a work of art what it is? Is the content crucial or even necessary or is the form and structure what matters? Many artists and philosophers (and others) have argued that content (as well as context) is crucial, while many others, often called formalists, have said that form is what is fundamental to art.

Form/Content

The issue of form versus content is an issue in the philosophy of art and aesthetics. The focus is a debate on the role and meaning of the form of artworks versus the content of artworks. This debate plays out in various ways. One way has to do with what is the very nature of something *as art*. Is it the specific content of the artwork that matters or is it the form that matters? For example, two poems might have the same form or structure, even though they have very different content. Or two films could have the same form (for example, the same plot structure and sequence of events and resolution of conflict), although they might have different specific content (for example, they might have different characters or take place in different times). Some artists and philosophers of art claim that what is fundamental about artworks *as art* is their form, not their content. This is especially true, they say, with abstract art, which has no obvious, identifiable content. Other artists and philosophers of art disagree. They claim that the content, perhaps even the contexts of that artwork, are crucial. Art, they say, is about something; it means something, so content always matters.

Another way this debate plays out has to do with the nature of an aesthetic experience. When people encounter a work of art—for example, seeing a painting or photograph, hearing a song, reading a poem, etc.—they have an experience (or various experiences). What makes that experience an aesthetic one has to do with the connection to the work of art *as art*. The producer or financial backer of a play might encounter that play, but experience it as a financial investment, not as a work of art. In other words, that person might only (or primarily) focus on whether the play is a financial or critical success, not on the aesthetic meaning or value of the play. That person's experience, then, is not an aesthetic experience. On the other hand, someone in the audience who is encountering the play as a work of art might have an aesthetic experience. The issue of form versus content has to do with what it is about a work of art that relates to one's aesthetic experience.

A third way this debate about form versus content plays out has to do with the interpretation of artworks. Formalists argue that art is not simply about specific things or events, so the specific content of a given artwork is not what is important. Even if an artwork says something about some particular thing or event, or even if it says something about, say, human existence generally, to understand and to appreciate an artwork involves focusing on *how* it says this, and that means to focus on form and structure, not on the specific content. Critics of formalism claim that an artwork does not exist in a vacuum and, therefore, to understand and appreciate it requires that the content and the contexts of it be considered.

Formalism

Formalism is the emphasis on form. This emphasis is usually understood to mean form as opposed to content. For example, the following two sentences have different content but the same form: (1) Mycroft likes cheese; (2) Karloff eats sticks. The common form of the two sentences is that each has a subject, a verb, and an object, and they are in the same relationship in each sentence (that is, the subject is followed by the verb, which is followed by the object). The issue of formalism—or the view called *formalism*—is relevant to various areas within philosophy.

One philosophical area that includes formalism is the philosophy of art. Here the notion of formalism is that it is form, and not content, that is fundamental to the nature and value of art. Formalism in art is the view that what is significant about art, indeed, what makes something art, are its formal features. For example, with poetry those formal features might be the rhythm of sounds or flow of images; with music they might be the movement and blend of time signatures or dynamics; with film they might be camera angles or lighting techniques. For formalists in art, what makes a poem about some event different than a mere description of that event is not the content (which is the event) but its form. What makes a poem art, and not simply a description, is its form. Many other artists and philosophers of art disagree.

Aesthetic Experience

Along with issues about who is the artist and about the nature of artworks, one other basic issue related to art that has long been of concern to aesthetics, but that became even more pronounced in the 20th century, was the issue of the nature of aesthetic experience. What is it to have an aesthetic experience? After all, we can encounter a work of art (say, read a poem or watch a movie or listen to a song) and simply be bored or find it tedious. Or we might encounter a work of art, for instance, a work of architecture or a statue, and find it merely to be an obstruction. Or some people claim that to experience a rose as a botanist would is to see it in a very different way than to experience it as an artist would. Or one person might see a play and be morally offended by the content of the play, while another person might see that same play and, even if also morally offended, might still experience it as a fine work of art. The moral experience for that second person is not the same thing as the aesthetic experience. So, what is the nature of an *aesthetic* experience? One answer to this question is that an aesthetic experience is a matter of having some sort of special sense. This is related to many of the historical views about art and aesthetics, especially those of the early modern period (roughly the 17th and 18th centuries). This is the notion that a person experiences, or perceives, an artwork in an aesthetic way because of having a refined or sensitive taste. It is like another sense, beyond or different than the senses of smell, sight, touch, etc. An aesthetic sense is another means of encountering things.

Another answer to the question of what makes an experience aesthetic is not that it involves some special sense or sensitivity but some special attitude or way of encountering an artwork. For instance, many people claim that there is an important difference between nudity and nakedness. Many paintings are said to be nudes, that is, the content portrays a person (almost always a woman) who is not wearing clothes. But, they say, there is a difference between a painting of a nude and a painting of someone who is merely naked. The difference, they say, is that there is a different attitude taken toward seeing a painting as a nude versus as a naked person. Or the difference in attitude or way of encountering might be that for an aesthetic experience, the encounter must be primarily on an emotional level. To see a play, for example, from the perspective of someone interested in optics and lighting might be to see it with an attention on the technical aspects of lighting the stage, etc. However, to see that same play from an aesthetic perspective is to feel the light, so to speak. The point is not optics but emotional effect. Related to this notion of an aesthetic experience as being a matter of special attitude is the view that an aesthetic experience involves a special focus on aesthetic features of the artwork. For example, one might focus (whether intellectually or emotionally) on, say, the unity or harmony of a painting or dance, not on, say, the color of the costume.

Or one might focus on the balance or intensity or complexity of elements in a painting rather than on the subject matter of that painting. All of these perspectives—special sense or attitude or focus—have been of concern to philosophers of art for a long time, but they became even more explicit in the 20th century because of the conscious activities and choices made by artists then to openly question and challenge what they saw as traditional artistic assumptions (such as who the artist is or what role the beholder has in determining the nature of the artwork or in what counts as an aesthetic experience).

Aesthetic Interpretation

One topic within the philosophy of art is aesthetic interpretation. Interpretation is related to the fact that art has meaning and that art is about something. That is, artworks—at least, most artworks—do not just happen but are the result of conscious decisions and planning by artists. In the process of creating a work of art, an artist tries to do something: express herself or communicate some thought or feeling to others through the artwork or, perhaps, arouse or provoke some thought or feeling in whoever might encounter that artwork. The point is that art does not just pop into existence but is the result of someone's efforts. In addition, that work of art is about something or other. It might be about some particular thing or event, as in the case of portraits; it might be about some sense of what it is to be human, as in the case of a poem or novel; it might be about getting people to see things in a new or different way, as in the case of a controversial photograph; it might be about focusing on forms or patterns rather than particular content, as in the case of abstract art. Again, the point is that art is the result of someone's efforts, and there is meaning to a work of art. Indeed, often people encounter some artwork and ask, "What does it mean?" because it is not common or obvious, but there is the assumption that—having been the result of someone's efforts—it does mean something or other (and perhaps it means many things). Aesthetic interpretation is the topic of explaining art *as art*.

Because interpretation is a form of explanation, it is not merely a matter of describing art. If someone simply described the colors and shapes in a particular painting, that would not be to give an interpretation. Even if someone described the painting in aesthetic terms—for example, said that the painting had balance or grace or movement—this would still be a description, not an explanation, and, so, not an interpretation. Because interpretation is not mere description, it is similar to (although not the same thing as) criticism or critique. In art criticism, there is clearly the element of evaluation. That is, in criticism, one does not simply describe features of an artwork but evaluates it; one assesses in what ways artwork is good or bad. Interpretation, then, is between mere description and evaluative criticism.

There are two broad goals or purposes of aesthetic interpretation. One is the goal of understanding. We might encounter some work of art but not understand it. Usually this means that we might not understand what the artist was intending by creating the artwork. For example, the painting *Guernica* by Pablo Picasso came about in response to the destruction of a town during the Spanish civil war in the 1930s. A person could see this painting and not know the history behind it, but knowing this history allows a person to understand it better. A second goal of aesthetic interpretation is appreciation. Understanding is a cognitive, intellectual notion. Knowing the history behind *Guernica* might help someone to understand it better (for example, why certain figures are portrayed or why certain colors were used) but would not necessarily mean that the person had a new or different appreciation of the painting. If someone were unmoved by it before learning this history, one might still be unmoved afterward, even if one were more informed. Appreciation, then, is different than understanding and a different goal of interpretation. With appreciation, the goal is to understand at an emotional level; it is to respond differently. With the aid of an interpretation (or, perhaps, multiple interpretations), one might come to perceive an artwork not only differently but also more fully and have an enhanced aesthetic experience. (Some people have argued that interpretations do not enhance one's aesthetic experience but actually diminish it, because an interpretation "pushes" one's understanding or appreciation in certain directions rather than in other directions.)

Besides the issue of the goals or purposes of aesthetic interpretation, there is also the issue of the process(es) or method(s) of interpretation. In other words, not *why*, but *how* should a work of art be interpreted? One common approach to interpretation is to focus on aspects of the artwork itself, ignoring everything else. For instance, with the painting *Guernica*, one might focus on the colors that were used (blacks and grays), as well as pointing out what was not used (bright colors); one might focus on the figures that are portrayed in the painting (people and animals in contorted positions with obvious pain and anguish). This approach is often associated with a view called formalism. A second common approach is not to ignore what are seen as relevant facts and contexts about the artwork. So, bringing in the historical events that prompted Picasso to paint *Guernica* would be one example. In addition, one might bring in information about Picasso's other paintings to see if there is any commonality with *Guernica*. One might include any information about what Picasso said in speeches or lectures or letters about *Guernica* in particular or about his views on art in general. This approach is often associated with a view called contextualism (namely, that contextual information that is relevant to the artwork is also relevant to interpreting it). This issue of *how* to interpret a work of art also speaks to *what* gets interpreted. Is it the artwork by itself or is it the artist's intentions, personal history, cultural events, etc?

An additional issue related to aesthetic interpretation is the question of what would count as (1) a correct or incorrect interpretation and also (2) a better or worse interpretation. At just a commonsense level, some interpretations seem to be incorrect. For example, if someone said that Shakespeare's play *Hamlet* was about snowboarding, that would seem clearly to be a misinterpretation. After all, Shakespeare did not know about snowboarding, so how could *Hamlet* be about it? However, this assumes that an artwork must be, or should be, interpreted in terms of the artist's intentions. Yet many people have argued that an artist's intentions are not the only factor that is relevant to interpreting a work of art (and, perhaps, are not relevant at all, since a work of art can mean many different things to different people). Among philosophers of art, there is a lot of disagreement about what standards or criteria are appropriate for evaluating aesthetic interpretation (that is, for saying what would count as a correct or incorrect interpretation, as well as a better or worse interpretation).

Art and Society

John Dewey

John Dewey (1859–1952) was an American philosopher. He is considered one of the most influential American philosophers, not only within academic philosophy but also in the broader American culture. Along with Charles Peirce (1839–1914) and William James (1842–1910), he is considered one of the "big three" philosophers associated with a school of thought called pragmatism. Dewey was born in Vermont and attended college at the University of Vermont. After teaching high school for several years in Vermont and Pennsylvania, he went on to receive his doctorate at Johns Hopkins University in Baltimore. This was followed by teaching positions at several universities over his professional career, beginning at the University of Michigan during the mid-1880s to the mid-1890s. He then went to the University of Chicago for 10 years. While there, he became closely associated with the social work of Jane Addams (1860–1935). From 1905 until his retirement in 1930, he taught at Columbia University in New York City. Following his retirement, he continued to write a great many works both for professional philosophers and for the general American public. The range of his writings was vast; it included works on logic, theory of knowledge, religion, art and aesthetics, and political philosophy. He had particular influence on the philosophy of education.

Within academic philosophy, Dewey is probably best known for his work on inquiry and logic. He claimed that all inquiry is conducted by agents and not merely by passive information processors, and he emphasized the experimental and instrumental nature of human conduct. What he meant by this is that people bump into a world in which they have goals and concerns and try to make their way in the world. People are not simply processors of information; rather, they have interests and goals to satisfy, which is why they inquire about things. They are agents, simply meaning that they act in the world, and their actions are purposeful actions. This emphasis on purposeful interaction between agents and environments points to Dewey's criticism of what he termed "the quest for certainty." Too much human activity (with philosophers being the primary culprits) has been a search for absolutes, for certainty. This, for Dewey, was mistaken. The world is filled with changes and uncertainty. Human inquiry should be a matter of purposeful action in response to, and ultimately in anticipation of, such change and uncertainty. Intelligence is experimental and evaluative; we learn by doing, by engaging with the puzzles and problems presented by a changing environment. While there might not be eternal, absolute standards or criteria for, say, moral judgment, it is also the case that there are standards and criteria that go beyond just subjective, personal preferences, since there are facts about the uncertainties and changes and problems that we face. Dewey often referred to his philosophical approaches as instrumentalist and naturalist as well as pragmatist. This is because he emphasized a learning-by-doing view of human conduct, where we do not simply discover eternal truths about the world, but we often work in a trial-and-error way to find out what works.

Dewey was greatly influenced by science generally and by Darwinian evolution particularly. What is good (or bad), he said, is relative to contexts and goals but at the same time is a matter of what helps an organism cope with and flourish in the world. Drawing from evolutionary theory and writing as an early supporter of what is now seen as evolutionary ethics, Dewey claimed that growth is the primary moral end. Adaptation and adjustment to different and changing environments, including social and moral environments, are the signs of appropriate action. In the interaction with one's environments, a person must decide among goals and choices of action, based on what he thinks likely will happen. Appraising situations and deliberating on likely outcomes is what Dewey refers to as valuation. This process of valuation, for Dewey, involves both facts about the world and values and goals that a person has. As a result, he rejected what is often called the fact/value dichotomy (that is, that there is a sharp separation between facts and values).

These broad philosophical stances and views that Dewey held carried over to his conception of art and aesthetics. In a word, he said, art is experience. Artworks should be thought of not so much as products but processes. From the perspective of the artist, art is the result of engaging with materials in certain contexts and against a background of beliefs, values, goals, expectations, etc. Likewise, from the perspective of the audience, or those who encounter the artwork, they, too, engage with art as a process of having an experience. They, too, engage with it against a background of beliefs, values, goals, expectations, etc. Art is, then, not a thing, but an interaction. When we experience a work of art, we both find meaning in it and also impose meaning upon it. (We think it is reasonable to ask, "What does it mean?" or "What did the artist intend?" and at the same time remark, "This is what it means to me," or "This is how I understand it.")

Besides the fact that art is experience, Dewey also emphasized that (especially today) art is social. Neither artists nor beholders of art live in isolation. People's beliefs, values, goals, expectations, etc., are shaped by their interactions with the world, especially the social world. Furthermore, said Dewey, art is particularly important because it extends feelings and imagination and, so, has the capability of uniting people. (Think of how people can appreciate and enjoy art from other cultures even if they do not understand or appreciate the customs or politics of those cultures.)

Art and Society

Art is connected to society in many ways. Especially today, because of technology, art is everywhere. Billions of songs are downloaded from the Internet every year, and billions of dollars are spent by moviegoers every year. The Harry Potter books were a worldwide phenomenon. Thousands, even millions, of people can and do encounter not only works of art every day but often the same works of art; that is, on any given day, thousands, perhaps millions, of people can be listening to the same song or watching the same movie or video. There are celebrity artists, such as pop singers or movie stars, who are known around the world and are recognized by billions of people. Because of the availability and presence of art that technology has made possible, philosophers (and others) have expanded their aesthetic focus to include issues relating art and society.

One such issue within the world of art itself was highlighted by the American philosopher Nelson Goodman (1906–98). Goodman pointed out that many works of art are unique, what he called autographic. There is only one painting that is the Mona Lisa and only one building (architectural artwork) that is the Eiffel Tower and only one musical composition that is Beethoven's Fifth Symphony. However, there are many other works of art that are not unique, in the sense of there being only one copy of them. Goodman called these allographic. Goodman's interest in speaking of autographic art versus allographic art was to ask what made something a forgery. We think of a forgery as an illicit copy of some original thing. Even if it were not created or produced in order to get money (such as someone trying to sell a forgery of a painting), it is seen as a forgery because it is not the original. Goodman claimed that this is true only of autographic art. With allographic art, there is the assumption that there are lots of copies, so it might be inaccurate to even say that there is an original. For example, the case of a particular movie that is shown in thousands of theaters at the same time does not mean that one of those copies is the original and all of the others are mere copies. In fact, it might be that thousands of copies are created or produced at exactly the same time in a factory (or group of factories). So, even just within the concerns of artists and aestheticians, new questions have arisen because of the relationship between art and technology and, so, between art and society at large.

Of course, in a social and legal sense, people speak of forgeries or illicit copies of, say, a movie, but this is because those copies were created or produced by someone other than the owner of the original. For instance, the Walt Disney Corporation might own the copyright for some movie (such as *The Lion King*), and even though they create and produce thousands of copies of that movie, other copies are said to be forgeries only if Disney did not authorize their creation or production. They are not forgeries simply because they are copies, but because they are created and produced by people other than the legal owner.

Nonetheless, this point of ownership of art points to other issues connected to art and society. An important issue here is the business of art and the role of art in business. We all recognize that art is fundamental to advertising. More people recognize musical jingles from television ads than they do major political figures. In 2004, more Americans voted for the winner of *American Idol* than for the president of the United States. Art is part of business because it is seen as affecting how people behave, in particular what they will spend their money on. Some philosophers argue that advertising jingles are not art because their purpose is to sell a product, not to be a work of art. However, many advertisements use recognizable musical compositions. It would be strange to claim that these stopped being songs (and art) because they are included within a television ad. The use of them might not be artistic, but they are still works of art. Indeed, they are used in advertisements because of their power as works of art; they speak to people (consumers), and businesses want their products to be associated with these works of art. It is this very commodification of art—that is, treating art as an economic commodity—that was the focus of some philosophers such as Walter Benjamin (1892–1940), who critiqued and criticized such uses of art.

Another significant area in which art is connected to society at large is with respect to social and political values. This is often spoken of in the context of questions about public funding for certain art and censorship issues. Should the government be in the role of funding art? Many people argue that this is not an appropriate use of taxpayer money (which is how the government can fund anything). This is usually because people say that such funds should go to other, more important matters, such as national defense or health issues. Others who might believe that there is some legitimate role for the government to fund art insist on accountability for such funding. They say, for example, that the National Endowment for the Arts needs to be responsive to public wishes and attitudes, so the government has a legitimate role in deciding and overseeing what particular artistic projects get funded.

This last point about accountability also speaks to the issue of censorship and the place and role of art in society, especially in connection to morality and social values. There is, of course, a spectrum of views about this issue. Some people argue that artistic expression is a matter of the right to free expression, so no censorship is appropriate, regardless of how offensive some artwork might be. This view is sometimes put forth with the sentiment that if you do not like what you see (or hear), then do not look at it! If some work of art offends you, they say, then walk away (or, if you do not like what you see on television, change the channel). Others, however, have argued that this view is too simplistic. Some things are too offensive to simply walk away from. More than that, however, they claim that some works of art are not merely offensive; they are harmful. For instance, pornography, they say, is not merely offensive, but it leads to women being harmed (either from direct assault or from promoting general attitudes that dehumanize women). Or, they say, works of art that glorify the degradation of certain people go beyond being offensive to being harmful. The general point, of course, is that to the extent that art is a social phenomenon, it is related to social, political, and moral values. Given the fact that art is so prevalent in today's society, these value issues have become more and more immediate and widespread.

Philosophy of art is the analysis and evaluation of basic concepts and issues within and about art. The term should actually be philosophy of *the arts,* since this area of philosophy deals with any and all of the arts. So, it includes a consideration of dance, music, film, architecture, literature, photography, etc., as well as painting and sculpture. It is very closely connected with aesthetics, although today aesthetics is treated as less broad than philosophy of art.

The first question that philosophers of art ask is: What is art? Different philosophers try to answer this question in different ways. One such way is to define *art* in terms of some features or properties that things have that makes them art. In other words, just as we would try to define other things by looking for features that those things have in common (and, perhaps, that other things do not have), so, too, we look for features that artworks have in common. There are two ways of trying to define things in terms of some features or properties. One way is to look for necessary and sufficient conditions. (A second way is to look for family resemblances.) Looking for necessary and sufficient conditions means that one looks for features that something must have in order for it to be art (that is, it is necessary for something to have in order to be art) or one looks for features that are good enough for something to be art (that is, as long as something has those features, then it is art). For example, some people claim that art is self-expression. So, as long as someone does something (speak, write, draw, move, etc.) with the intention of expressing some feeling or thought, then that is art.

Not everyone agrees. A screaming child who is throwing a tantrum, for instance, is certainly expressing some feeling or thought, but that probably is not art. Or, another example, some people claim that art must be created by people, that is, to be created by a person is a necessary feature for something (whether it is an object or a set of sounds or movements, etc.) to be art. Once again, not everyone agrees. Some people speak of found art, such as naturally formed patterns or objects. The point is that many philosophers (and people in general) have tried to define art in terms of some features that things must have in order to be art.

Others have said that art should be defined not in terms of some features that things must have but in terms of some relations that they have. This means that there is nothing about objects (including sounds or movements) that by themselves, or by some features they have, makes them art. Instead, what makes something art is that it is related to other things in some way or other. For example, an object might be considered by people just to be sturdy and function as a good jug for carrying water. However, someone else might not care about its function for carrying water and, rather, focus on other aspects of the object, so as to consider it beautiful or balanced. For that person, it is seen as art. The point is that what makes it art is how it is related to someone or something else. Or, another example, a can of soup in the grocery store might not be considered art, but that same can of soup mounted in an art gallery might be considered art, not because the can or its features have changed, but because its presence in the art gallery leads people to think about the can in different ways than they thought about it in the grocery store. The point here is that what makes something art is that it is related in certain ways to something or someone outside of it.

When considering art, philosophers often focus on four different aspects: (1) artist-centered issues, (2) viewer-centered issues, (3) artwork-centered issues, and (4) social and ethical issues. Artist-centered issues deal with basic aspects of art from the perspective of artists, that is, from the creators of art. One such aspect was mentioned above, namely, expression. That is, one issue about the nature of art is that it involves some form of expression by the artist. But this issue of expression is not simple. For instance, there is the question of what, exactly, is expressed in the act of creating art. One might express some feeling or some thought or some value. While it might be the case that during the creation of the work of art, an artist is feeling something and expressing it, that might not necessarily be the case. An artist can express, say, sadness, even if she does not feel sad at that moment. Indeed, we assume that good actors do this all the time. One way that philosophers speak of this is to distinguish the *expression of* something versus the *expressiveness in* something. That is, there might well be expressiveness in some work of art that makes people feel sad or think of sadness, but that is not necessarily the same thing as the work of art itself being an expression of sadness. Again, one person might hear a particular song and feel sad because of having heard that song, while another person might not, so the sadness might be expressed to one person, but not because the song itself was sad.

Another aspect of expression has to do with the further issue of communication. That is, many philosophers (and artists) claim that what is fundamental to art is not so much that something is expressed but that something is communicated. For example, if an artist created a work of art with the intention of expressing, say, sadness, but everyone who encountered that work of art felt bored or laughed or was disgusted, then—at least many philosophers and artists say—the artist has failed and failed because the sadness was not communicated, regardless of whether or not it was expressed.

This issue of communication points to the second broad aspect of art that philosophers deal with, namely, viewer-centered issues. These issues focus on the experience of art by nonartists (that is, by anyone who is not creating the work of art). This issue of artistic experience includes the question of *how* something is experienced artistically (or aesthetically). Someone might experience a film or a poem, for instance, and be moved emotionally by it. This is usually said to be an aesthetic experience. However, someone else might experience that same film or poem, but being a filmmaker or being a poet, that second person might experience it from a professional, critical point of view. As a result, that person's experience might not be aesthetic, but might be based on looking at the technical details of the work of art. Many philosophers speak of an artistic experience as a matter of having a special attitude toward works of art, namely, an attitude of being receptive to aesthetic feelings or thoughts. This is related to an older term: taste. That is, in the past (and even still today) people spoke of having a refined taste for art. Just like some people who are said to have a refined taste for fine wines and can distinguish very subtle features of different wines, so some people speak of having refined artistic taste and can appreciate fine and subtle features of artworks while others cannot (or are not trained to do so).

Beyond the issue of having some developed sense or taste, many people speak of artistic experience as being based on understanding. Most people have had the experience of seeing some painting and thinking, "What is that supposed to be?" Or the experience of a trained musician is quite different than that of a young child when they are both listening to some complicated composition of classical music. The trained musician can understand—and therefore appreciate and experience—the complicated aspects of the composition that the young child cannot. Because of the nature of artistic experience as being, at least in part, a matter of one's understanding and attitude, this raises the question of how to evaluate works of art and even how to evaluate experiences of works of art. Is the experience that the young child has of the complicated musical composition less of an artistic experience than that of the trained musician? (The musician's experience might be so focused on technical elements of the music that the young child might "feel" the expressiveness of the composition even more than the musician.)

A third aspect of art that philosophers focus on involves artwork-centered issues. These are issues that center on features of works of art themselves, not around artists or viewers (listeners, etc.) of art. For example, when looking at a painting, someone might focus on describing it in terms of the colors in the painting or the shapes or how light or dark it is, etc. However, someone might also speak of the painting as having unity or harmony or balance or intensity, etc. The latter terms (such as unity and harmony) are aesthetic features, as opposed to being merely descriptive features (such as its colors or shapes). A question arises about the relationship between the descriptive features and the aesthetic features. After all, the painting "just is" the colors and shapes, etc., yet there is unity or harmony, etc., in some paintings and not in others. How is this to be explained?

Another artwork-centered issue that is dealt with is the issue of form versus content. Philosophers (and artists) often speak of the form of a work of art as being separate from its content. For example, one might look at the rhyme scheme of a poem and disregard the actual content of the poem (that is, what the words say). Or someone might focus on patterns of movement in a dance and disregard some particular content if, say, the dance was supposed to express or represent something. The point is that often people distinguish form and content. This leads to questions about what really makes the work of art what it is—is it the form or the content?—as well as to the evaluation of the work of art (for instance, whether or not the work of art succeeds in communicating sadness by its form or content). In addition, there is also the issue of form versus context. Some people have claimed that unless a person knows the context in which a work of art was created, one cannot really understand or appreciate that work of art. Also, they claim, the more one knows about the context of some work of art, the more one can appreciate and properly evaluate it. For example, if one comes upon a painting, it would make a major difference in one's experience of it (including one's evaluation of it) if one knew that it was created by a trained professional as opposed to being created by a young child. Likewise, they say, if one knew that an author had lived in certain conditions and had certain life experiences that came out in his written work, knowing this versus not knowing it would lead to different understandings and evaluations of that work. Others disagree and say that context is not important or even relevant to one's aesthetic experience of a work of art.

This point of form versus context points to the issue of interpretation and criticism of art, which, in turn, points to the fourth broad aspect of art that philosophers deal with, namely, social and ethical issues. What makes good art or bad art? There are various issues of evaluating art. One of them has to do with interpretation and criticism. What would it mean to have a correct, or an incorrect, interpretation of a work of art? How could an interpretation of a work of art be wrong, or be right? It is tempting for many people to say that the meaning of a work of art lies with the viewer (or listener, etc.). For these people, there can be no wrong or mistaken interpretation because art means whatever anyone takes it to mean. Others strongly disagree and claim that at least part of the meaning of a work of art depends upon what the artists was trying to express or communicate. Although there might be many interpretations, say, of Shakespeare's *Macbeth*, these people claim, any interpretation that says the play was about the evils of snowboarding or nuclear weapons is simply wrong (because Shakespeare did not know about snowboarding or nuclear weapons). On what criteria, then, can and should interpretation and critique of artworks be made? This is a major area of philosophical concern within the philosophy of art.

Besides questions of good and bad art in terms of interpretation, there are questions about good and bad art in terms of social and ethical concerns. There are many issues relating art and society/morality. For example, when, if ever, is censorship of art appropriate? As everyone knows, different people respond differently to works of art. If a work of art is experienced by some people as being offensive, is that good enough grounds for censoring it, at least in certain contexts? For instance, some art might glorify demeaning certain people, or the artist might have the intention to offend and upset some people (say, by showing a racial group in demeaning ways). Is it appropriate to censor (or remove) such art if it is placed in public? Should taxpayers' money fund artworks if those taxpayers find the art offensive? Of course, many people argue that one of the major values of art is that it provokes people; it forces them to be uncomfortable and to examine their beliefs and values. Critics, however, claim that even if this is true, people should not be forced to pay to be insulted or offended. Just what are the values *of* art (not simply the values *within* art) is a significant area of concern for philosophers of art.

Concluding Discussion Questions

1. Why did Plato believe that art is merely a shadow of what is truly real? Was he correct? What did he see as the source and power of art?
2. Why did Aristotle disagree with Plato's assessment of art? What did Aristotle see as the source and power of art?
3. What did philosophers in the 18th and 19th centuries see as being objective about art and what did they see as being subjective about art?
4. What are the arguments that art is essentially a mode of perception, that is, a way of experiencing things? Is there an aesthetic sense?
5. What are the arguments in favor of expression as the basic nature of art and the arguments against this view?
6. Does technology really make a difference with respect to the meaning and power of art? Are we desensitized to the meaning and power of art because it is everywhere?

Further Reading

Adams, Laurie Schneider. *The Methodologies of Art: An Introduction.* Boulder, Colo.: Westview Press, 1996.

Barrett, Terry. *Why Is That Art?: Aesthetics and Criticism of Contemporary Art.* Oxford: Oxford University Press, 2007.

Eaton, Marcia Muelder. *Basic Issues in Aesthetics.* Long Grove, Ill.: Waveland, 1988.

Eldridge, Richard. *An Introduction to the Philosophy of Art.* Cambridge: Cambridge University Press, 2003.

Freeland, Cynthia. *Art Theory: A Very Short Introduction.* Oxford: Oxford University, 2007.

Gilbert, Katharine Everett, and Helmut Kuhn, eds. *A History of Esthetics.* New York: Dover, 1972.

Goldblatt, David, and Lee B. Brown, eds. *Aesthetics: A Reader in Philosophy of the Arts.* 2nd ed. Englewood Cliffs, N.J.: Prentice Hall, 2004.

Graham, Gordon. *Philosophy of the Arts: An Introduction to Aesthetics.* 3rd ed. New York: Routledge, 2005.

Herwitz, Daniel. *Aesthetics (Key Concepts in Philosophy).* New York: Continuum, 2008.

Richter, Peyton E., ed. *Perspective in Aesthetics: Plato to Camus.* Indianapolis: Bobbs-Merrill, 1967.

Sheppard, Anne. *Aesthetics: An Introduction to the Philosophy of Art.* Oxford: Oxford University Press, 1987.

Townsend, Dabney, ed. *Aesthetics: Classic Readings from the Western Tradition.* 2nd ed. Belmont, Ky.: Wadsworth, 2000.

Glossary

aesthetics the philosophical study of art, usually focused on the perspective of the artist, the audience (or beholder of art), and artworks themselves.

Apollo/Dionysus two Greek gods, representing orderliness and aspiration (Apollo) and passion and inspiration (Dionysus). They were used by Friedrich Nietzsche as metaphors for the meaning and power of art.

autographic/allographic two types of art; autographic art is art in which there is one original work, such as Mona Lisa (with perhaps copies of that original), while allographic art is art in which there is not one original work but many copies, such as many instances of a particular movie.

beauty a quality that is defined in many different ways; a common conception is that it is a sensible condition of aesthetic excellence (that is, some sensory feature that is of great positive value and quality).

catharsis a purging or purification; in aesthetics it is most commonly associated with the views of Aristotle, who claimed that an effect and value of tragedy is that it purged its audience of powerful negative emotions.

contextualism in aesthetics, the view that the meaning of an artwork depends upon the contexts in which it exists; those contexts are multiple and can include the personal history of the artist, the time and place of the inception and creation of the artwork, etc.; similar contexts would be relevant for the beholder (audience) of the artwork.

critique the evaluation of an artwork; related to, but not the same as the interpretation of an artwork, because the goal of interpretation is understanding and comprehension, while the goal of critique is assessment.

disinterestedness the notion that art is to be understood and experienced independently of interests; also the notion that an aesthetic experience (as opposed to some other kind of experience) requires that the beholder of art have an appropriate distance or separation from the artwork to truly appreciate it as art.

expressivism   the view that art is fundamentally a matter of the artist expressing something through the process of creating an artwork and through the product that is created; some artists and philosophers claim that what matters is that the artist expresses some feeling or idea, while others claim that what matters is that the artist actually communicates or even evokes some feeling or idea (and does not merely express it).

family resemblance   the view that things that are categorized together do not have some common essence but instead share various overlapping threads in common, much like members of a biological family might resemble one another without having some single feature that they all have in common.

formalism   the view that form, not content or context, is what is fundamental to art.

intention   in aesthetics, the notion that the intentions (beliefs, feelings, desires, etc.) of an artist are fundamental to the meaning of an artwork; artists and philosophers disagree on whether the artist's intentions are crucial, or even relevant, to the nature and meaning of an artwork.

mimesis   imitation, copying, or representation; for some artists and philosophers, mimesis was seen as a basic aspect of art, with Plato denouncing it (for being a pale copy of reality), and Aristotle embracing it (as allowing for and even promoting catharsis).

moralism   in aesthetics, the view that aesthetic value is directly related to moral value, so an artwork that depicted something morally bad could not be aesthetically good (and vice versa).

performance   an action; in aesthetics, the notion that some works of art are not products (such as a painting or a sculpture) but are events and actions (such as a performance of a dance or a particular playing of some musical composition).

representation   in aesthetics, the notion of art as re-presenting something; it is related to, but not the same thing as, copying or resembling, since, for example, a dog in a painting might represent loyalty not a particular dog.

sublimity the notion of greatness or awesomeness; also the feeling of experiencing something that is great or awesome; in aesthetics, many philosophers spoke of art as striving to approach or capture the sublime.

taste in aesthetics, the notion that there is an aesthetic sense, much like there are the usual five senses (sight, touch, smell, hearing, and taste); an ability or capacity for people to experience aesthetic features or qualities.

Key People

Aristotle (384-322 B.C.E.) Greek philosopher who greatly influenced philosophy, science, and art. In his book Poetics, he provided the first sustained analysis and evaluation of art (particularly poetry and tragic drama). He claimed that an important function and value of art was that it permitted the purging of strong emotions and promoted discovery. In the passage below, Aristotle claims that art (poetry) represents what is universal and what is possible, not simply particular things or events, and this feature of art is of great value.

> From what we have said it will be seen that the poet's function is to describe, not the thing that has happened, but a kind of thing that might happen, i.e. what is possible as being probable or necessary. The distinction between historian and poet is not in the one writing prose and the other verse—you might put the work of Herodotus into verse, and it would still be a species of history; it consists really in this, that the one describes the thing that has been, and the other a kind of thing that might be. Hence poetry is something more philosophic and of graver import than history, since its statements are of the nature rather of universals, whereas those of history are singulars. By a universal statement I mean one as to what such or such a kind of man will probably or necessarily say or do—which is the aim of poetry, though it affixes proper names to the characters; by a singular statement, one as to what, say, Alcibiades did or had done to him.
>
> In comedy this has become clear by this time; it is only when their plot is already made up of probable incidents that they give it a basis of proper names, choosing for the purpose any names that may occur to them, instead of writing like the old iambic poets about particular persons. In tragedy, however, they still adhere to the historic names; and for this reason: what convinces is the possible; now whereas we are not yet sure as to the possibility of that which has not happened, that which has happened is manifestly possible, else it would not have come to pass. Nevertheless even in tragedy there

are some plays with but one or two known names in them, the rest being inventions; and there are some without a single known name, e.g., Agathon's *Antheus,* in which both incidents and names are of the poet's invention; and it is no less delightful on that account. So that one must not aim at a rigid adherence to the traditional stories on which tragedies are based. It would be absurd, in fact, to do so, as even the known stories are only known to a few, though they are a delight none the less to all.

It is evident from the above that, the poet must be more the poet of his stories or plots than of his verses, inasmuch as he is a poet by virtue of the imitative element in his work, and it is actions that he imitates. And if he should come to take a subject from actual history, he is none the less a poet for that; since some historic occurrences may very well be in the probable and possible order of things; and it is in that aspect of them that he is their poet.

[*Aristotle and the Art of Poetry.* Translated by Ingram Bywater. Oxford: Oxford University Press, 1920.]

Dewey, John (1859–1952) *American philosopher who wrote extensively on most areas of philosophy, including aesthetics. In his writings on art and aesthetics, he argued that art should be understood not as a product but as a process. In his words, art is experience. It is both interactive and social. The selection below is from his book* Art as Experience *and speaks to the interactive, experiential nature of art for both the artist and the audience.*

In short, art in its form, unites the very same relation of doing and undergoing, outgoing and incoming energy, that makes an experience to be an experience . . . Man whittles, carves, sings, dances, gestures, molds, draws, and paints. The doing and making is artistic when the perceived result is of such a nature that *its* qualities *as perceived* have controlled the question of production . . . But with the perceiver, as with the artist, there must be an ordering of the elements of the whole that is in form, although not in details, the same as the process of organization the creator of the work consciously experienced. Without an act of recreation the object is not perceived as a work of art. The artist selected, simplified, clarified, abridged and condensed according to his interest. The beholder must go through these operations according to his point of view and interest. In both, an act of abstraction, that is of extraction of what is significant, takes place.

[Dewey, John. *Art as Experience*. New York: Putnam, 1934.]

Hegel, Georg Wilhelm Friedrich (1770–1831)   *German Idealist philosopher. Hegel sought to construct a theoretical system to explain all of reality. He defended the view that history is the developmental process of Mind coming to self-consciousness and recognizing that it is reality; Hegel thought that the ultimate product of this process is freedom. Art, for Hegel, aims at beauty, which itself is one means of the expression of freedom and truth (what he termed Idea). The passage below is taken from his* Philosophy of Fine Art. *Here he states that art is, along with philosophy and religion, an important stage in the full realization of freedom and truth.*

. . . [It] is no doubt the case that art can be employed as a fleeting pastime, to serve the ends of pleasure and entertainment, to decorate our surroundings, to import pleasantness to the external conditions of our life, and to emphasize other objects by means of ornament. In this mode of employment art is indeed not independent, not free, but servile. But what we mean to consider, is the art which is free in its end as in its means . . .

Fine art is not real art till it is in this sense free, and only achieves its highest task when it has taken its place in the same sphere as religion and philosophy, and has become simply a mode of revealing to consciousness and bringing to utterance the Divine Nature, the deepest interests of humanity, and the most comprehensive truths of the mind. It is in works of art that nations have deposited the profoundest intuitions and ideas of their hearts; and fine art is frequently the key—with many nations there is no other—to the understanding of their wisdom and of their religion . . .

The universal need for expression in art lies, therefore, in man's rational impulse to exalt the inner and outer world into a spiritual consciousness for himself, as an object in which he recognizes his own self. He satisfies the need of this spiritual freedom when he makes all that exists explicit for himself *within*, and in a corresponding way realizes thus his explicit self *without,* evoking thereby, in this reduplication of himself, what is in him into vision and into knowledge for his own mind and for that of others. This is the free rationality of man, in which, as all action and knowledge, so also art has its ground and necessary origin . . .

In art . . . sensuous shapes and sounds present themselves, not simply for their own sake and for that of their immediate structure, but with the purpose of affording in that shape satisfaction to higher spiritual interests, seeing that they are powerful to call forth a response and echo in the mind from all the depths of consciousness. It is thus that, in art, the sensuous is *spiritualized,* i.e., the spiritual appears in sensuous shape.

[Hegel, G. W. F. *The Introduction to Hegel's Philosophy of Fine Art.* Translated by Bernard Bosanquet. London: Kegan Paul, Trench & Co., 1886.]

Hume, David (1711–1776) *Scottish empiricist philosopher who was famous for defending an empiricist view in which all knowledge comes from the senses. With respect to art and aesthetics, he also saw these as being derived from the senses, with people having an aesthetic sense, or taste, much like other senses (such as sight or smell). In the selection below, from his essay "Of the Standard of Taste," he argues that although taste is a matter of people's experiences, there are objective standards to taste.*

It appears, then, that amidst all the variety and caprice of taste, there are certain general principles of approbation or blame, whose influence a careful eye may trace in all operations of the mind. Some particular forms or qualities, from the original structure of the internal fabric are calculated to please, and others to displease; and if they fail of their effect in any particular instance, it is from some apparent defect or imperfection in the organ. A man in a fever would not insist on his palate as able to decide concerting flavors; nor would one afflicted with the jaundice pretend to give a verdict with regard to colors. In each creature there is a sound and a defective state; and the former alone can be supposed to afford us a true standard of taste and sentiment. If, in the sound state of the organ, there be an entire or a considerable uniformity of sentiment among men, we may thence derive an idea of the perfect beauty; in like manner as the appearance of objects in daylight, to the eye of a man in health, is denominated their true and real color, even while color is allowed to be merely a phantasm of the senses.

[Hume, David. *Of the Standard of Taste and Other Essays.* London: Allyn and Bacon, 1918.]

Hutcheson, Francis (1694–1746) *Scottish philosopher who wrote of knowledge and experience as being the result of people having multiple senses, including not only the usual five senses (sight, touch, smell, hearing, taste) but also a moral sense, an empathetic sense, and an aesthetic sense. The passage below, taken from his book* An Inquiry into the Original of Our Ideas of Beauty and Virtue, *states that we have an inner sense by which we experience beauty that is in the world independently of us.*

Let it be observ'd . . . the Word Beauty is taken for the Idea rais'd in us, and a Sense of Beauty for our Power of receiving this Idea. Harmony also denotes our pleasant Ideas arising from Composition of Sounds, and a good Ear (as it is generally taken) a Power of perceiving this Pleasure. In the following Section, an attempt is made to discover "what is the immediate Occasion of these pleasant Ideas, or what real Quality in the Objects ordinarily excites them."

It is of no consequence whether we call these Ideas of Beauty and Harmony, Perceptions of the External Senses of Seeing and Hearing, or not. I should rather choose to call our Power of perceiving these Ideas, an *internal sense,* were it only for the Convenience of distinguishing them from other Sensations of Seeing and Hearing, which Men may have without Perception of Beauty or Harmony. It is plain from Experience, that many Men have in the common meaning, the Senses of Seeing and Hearing perfect enough; they perceive all the simple Ideas separately, and have their Pleasures . . . and may be as capable of hearing and seeing at great distances as any Men whatsoever; And yet perhaps they shall find no Pleasure in Musical Compositions, in Painting, Architecture, natural Landskip; or but a very weak one in comparison of what others enjoy from the same Objects. This greater Capacity of receiving such pleasant Ideas we commonly call a fine Genius or Taste; in Musick we seem universally to acknowledge something like a distinct Sense from the External one of Hearing, and call it a good Ear; and the like distinction we should probably acknowledge in other Objects, had we also got distinct Names to denote these Powers of Perception by.

There will appear another Reason perhaps hereafter, for calling this Power of perceiving the Ideas of Beauty, an Internal Sense, from this, that in some other Affairs, where our External Senses are not much concern'd, we discern a sort of Beauty, every like, in many respects, to that observ'd in sensible Objects, and accompany'd with like Pleasure: Such is that Beauty perceiv'd in Theorems, or universal Truths, in general Causes, and in some extensive Principles of Action.

[Hutcheson, Francis. *An Inquiry into the Original of Our Ideas of Beauty and Virtue*. London: Ware, 1753.]

Kant, Immanuel (1724–1804) *German philosopher who made what he called the Copernican revolution, arguing that objects conform to our knowledge, rather than knowledge conforming to objects; he believed that the mind structures experience according to certain categories. With respect to art and aesthetics, he claimed that art is a bridge between the determinism of the natural world and the freedom of human action. His major work on art and aesthetics was* The Critique of Judgment, *from which the following selection is taken. In this selection, he claims that although art and what is beautiful are based on feeling, they are not merely subjective, because there are aspects of beauty that cause those feelings in us, and so there is something nonsubjective about it.*

As regards the Pleasant everyone is content that his judgment, which he bases upon private feeling, and by which he says of an object that it pleases him, should be limited merely to his own person. Thus he is quite contented that if he says, "Canary wine is pleasant," another man may correct his expression and remind him that he ought to say "It is pleasant *to me*." And this is the case not only as regards the taste of the tongue, the palate, and the throat, but for whatever is pleasant to any one's eyes and ears . . .

The case is quite different with the Beautiful. It would (on the contrary) be laughable if a man who imagined anything to his own taste, thought to justify himself by saying: "This object (the house we see, the coat that the person wears, the concert we hear, the poem submitted to our judgment) is beautiful *for me*." For he must not call it *beautiful* if it merely pleases him. Many things may have for him charm and pleasantness; no one troubles himself at that; but if he gives out anything as beautiful, he supposes in others the same satisfaction—he judges not merely for himself, but for everyone, and speaks of beauty as if it were a property of things. Hence he says "the *thing* is beautiful;" and he does not count of the agreement of others with this his judgment of satisfaction, because he has found this agreement several times before, but he *demands* it of them. He blames them if they judge otherwise and he denies them taste, which he nevertheless requires from them. Here then we cannot say that each man has his own particular taste. For this would be as much as to say that there is no taste whatever, i.e. no aesthetic judgment, which can make a rightful claim upon every one's assent.

[Kant, Immanuel. *Critique of Judgment*. Translated by J. H. Bernard. London: Macmillan & Co., 1892.]

Nietzsche, Friedrich (1844–1900) *German philosopher who wrote, often in an unconventional style, on topics ranging from aesthetics and ethics to epistemology and metaphysics. Nietzsche is famous for his pronouncement that God is dead. With the death of God, Nietzsche believed humans needed to create their own values. Central to Nietzsche's views is what he called the will to power, that is, our natural drive toward creative autonomy. This carried over to his remarks about art and aesthetics, as the passage below (from his book* Twilight of the Idols*) indicates.*

Beautiful and ugly ["fair and foul"]. Nothing is more conditional—or, let us say, narrower—than our feeling for beauty. Whoever would think of it apart from man's joy in man would immediately lose any foothold. "Beautiful in itself" is a mere phrase, not even a concept. In the beautiful, man posits himself as the measure of perfection; in special cases he worships himself in it. A species cannot do otherwise but thus affirm itself alone. Its lowest instinct, that of self-preservation and self-expansion, still radiates in such sublimities. Man believes the world itself to be overloaded with beauty—and he forgets himself as the cause of this. He alone has presented the world with beauty—alas! only with a very human, all-too-human beauty. At bottom, man mirrors himself in things; he considers everything beautiful that reflects his own image: the judgment "beautiful" is the vanity of his species. For a little suspicion may whisper this question into the skeptic's ear: Is the world really beautified by the fact that man thinks it beautiful? He has humanized it; that is all. But nothing, absolutely nothing, guarantees that man should be the model of beauty. Who knows what he looks like in the eyes of a higher judge of beauty? Daring perhaps? Perhaps even amusing? Perhaps a little arbitrary?

Nothing is beautiful, except man alone: all aesthetics rests upon this *naïveté*, which is its first truth. Let us immediately add the second: nothing is ugly except the degenerating man—and with this the realm of aesthetic judgment is circumscribed. Physiologically, everything ugly weakens and saddens man. It reminds him of decay, danger, impotence; it actually deprives him of strength. One can measure the effect of the ugly with a dynamometer. Wherever man is depressed at all, he senses the proximity of something "ugly." His feeling of power, his will to power, his courage, his pride—all fall with the ugly and rise with the beautiful. In both cases we draw an inference: the premises for it are piled up in the greatest abundance in instinct. The ugly is understood as a sign and symptom of degeneration: whatever reminds us in the least of degeneration causes in us the judgment of "ugly." Every suggestion of exhaustion, of heaviness, of age, of weariness; every kind of lack of freedom, such as cramps, such as paralysis; and above all, the smell, the color, the form of dissolution, of decomposition—even in the ultimate attenuation into a symbol—all evoke the same reaction, the value judgment, "ugly." A hatred is aroused—but whom does man hate then? There is no doubt: the decline of his type. Here he hates out of the deepest instinct of the species; in this hatred there is a shudder, caution, depth, farsightedness—it is the deepest hatred there is. It is because of this that art is deep.

[Nietzsche, Friedrich Wilhelm. *The Complete Works of Friedrich Nietzsche*. Vol. 16. Translated by Oscar Levy et al. London: T. N. Foulis, 1911.]

Plato (ca. 428–348 B.C.E.) *Extremely influential philosopher who shaped much of later Western thought and who argued that there are levels of reality, with the world of Ideas as the most real. Art, he claimed, was merely an imitation of what is (most) real. The selection below is from his most famous work* The Republic. *In this selection, Socrates questions Glaucon, who admits that art is merely imitation and therefore suspect.*

Well then, [said Socrates] shall we begin our inquiry in our usual manner: Whenever a number of individuals have a common name, we assume them to have also a corresponding idea or form . . . Let us take any common instance; there are beds and tables in the world—plenty of them, are there not?

Yes [said Glaucon].

But there are only two ideas or forms of them—one the idea of a bed, the other of a table.

True.

And the maker of either of them makes a bed or he makes a table for our use, in accordance with the idea—that is our way of speaking in this and similar instances—but no artificer makes the ideas themselves: how could he?

Impossible.

And there is another artist . . . who is able to make not only vessels of every kind, but plants and animals, himself and all other things—the earth and heaven, and the things which are in heaven or under the earth; he makes the gods also.

What an extraordinary man! . . . He must be a wizard and no mistake.

Oh, you are incredulous, are you? . . . Do you see that there is a way in which you could make them all yourself?

What way?

Any easy way enough; or rather, there are many ways in which the feat might be quickly and easily accomplished . . . in the mirror.

Yes, [Glaucon] said; but they would be appearance only.

Very good, [Socrates] said, you are coming to the point now. And the painter too is, as I conceive, just another—a creator of appearances, is he not?

Of course.

But then I suppose you will say that what he creates is untrue, and yet there is a sense in which the painter also creates a bed?

Yes, he said, but not a real bed . . .

But would you call the painter a creator and maker?

Certainly not.

Yet, if he is not the maker, what is he in relation to the bed?

I think, he said, that we may fairly designate him as the imitator of that which the others make.

Good, I said; then you call him who is third in the descent from nature an imitator?

Certainly, he said.

And the tragic poet is an imitator, and therefore, like all other imitators, he is thrice removed from ... the truth.

[Plato. *The Republic*. Book X. Translated by Benjamin Jowett. Oxford: Oxford University Press, 1892.]

Schopenhauer, Arthur (1788–1860) *German philosopher who claimed that will (that is, longing and desire) was more real and fundamental than intellect, with all things sharing a will to live. Art, he claimed, was more important than science because art was more directly connected to the will and because engaging in the world with an aesthetic attitude was the best means of living a good life. He presented this view in his most famous work,* World as Will and Idea. *In the following selection he claims that music is the highest form of art because it is the most directly connected to feeling and will.*

Music is as *direct* an objectification and copy of the whole *will* as the world itself, nay, even as the [Platonic] Ideas, whose multiplied manifestation constitutes the world of individual things. Music is thus by no means like the other arts, the copy of the Ideas, but the *copy of the will itself,* whose objectivity the Ideas are. This is why the effect of music is so much more powerful and penetrating than that of the other arts, for they speak only of shadows, but it speaks of the thing itself ...

According to all this, we may regard the phenomenal world, or nature, and music as two different expressions of the same thing, which is therefore itself the only medium of their analogy, so that a knowledge of it is demanded in order to understand that analogy. Music, therefore, if regarded as an expression of the world, is in the highest degree a universal language, which is related indeed to the universality of concepts, much as they are related to the particular things ...

The unutterable depth of all music by virtue of which it floats through our consciousness as the vision of a paradise firmly believed in yet ever distant from us, and by which also it is so fully understood and yet no inexplicable, rests on the fact that it restores to us all the emotions of our inmost nature, but entirely without reality and far removed from their pain. So also the seriousness which is essential to it, which excludes the absurd from its direct and peculiar province, is to be explained by the fact that its object is not the idea, with reference to which alone deception and absurdity are possible; but its object is directly the will, and this is essentially the most serious of all things, for it is that on which all depends.

[Schopenhauer, Arthur. *The World as Will and Idea.* Translated by R. B. Haldane and J. Kemp. London: Trübner & Co., 1883.]

Shaftesbury, third earl of (Anthony Ashley Cooper) (1671–1713)

English thinker of the Enlightenment who resurrected Plato's views that Beauty, Goodness, and Truth are all one and the same. He claimed that nature is beautiful and good because it comes from God, with orderliness and harmony as basic values; artistic creation is the closest that humans come to mirroring or capturing this orderliness and harmony, and, so, aesthetic value is primary. The selection below is taken from his work Characteristics, *in which he makes the point that art should strive to go beyond specifics and particulars to connecting up with what is universal.*

And thus, after all, the most natural beauty in the world is honesty and moral truth. For all beauty is truth. True features make the beauty of a face; and true proportions the beauty in architecture; as true measures that of harmony and music. In poetry, which is all fable, truth still is the perfection . . .

A painter, if he has any genius, understands the truth and unity of design; and knows he is even then unnatural when he follows Nature too close, and strictly copies Life. For his art allows him not to bring all nature into his piece, but a part only. However, his piece, if it be beautiful, and carries truth, must be a whole, by itself, complete, independent, and withal as great and comprehensive as he can make it. So that particulars, on this occasion, must yield to the general design, and all things be subservient to that which is principle; in order to form a certain easiness of sight, a simple, clear, and united view which would be broken and disturbed by the expression of any thing peculiar or distinct.

[Cooper, Anthony Ashley. *Characteristicks of Men, Manners, Opinions, Times*. 3 vols. Vol. 1. Edited by Douglas den Uyl. Indianapolis, Ind.: Liberty Fund, 2001. Available online. URL: http://oll.libertyfund.org/title/811. Accessed July 28, 2011.]

Tolstoy, Leo (1828–1910) *Russian author who forcefully argued in favor of the expressivist view of art. In particular, he claimed that the essence of art is the transmission of feeling from the artist through the artwork to the audience, or beholder, of the artwork. His most famous works were his novels* War and Peace *and* Anna Karenina, *but his most important work on aesthetics was his book* What Is Art? *The following passage is taken from this book.*

Photograph of Leo Tolstoy from the late 19th century

To evoke in oneself a feeling one has once experienced, and having evoked it in oneself, then, by means of movement, lines, colors, sounds, or forms expressed in words, so to transmit that feeling that others may experience the same feeling—this is the activity of art.

Art is a human activity, consisting in this, that one man consciously, by means of certain external signs, hands on to others feelings he has lived through, and that other people are infected by these feelings, and also experience them.

Art is not, as the metaphysicians say, the manifestation of some mysterious Idea of beauty, of God; it is not, as the aesthetical physiologists say, a game in which man lets off his excess of stored-up energy; it is not the expression of man's emotions by external signs; it is not the production of pleasing objects; and, above all, it is not pleasure; but it is a means of union among men, joining them together in the same feelings, and indispensible for the life and progress toward well-being of individuals and of humanity.

[Tolstoy, Leo. *What Is Art?* Translated by Aylmer Maude. New York: Thomas Y. Crowell & Co., 1899.]

Weitz, Morris (1916–1981) *American philosopher who advocated the view that art has no essence and cannot be defined precisely. Drawing from the work of Ludwig Wittgenstein, he claimed that art is an open concept, without distinct features. The passage below is from his most famous article, "The Role of Theory in Aesthetics."*

Card games are like board games in some respects but not in others . . . Some games resemble others in some respects—that is all . . . The problem of the nature of art is like that of the nature of games, at least in these respects: If we actually look and see what it is that we call "art," we will also find no common properties—only strands of similarities. Knowing what art is is not apprehending some manifest or latent essence but being able to recognize, describe, and explain those things we call "art" in virtue of those similarities . . .

"Art," itself is an open concept. New conditions (cases) have constantly arisen and will undoubtedly constantly arise; new art forms, new movements will emerge, which will demand decisions on the part of those interested, usually professional critics, as to whether the concept should be extended or not. Aestheticians may lay down similarity conditions but never necessary and sufficient ones for the correct application of the concept.

[Weitz, Morris. "The Role of Theory in Aesthetics." In *Journal of Aesthetics and Art Criticism* 15 (1956): 27–35.]

INDEX

A

abortion 76–79
Absolute (Hegel) 165–166
active euthanasia 73
act utilitarianism 38–40
Addison, Joseph 236–238, *237*
advertising 96–97, 272
aesthetic disinterestedness 238–240, 281–282
aesthetic experience 227–229, 263–265, 275–276, 285–286
    Enlightenment and 236
    form v. content and 262
aesthetic impulse 243
aesthetic interpretation 262–263, 265–267, 277–278
aesthetic properties 227
aesthetics 225–229. *See also* art
    definition of 281
    epistemological issues of 228
    metaphysical issues of 228
    origin of term 225–226
aesthetic taste 235–240, 275–276
    definition of 283
    Hume on 287–288
    Hutcheson on 288–289
affirmative action 190
agent 8, 43
agent-neutral view 43
agent-relative view 43
Age of Reason 235
aistheta 225
allographic art 271, 281
altruism 58
Anarchy, State, and Utopia (Nozick) 197, 215–216

animal ethics 87–93
    Aquinas on 87
    Aristotle on 87
    Cohen on 93
    Descartes on 87–88
    Kant on 88
    metaethics on 7, 8–9, 87
    Narveson on 93
    Regan on 92–93
    Singer on 89–90, 116–117
    utilitarianism on 40, 89–90
animal rights 89–93
Anscombe, G. E. M. (Elizabeth) 28, 47
anthropocentric view 85
antithesis (Hegel) 166–167
Apollo 281
Apollonian impulses 253
applied ethics 5, 66–93. *See also* specific issues
    definition of 66, 104
    method of 67–69
    subfields of 66–67
    topics for analysis under 67
appreciation, aesthetic 266
Aristotle *22,* 106, *136,* 207–208
    on animal ethics 87
    on art and aesthetics 232–234, 284–285
    on cause 138–139
    on eudaemonia 30, 137–138
    on political philosophy 137–140, 207–208
    and Rand 198
    on virtue ethics 28–30, 106, 137–138
art
    Addison on 236–238
    Aristotle on 232–234

artist-centered issues in 274–275
artwork-centered issues in 274, 276–278
business of 271–272
censorship of 272–273
Cooper on 240, 294–295
definition of 273–274
Dewey on 270, 285–286
Enlightenment on 235–240
expressivism on 254–256, 273–275, 282, 295–296
family resemblance and 256–259
formalism on 262–263
form v. content in 261, 262–263, 276–277
Goodman on 271
Hegel on 247–249, 286–287
Hume on 236, 287–288
Hutcheson on 238–240, 288–289
interpretation of 262–263, 265–267, 277–278
Kant on 241–242, 289–290
language and 225
Nietzsche on 252–253, 290–291
philosophy of 225–229, 273–278
Plato on 230–231, 233–234
public funding of 272
Romanticism on 245–253
Schelling on 246–247
Schiller on 242–244
Schopenhauer on 251–252, 293–294
social and ethical issues in 277–278
and society 225, 270–278
Tolstoy on 254, 295–296
20th-century challenges in 260–267
viewer-centered issues in 274, 275–276
Weitz on 258–259, 296–297
Art as Experience (Dewey) 285–286
artificial virtues 17
artist-centered issues 274–275
artwork-centered issues 274, 276–278
Atlas Shrugged (Rand) 198
authority, political 124–127
autographic art 271, 281
Ayer, A. J. 14

B

beauty 225–229. *See also* art
definition of 281
descriptive 226
epistemological issues of 228
evaluative 226
metaphysical issues of 228
nature of 226–229
as relation 227
sublime in 229
becoming, Hegel on 166
being, Hegel on 166
Benjamin, Walter 272
Bentham, Jeremy 37, 41, 89, 107, 176–178, 208–209
biocentric view 85
biodiversity 85
bioethics 66–67, 69–75
The Birth of Tragedy (Nietzsche) 253
"boo-hurrah" theory 13–14
bourgeoisie 171–172
business of art 271–272
business ethics 66, 94–98

C

Cage, John 260
capitalism 48–49, 94–95, 168–172
capital punishment 75–76
care, ethics of 63–65, 104
cared-for 63
Carnap, Rudolf 13
categorical imperative 44–48, 110–111
category mistake 226–227
catharsis 232–234, 281
causal agent 8
cause, Aristotle on 138–139
caveat emptor 96
censorship 272–273
certainty, quest for (Dewey) 269
Channing, William Ellery 246
Christianity
    Nietzsche on 51
    Rand on 199
civil disobedience 204
civil law 126–127, 157–160
classical art 248
classical liberalism 184, 186–187, 195
cognitivism 18–20

definition of 12, 105
   Plato on 21–25
Cohen, Carl 93
commodification, of art 271–272
commons, tragedy of 200–201, 206
communication
   through art 256, 275
   through media 98
A Communist Manifesto (Marx) 212
communitarianism 56–58, 104, 204
   v. liberalism 56–58, 173–175, 187
   v. libertarianism 196
   as political philosophy 172–175
confidentiality
   in health care 72
   for media sources 101
consciousness, Hegel on 167–169
consent, informed 72
consequentialism 36–37
   deontology v. 43–44, 129
   utilitarianism as 36
Constitution, U.S. 75–76, 142, 151
consumers, business ethics and 96–97
content v. form, in art 261, 262–263, 276–277
contextualism 261, 267, 281
A Contribution to the Critique of Political Economy (Marx) 112–113, 212–213
Cooper, Anthony Ashley 239, 240, 294–295
corrective justice 189–190
courage
   as ancient virtue 29
   doctrine of mean and 31
critical legal studies 159
critique 266, 281
The Critique of Judgment (Kant) 241, 243, 289–290
The Critique of Practical Reason (Kant) 241
The Critique of Pure Reason (Kant) 241
cruel and unusual punishment 75–76
cultural relativism 9–11, 104

D

death and dying 72–75
death penalty 75–76
Declaration of Independence, U.S. 151
deep ecology 84

deontology 42–51, 129
   advantages of 42–43
   consequentialism v. 43–44, 129
   definition of 42, 104
   Kant on 42, 44–48, 110–111, 129
   Marx on 48–49
   Nietzsche on 49–51
Descartes, René 87–88, 149, 235
descriptive beauty 226
descriptive cultural relativism 9–11
deterrence 162, 190
Dewey, John 268–270, 285–286
dialectical materialism 204
Diderot, Denis 154
difference principle (Rawls) 55, 147, 192–193
Dionysian impulses 253
Dionysus 281
disinterestedness 238–240, 281–282
distributive justice 188–189, 190
divine command ethics 33–35
divine rights of kings 142–144
Dog, Idea of (Plato) 23
dominion, over environment 85
drama, tragic 233–234, 253
Duchamp, Marcel 260
duty theory 42–51. *See also* deontology

E

economy
   business ethics in 66, 94–98
   liberalism on 185–186
   Marx on 48–49, 94–95, 168–172, 212–213
education ethics 66
Edwards, Jonathan 235
efficient cause 138–139
egoism 26–27, 58–60
   ethical 26, 58–60, 104
   psychological 26–27, 58
Eighth Amendment 75–76
Emerson, Ralph Waldo 246
emotions
   beauty and 228–229
   virtue ethics on 29
emotivism 13–15, 104
employee rights 97–98
empowerment 131
end-of-life issues 72–75
engrossment 64

Enlightenment 235–240
environmental ethics 83–86
    feminism on 65
    metaethics on 7, 8–9
    tragedy of the commons in 200–201
    utilitarianism on 86
environmental philosophy 83
environmental sustainability 95–96
Epicurus 108, *136*
equality 127, 193–194, 204
equality principle (Rawls) 54–55, 147, 192–193
equal opportunity principle (Rawls) 193
ethical egoism 26, 58–60, 104
ethical hedonism 26, 104
ethics
    applied 5, 66–93, 104. *See also* specific issues
    definition of 5
    divine command 33–35
    feminist 61–65
    metaethics 5, 6–11
    normative 5, 26–27, 105
    subareas of 5
eudaemonia 30, 137–138
euthanasia 73–75
Euthyphro (Plato) 33, 117
evaluative beauty 226
evolutionary ethics 70, 269
existentialism 252
expressivism 254–256, 273–275, 282, 295–296

F
facts, moral 18–20
fact/value dichotomy 270
fairness doctrine 100
family resemblance 256–259, 282
Faust (Goethe) 246
feminist ethics 61–65, 148
    Gilligan on 62–63
    Jaggar on 61–62
    Mill on 180
    Noddings on 62, 63–65
feminist jurisprudence 159
Fichte, Johann Gottlieb 247
First Amendment 142
Fisher, John *144*
forces of production (Marx) 169–172
forgery 271

formal cause 138–139
formal impulse 243
formalism 52, 262–263, 282. *See also* social contract theory
form v. content, in art 261, 262–263, 276–277
The Fountainhead (Rand) 198
freedom 133–134
    communitarianism on 174
    harm principle on 180–183, 185
    Hegel on 166, 167–168
    Hobbes on 149–150, 209–211
    liberalism on 184
    Locke on 153–154
    neutralism on 185
    paternalism principle on 182
    Rousseau on 156–157, 218
    welfare principle on 183
"freedom from" 133–134
"freedom to" 133–134
free will 133
Freud, Sigmund 62, *62*
Fuller, Margaret 246
Fundamental Orders of Connecticut 141

G
Galen *22*
Gauthier, David 54
gay ethics and rights 65, 79–80
The Gay Science (Nietzsche) 49
Gersdorff, Carl von *50*
Gilligan, Carol 62–63
God
    divine command ethics on 33–35
    Hegel on 165–166
    Mawdudi on 142
    Nietzsche on 49, 51, 252–253
    political philosophy on 141–144
    Romanticism on 246
    Socrates on 117
Goethe, Johann Wolfgang von 243, 246–247, 253
good
    Aristotle on 137
    communitarianism on 58, 174–175
    metaethics on 7
    moral realism on 19
    Nietzsche on 49, 114
    Plato on 21, 23–25
    Socrates on 117

good life, virtue ethics on 28–32
Goodman, Nelson 271
good will, Kant on 46–47, 110–111
The Grounding of the Metaphysics of Morals (Kant) 110–111
Guernica (Picasso) 266–267

H

happiness. *See also* pleasure
    Aristotle on 30, 137–138
    utilitarianism on 37–41, 176–180
    virtue ethics on 30
harassment, workplace 97
Hardin, Garret 200
Hare, R. M. 13
harm principle 180–183, 185, 204
health care, ethics in 69–75
health care providers, ethics of 71
health resources, allocation of 71
hedonic calculus 37
hedonism
    egoism on 58–59
    ethical 26, 104
    normative ethics on 26–27
    psychological 26–27, 37
    utilitarianism on 37–41, 129, 179
Hegel, Georg W. F. 48, 164–168, *165,* 209
    on art and aesthetics 247–249, 286–287
    and Marx 168–169
    on master/slave relationship 167–168
    and Schelling 246
Hegelian dialectic 166, 247–248
Henry VIII (king of England) 143
Heraclitus *136*
herd (Nietzsche) 50
hierarchy of rights 78, 132
Hobbes, Thomas 52–53, 108–109, 145–146, 149–151, 154, 209–211
Hölderlin, Friedrich 164, 246
homosexuality 65, 79–80
Hooper, Ellen 245
hostile workplace 97
Hume, David 16–17, 109–110
    on art and aesthetics 236, 287–288
    Rousseau and 154
Hutcheson, Francis 238–240, 288–289
hypothetical imperative 44

I

Ideas (Plato) 23–24, 226, 230–231
identity politics 204
ideological superstructure 48
ignorance, veil of 54–55, 147, 192–193, 206
imitation, art as 230, 232–234, 282, 291–293
immunity 131
impartiality principle 59–60
In a Different Voice: Psychological Theory and Women's Development (Gilligan) 62
incest 79
informed consent 72
infotainment 99
inquiry, Dewey on 268–269
An Inquiry into the Original of Our Ideas of Beauty and Virtue (Hutcheson) 288–289
intention, in aesthetics 282
interests, in utilitarianism 40
interpretation, aesthetic 262–263, 265–267, 277–278
An Introduction to the Principles of Morals and Legislation (Bentham) 208–209
involuntary euthanasia 73

J

Jaggar, Alison 61–62
James, William 268
Jefferson, Thomas 142, 151, 235
Jesus 143
jurisprudence 157–160
justice 127, 187–190
    as ancient virtue 29
    Bentham on 176–178
    corrective 189–190
    definition of 204
    distributive 188–189, 190
    in economic systems 95
    equality and 194
    philosophy of law on 159–160
    Plato on 21–25, 114–115, 127, 135, 187, 189
    procedural 187–188
    punishment in 162
    Rawls on 54–55, 115, 147, 189, 191, 217

substantive 187, 188–190
utilitarianism on 188, 189–190
justification, of rights 132

K

Kant, Immanuel 110–111, 235
   on animal ethics 88
   on art and aesthetics 241–242, 289–290
   criticism of 47–48
   on deontology 42, 44–48, 129
   on good will 46–47
   on human value 45–46, 79
   Rand on 198–199
   and Schopenhauer 249
   on women 61
Das Kapital (Marx) 168, 212
Kierkegaard, Søren 246
King, Martin Luther, Jr. 158
kings
   divine rights of 142–144
   philosophers as 25, 136–137, 216–217
knowledge
   in art and aesthetics 225–229
   family resemblance and 258
   Plato on 23–24, 226
   Rand on 198
   virtue as 30
Kohlberg, Lawrence 62–63

L

language
   art and 225
   cognitivism on 12, 18
   emotivism on 13–15
   Hume on 16–17
   metaethics on 6–7
   noncognitivism on 12
   prescriptivism on 12–13
law
   Bentham on 176–178
   bindingness of 157–159
   feminist perspective on 159
   natural 143, 153, 157–159, 205
   philosophy of 157–160
   punishment under 160–163
legal positivism 158, 204
legal realism 158–159

legitimacy, political 124–127, 205
lesbian ethics 65
A Letter Concerning Toleration (Locke) 152
The Leviathan (Hobbes) 150, 209–211
liberalism 184–187, 194–195, 205
   classical 184, 186–187, 195
   communitarianism v. 56–58, 173–175, 187
   Locke on 184
   Mill on 180
   modern 184, 186–187, 195, 196
   Rawls on 184
libertarianism 194–197, 205
   classical liberalism as 186–187
   communitarianism v. 56–58, 173–175, 187, 196
   criticism of 196–197
   modern liberalism v. 196
   Nozick on 197, 215–216
   as political philosophy 194
   Rand and 197, 199
liberty. *See* freedom
liberty principle (Rawls) 192–193
Locke, John 111–112, 151–154, 211–212, 235
   on freedom 153–154
   on liberalism 184
   on social contract theory 52–53, 145–147, 151–154, 211–212
   on state of nature 146, 152–154, 211–212
logic, Dewey on 268–269
The Lord of the Rings (Tolkien) 21
love, ethics of 79–83

M

Mackie, J. L. 20
majority, tyranny of (Mill) 180
The Manifesto of the Communist Party (Marx) 168
"man is an end in himself" (Rand) 198
marginal cases, argument from 88–89
Marx, Karl 48–49, 112–113, 168–172, *171*, 212–213
Marxism 205
master/slave morality (Nietzsche) 49–51
master/slave relationship (Hegel) 167–168
material cause 138–139
material impulse 243

materialism
   dialectical 204
   Hobbes on 149
Mawdudi, Abu'l A'la 142
maxim 45
Mayflower Compact 141
mean, doctrine of 31
media ethics 66–67, 98–101
medical ethics 69–75
metaethics 5, 6–11
   agent and patient in 8–9
   cultural relativism in 9–11
   definition of 6, 105
   distinction between good and right in 7
   language in 6–7
   moral standing in 7–8
metaphysical freedom 133
metaphysics
   aesthetics and beauty in 228
   Aristotle on 137
   Hegel on 164–166
   Hobbes on 149
   Schopenhauer on 249–251
Mill, John Stuart 37–38, 113, 178–180, 213–214
   on harm principle 180–183
   on liberalism 180, 184
   on women 180
Milton, John 235
mimesis (imitation), art as 230, 232–234, 282, 291–293
Mind (Hegel) 165–166
modern liberalism 184, 186–187, 195, 196
"Modern Moral Philosophy" (Anscombe) 28
Moore, G. E. 19
moral agent 8, 43
moral facts 18–20
moralism 282
morality, ethics as study of 5
moral patients 8–9
   animals as 8–9, 87
   ecosystems as 8–9, 84
moral philosophy. *See* ethics
moral realism 18–20, 105
moral relativism 9, 105
moral standing 7–8
More, Thomas 143–144, *144,* 214–215, *215*

motivation
   emotivism and 14
   moral facts and 20
   psychological hedonism and 37
motivational displacement 64

N

Narveson, Jan 93
nation, concept of 123–124
naturalist approach, in moral realism 19
natural law theory 143, 153, 157–159, 205
natural rights 53, 146, 153, 178
natural virtues 17
nature
   state of. *See* state of nature
   value of 83–84
necessary and sufficient conditions, of art 273–274
negative freedom 133–134
negative rights 131, 186
neutralism 185
news media. *See* media ethics
Newton, Isaac 235
Nietzsche, Friedrich 49–51, *50,* 113–114
   on art and aesthetics 252–253, 290–291
   on God 49, 51, 252–253
Noddings, Nel 62, 63–65
noeta 225
noncognitivism 12–15
   definition of 12, 105
   Hume on 16–17, 109–110
normative ethics 5, 26–27
   definition of 105
   and politics 128–134
normative hedonism 37, 41
normativity 128–129, 205
nothing, Hegel on 166
Nozick, Robert 197, 215–216
numeric equality 193

O

obedience, in divine command ethics 35
objectivism 197–199
Objectivist Newsletter 198
objectivity
   in media 101
   in metaethics 6
objects of moral acts 8

one-caring 63
On Liberty (Mill) 180, 213–214
On the Aesthetic Education of Man in a Series of Letters (Schiller) 243
On the Genealogy of Moral (Nietzsche) 49
original position (Rawls) 54, 147, 191
"ought implies can" 26
Oversoul (Emerson) 246

P

panopticon (model prison) 176
paparazzi 101
passion
    Plato on 231
    Romanticism on 246
passive euthanasia 73
paternalism principle 182
paternalistic laws 196
patients, medical 72
patients, moral 8–9
    animals as 8–9, 87
    ecosystems as 8–9, 84
Peirce, Charles 268
perfect duties 45
performance 282
Phenomenology of Spirit (Hegel) 164
philosopher-king 25, 136–137, 216–217
Les Philosophes 235
philosophical cultural relativism 9–11, 104
Philosophy of Fine Art (Hegel) 286–287
Philosophy of Right (Hegel) 209
physician-assisted suicide 73–74
Picasso, Pablo 266–267
Plato 22, 114–115, *136*, 216–217, 291–293
    on art and aesthetics 230–231, 233–234, 291–293
    on cognitivism 21–25
    on divine command ethics 33–34
    on Ideas 23–24, 226, 230–231
    on justice 21–25, 114–115, 127, 135, 187, 189
    on knowledge 226
    on political philosophy 24–25, 123, 135–137, 216–217
    Rand on 198–199
    on reality 23
    and Schopenhauer 249
    on soul 24, 135

    on state 24–25
    on virtue ethics 30
pleasure
    Addison on 236–238
    Bentham on 37, 107, 176–177
    egoism on 58–59
    Epicurus on 108
    Mill on 37–38, 113, 179–180
    utilitarianism on 37–41, 176–177
Poetics (Aristotle) 232–234, 284
poetry 232–234, 284–285
political philosophy 123–127. *See also* specific philosophies
    Aristotle on 137–140, 207–208
    freedom in 133–134
    legitimacy and authority in 124–127
    normative ethics in 128–134
    Plato on 24–25, 123, 135–137, 216–217
    political unit in 123–124
    representation in 125–126
    rights in 126–127, 130–132
political unit 123–124
Politics (Aristotle) 207–208
polygamy 79
pornography 80–83
positive freedom 133–134
positive rights 131, 186
positivism, legal 158, 204
practical wisdom 29
pragmatism 268
prescriptivism 12–13, 105
principle-based ethics, virtue ethics v. 28–29
privacy
    employee right to 97–98
    in political philosophy 127
procedural justice 187–188
production, forces of (Marx) 169–172
progressives 186–187
proletariat 171–172
property rights 195–196
psychological egoism 26–27, 58
psychological hedonism 26–27, 37
punishment
    Bentham on 177–178
    capital 75–76
    justice and 189–190
    legal concept of 160–163
    utilitarianism on 76, 162, 177–178, 190
Pythagoras *136*

Q

quest for certainty (Dewey) 269

R

Rand, Ayn 58, 197–199
rationality
   Aristotle on 30, 138
   Hegel on 165–166
   Kant on 44, 110–111
   Rand on 198
Rawls, John 54–55, 115, 147, 191–193, 217
   on justice 54–55, 115, 147, 189, 191, 217
   on liberalism 184
realism
   legal 158–159
   moral 18–20, 105
reality
   Aristotle on 137
   Hegel on 164–166
   Hobbes on 149
   Plato on 23
   Schopenhauer on 249–251
reason (rationality)
   Aristotle on 30, 138
   Hegel on 165–166
   Kant on 44, 110–111
   Rand on 198
"reasonable man" standard 159
Regan, Tom *92*, 92–93
relativism
   cultural 9–11, 104
   moral 9, 105
religion
   divine command ethics on 33–35
   Hegel on 165–166
   political philosophy on 141–144
   Rand on 199
   Romanticism on 246
reparation 190
representation
   aesthetic 282
   political 125–126
The Republic (Plato) 21, 24, 127, 135, 187, 216–217, 291–293
responsibility
   communitarianism on 173–175
   philosophy of law on 160, 162
restitution, v. punishment 163
retributivism 76, 162–163, 189–190

right (right action)
   communitarianism on 58, 174–175
   consequentialism on 36–37
   deontology on 42
   divine command ethics on 33–35
   metaethics on 7
   utilitarianism on 36–41
rights (human or political) 53, 126–127, 130–132
   communitarianism on 173–175
   definition of 205
   harm principle on 180–183
   hierarchy of 78, 132
   liberalism on 185, 186–187
   libertarianism on 195
   natural 53, 146, 153, 178
   philosophy of law on 159–160
rights, animal 89–93
Ring of Gyges (Plato) 21–22
Rohde, Erwin *50*
romantic art 248–249
Romanticism 245–253
Rosenbaum, Alisa. *See* Rand, Ayn
Ross, W. D. 42
Rousseau, Jean-Jacques 52, 115–116, 145–146, 154–157, *155*, 218–219, 235
rule utilitarianism 38–40

S

Schelling, Friedrich Wilhelm Joseph von 164, 246–247
Schiller, Friedrich 242–244, *243*
The School of Athens (Raphael painting) *136*
Schopenhauer, Arthur 249–252, *250*, 293–294
Second Treatise of Government (Locke) 152–153, 211–212
self, unencumbered 173–175
self-consciousness, Hegel on 167–168
self-expression, art as 254–256, 273–275
self-interest
   in egoism 58–60
   Rand on 198
   Rawls on 191–193
   in social contract theory 52–56, 145–148
selfishness, virtue of 58, 198
separation of church and state 142
sexual ethics 79–83
sexual harassment 97

Singer, Peter 39, 90, 116–117
    on animal ethics 89–90, 116–117
    on utilitarianism 40
slave/master relationship (Hegel) 167–168
slave morality (Nietzsche) 49–51
Smith, Adam 235
social contract, definition of 205
social contract theory 52–56, 105, 130, 145–148
    animal ethics in 93
    criticism of 55–56, 148
    in ethics 52, 145, 152
    Gauthier on 54
    Hobbes on 52–53, 108–109, 145–146, 150–151, 209–211
    influence of 148
    liberalism in 184–185
    Locke on 52, 53, 111–112, 145–147, 151–154, 211–212
    in political philosophy 52, 145, 152
    Rawls on 54–55, 115, 147, 191–193, 217
    Rousseau on 52, 115–116, 145–146, 154–157, 218–219
social ethics 75
    abortion in 79
    capital punishment in 75–76
    media ethics in 98
socialism 164–175
society, art and 225, 270–278
Socrates 117, *136. See also* Plato
    on divine command ethics 33–34
    on virtue ethics 30
soul
    Nietzsche on 51
    Plato on 24, 135
species-being (Marx) 169
speciesism 89
sports ethics 66
state. *See also* political philosophy
    concept of 123–124
    Plato on 24–25, 135–136
    social contract theory on 52–53
statements
    cognitivism on 12, 18
    emotivism on 13–15
    Hume on 16–17
    metaethics on 6–7
    noncognitivism on 12
    prescriptivism on 12–13

state of nature 145–146, 206
    Hobbes on 146, 150, 154
    Locke on 146, 152–154, 211–212
    Rousseau on 154–156
Stevenson, Charles L. 14–15
stewardship, of environment 85
Stocker, Robert 29
Stoics 138
The Subjection of Women (Mill) 180
subjectivity 6, 16, 245–246
sublimity 229, 238, 283
substantive justice 187, 188–190
supererogatory actions 43
superman (Nietzsche) 252–253
surrogate pregnancy 72
sustainability 95–96
symbolic art 248
synthesis (Hegel) 166–167, 247–248

T

taste, aesthetic 235–240, 275–276
    definition of 283
    Hume on 287–288
    Hutcheson on 288–289
techné 230
teleology 139
temperance, as ancient virtue 29
theocracy 141–144, 206
therapy, v. punishment 163
thesis (Hegel) 166–167
Thomas Aquinas 87, 143
Thoreau, Henry David 245
threshold deontology 48
Thus Spoke Zarathustra (Nietzsche) 49
Tolkien, J. R. R. 21
Tolstoy, Leo 254, *255, 295,* 295–296
tragedy of the commons 200–201, 206
tragic drama 233–234, 253
truth-value 12
Twilight of the Idols (Nietzsche) 290–291
tyranny of the majority (Mill) 180

U

understanding, aesthetic 266
unencumbered self 173–175
utilitarianism 36–41, 105, 206
    on animal ethics 40, 89–90
    Bentham on 37, 107, 176–178, 208–209
    criticism of 40–41

on environment 86
impact of 40
on justice 188, 189–190
Mill on 37–38, 113, 178–180, 213–214
as political philosophy 129–130, 176–183
on punishment 76, 162, 177–178, 190
Singer on 40
Utopia (More) 143–144, 214
utopianism 206

V

valuation (Dewey) 269–270
veil of ignorance 54–55, 147, 192–193, 206
viewer-centered issues, in art 274, 275–276
virtue(s)
    conflict between 31–32
    definition of 29
    four ancient 29
    Hume on 16–17
    of selfishness 58, 198
virtue ethics 28–32, 105
    Anscombe on 28
    Aristotle on 28–30, 106, 137–138
    criticism of 31–32
    doctrine of mean in 31
    emotion in 29

eudaemonia in 30
Plato on 30
Socrates on 30
The Virtue of Selfishness (Rand) 198
voluntary euthanasia 73

W

Warhol, Andy 260
watchdog role, of media 99
Weitz, Morris 258–259, 296–297
welfare laws 196
welfare principle 183
What Is Art? (Tolstoy) 295–296
will, Schopenhauer on 251, 293–294
wisdom, practical 29
Wittgenstein, Ludwig 257–258
women
    feminist ethics on 61–65
    jurisprudence and 159
    Kant on 61
    Mill on 180
    pornography and 82
working conditions 97
World as Will and Idea (Schopenhauer) 249, 293–294

Z

Zeno of Citium *136*

JAN 2013